The Russian City between Tradition and Modernity, 1850–1900

The Russian City between Tradition and Modernity, 1850–1900

Daniel R. Brower

University of California Press

Berkeley   Los Angeles   Oxford

University of California Press

Berkeley and Los Angeles, California

University of California Press, Ltd.
Oxford, England

Library of Congress Cataloging-in-Publication Data

Brower, Daniel R.
The Russian city between tradition and modernity,
1850–1900 /
Daniel R. Brower.
    p. cm.
  Includes bibliographical references.
  ISBN 0-520-06764-9 (alk. paper)
    1. Cities and towns—Soviet Union—History—
19th century.   2. Soviet Union—Social
conditions—1801–1917.   I. Title.
HT145.S58B76   1990
307.76'0947'09034—dc20   89-20442
                                               CIP

Printed in the United States of America

1   2   3   4   5   6   7   8   9

The paper used in this publication meets the
minimum requirements of American National
Standard for Information Sciences—Permanence of
Paper for Printed Library Materials, ANSI
Z39.48-1984.   ∞

To the memory of my father,
Daniel R. Brower, 1905–1987

Contents

List of Illustrations

List of
Tables and Chart

Acknowledgments

During the years of researching and writing this work I have accumulated a host of debts, both institutional and personal. At an early stage in this book's formulation I found a place of nurturing in a seminar at the Centre des Hautes Etudes of the University of Paris, where professors Louis Bergeron and Marcel Roncayolo broadened their discussion of urban history to include historical trends in distant Russia. I went through a difficult period of reexamination and reconceptualization at about the time Professor Michael Hamm was organizing a research group to study the history of Russia's largest cities in the late imperial period. This fortuitous event, together with Professor Hamm's readiness to include among the participants a scholar without a city of his own, gave my project a much-needed rooting in the expertise of this group of scholars. More recently, colleagues in the Social Theory and Comparative History Colloquium at the University of California, Davis, applied their critical skills to a paper I wrote discussing important themes in Russian urban history. In various verbal and manuscript forms this book has received a thoughtful reception from individual scholars, including Joseph Bradley, Fred Carstensen, Adele Lindenmyer, Reginald Zelnik, Kay Flavell, Ben Eklof, and Michael Hamm. Their interest and assistance have helped my project survive to see the light of day. At the University of California Press, Sheila Levine provided encouragement and sound advice and Jay Plano brought his many talents to bear in giving clarity and coherence to my rough-hewn manuscript.

This book is pieced together in good measure from materials that are accessible only in Soviet historical archives. I was fortunate to be selected twice by the International Research and Exchange Board to pursue research on this project as a member of the Soviet-American cultural exchange program. During these trips I worked in the Central State Archives of the October Revolution and the Central State Historical Archives in Leningrad. By the count of Soviet archivists I consulted an immoderate number of archival files. For her patience and help Serafima Grigorevna Sakharova is especially deserving of my gratitude. I was able to consult with several Soviet historians, among whom I would particularly like to thank Boris Nikolaevich Mironov, Vera Romanovna Leikina-Svirskaia, Valeriia Antonovna Nardova, and A. S. Nifontov.

Financial support for research and writing has come from a variety of sources, including grants from the University of California, Davis, the American Academy of Learned Societies, and the International Research and Exchange Board.

Parts of this book have appeared in print previously. Permission to use this material has come from the editors of *Annales (Economies, Sociétés, Civilisations)* ("L'urbanisation russe à la fin du 19e siècle," vol. 32 [January-February 1977]); *Russian Review* ("Urbanization and Autocracy: Russian Urban Development in the First Half of the Nineteenth Century," vol. 42 [October 1983]); and *Slavic Review* ("Labor Violence in Russia in the Late Nineteenth Century," vol. 41 [September 1982]).

Introduction

This history of Russian cities examines the transformation of urban life in the late tsarist period. Specifically, it looks at the changes under way in European Russia in the decades between the reforms of Alexander II and the Revolution of 1905. These years saw innovations in all areas of Russian life, but they also saw debate over the desirability and pace of these trends. Russian urban society was a key part of both developments; it was an arena of reform and a symbol of both the promises and the dangers of reform. The inhabitants of the capitals, St. Petersburg and Moscow, could no longer lay claim to live in the only civilized cities in the land. Provincial towns were becoming centers of trade, manufacturing, education, and print culture. The past and the future served as points of reference by which urban progress could be measured—from ignorance in the past to enlightenment in the future, from poverty to wealth, backwardness to civilization, and, in very muted tones, servility to freedom. These standards of change were judgmental and inspirational in intent. They were pervasive among educated townspeople and are as important to this history as are the indicators of population growth, economic development, the municipal statutes, and the police regulations. In other words, my study is as much about the changing ideas of the Russian city as it is about the processes of institutional and social change in Russian urban life.

My approach to these topics is informed by what might loosely be termed "the methodology of urban history." Although the city has frequently provided a background for the analysis of particular political, social, and economic topics, the methodology of urban history is of recent origin. It is best understood not as a distinct discipline but rather as "a strategy for illuminating historical understanding" that is particularly relevant for modern history.[1] The modesty of this claim to scholarly identity is owing to the multiple historical perspectives on the city and to the complex patterns of change occurring in urban centers in modern times. The concept of urbanization, that is, the process of population concentration, is especially popular among scholars who are attracted by the apparent precision and interdependence of the data on the geographical location of towns, population movements, and urban economic activities. It relies heavily on this quantitative material to uncover distinct urban "systems."[2] I use urbanization to refer specifically to the patterns created by changes in urban location, population movements, and the production and distribution of economic resources.

Although useful in defining the demographic and social context of urban history, this particular methodology of urban history neglects topics that are related to the practices and attitudes by which populations give meaning to their urban experience. In an anthropological perspective the city is a cultural creation that is put together through efforts to implement political and social objectives and ideals. The city is also the product of the particular practices, that is, the meaningful actions, by which urban inhabitants make the city in some measure their own place. This cultural approach assumes that urban dwellers understand and shape the city in ways that the American historian Sam Bass Warner has called "multiple urban images."[3] These images are found in policies and plans, in fiction and the urban press, in discourse, and in practices. In my opinion they represent a significant and rewarding manner of understanding the Russian city.

The interplay of urban perceptions and practices defines the concept of urbanism as I employ it in this study. This concept is not a predictive model because it makes no assumptions about the structural determinants that control urban images and functions. As I already suggested, it serves to "illuminate our understanding" of the key actors in the transformation of the Russian city in the nineteenth century. Russian cities included merchants and migrants, the two social types who appeared to typify the

---

1. Derek Fraser and Anthony Sutcliffe, Introduction, to *The Pursuit of Urban History*, ed. Derek Fraser and Anthony Sutcliffe (London, 1983), 1.
2. See, for example, Jan de Vries, *European Urbanization, 1500–1800* (Cambridge, Mass., 1984).
3. Sam Bass Warner, "Slums and Skyscrapers: Urban Images, Symbols, and Ideology," in *Cities of the Mind: Images and Themes of the City in the Social Sciences*, ed. L. Rodwin and R. Hollister (New York, 1984), 183.

industrious population and whose activities gave special meaning to the city as a workplace. Russian cities included medical personnel and educators, for whom Western models of the progressive city were the standard by which they judged—usually unfavorably—the qualities of their own towns. And Russian cities also housed tsarist administrators and civic leaders, who assumed in differing degrees power over the urban population and sought to impose public order on the chaotic processes of city building.

In a larger sense urbanism was present as an assumption, which was shared by many educated Russians as well as by officials, that the city ought to develop according to an ideal model. This objective guided tsarist administrators, who elaborated city plans in the eighteenth and early nineteenth centuries. The character of the ideal model changed in later years but not the intent. Ideal models were also present in other parts of the Western world. A very precise definition and declaration of purpose came from a French colonial administrator who proclaimed "urbanism" to be "the art and science of developing human agglomerations."[4] His belief in the malleability of the city, which was drawn from his work in a colonial territory, is equally applicable to the activities of urban leaders in Russia, many of whom considered their country to be a borderland of Europe.

The European core of nineteenth-century Western civilization plays an important supporting role in the story of Russian urbanism. It was present in the form of markets for Russian goods, whose sale enriched and expanded Russian urban commerce. European standards of sanitation, public health, cleanliness, and hygiene in the cities offered a tangible model for civic leaders in Russia to emulate. Generalized elementary schooling and nearly universal literacy among the urban population were goals for educators in Russian cities. For some, however, the Western city also represented forces of decadence and disorder; depending on the point of view of the observer, these forces ranged from the capitalist factory to the rebellious proletariat, from bourgeois materialism to the urban mob. Whether progressive or destructive, European urban centers epitomized the city of the future and, as such, served as a useful device by which to condemn any conditions in Russian towns that observers found intolerable. Contemporary attitudes toward Russian urbanism reflected, explicitly or implicitly, the positions adopted by Russians toward both the idealized future, or "modernity," and the imaginary past, or "tradition." The bitter conflicts provoked by Russian urbanism revealed how profound this dichotomy was.

4. Cited by Paul Rabinow, "Representations Are Social Facts," in *Writing Culture*, ed. J. Clifford (Berkeley, 1986), 260.

In a formal sense the city had a clearly defined place in the laws and regulations of the tsarist state. Its juridical form emerged in statutes that defined the responsibilities and leadership of the municipalities. Its population received rank and status in the system of legal estates (*sosloviia*) that was in existence (although somewhat reformed) until the 1917 revolution. Its economic activities were taxed and regulated by the state, and according to tsarist regulations its migrant population had to possess the proper travel documents and to register with the police. In other words, the state's extensive powers created an "official city" of institutions, residents, and activities.

Tsarist statutes and administrative reports reveal official assumptions and expectations toward the city. However, these documents must be used with caution. They give voice to a statist view of urbanism, and this view is as distant from the practices of the population as are other idealized versions of the city. Gregory Freeze has argued that in the mid nineteenth century the "*soslovie* system" was "amorphous, plastic, and complex."[5] This observation is a warning that the estates may not be a meaningful way to describe the social identity of the urban population. The questions of whether well-to-do manufacturers and traders viewed themselves as "merchants"—as required by state decrees—and whether urban migrants remained "peasants," as their passports indicated, raise complex issues of social relations and cultural values that cannot be resolved by reference to either formal documentation or the observations of intellectuals. In the same way, municipal statutes reveal only one small part of the civic practices that shaped the public sphere of the city. A struggle over order and domination was an integral part of Russian urban history, and although the state was an important player in this struggle, it was not the only one.

In many respects this study is a work of synthesis. It incorporates economic, political, social, and cultural perspectives on the Russian city and attempts an interdisciplinary interpretation of the history of Russia in those years. Few such broad studies in the field of social history have as yet appeared. My findings are thus necessarily tentative and the chapters that follow might best be read as essays in Russian urban history. In my search for meaningful generalizations I have relied on the abundant tsarist archival and published materials on the cities. In particular, I use the imperial census of 1897 to construct a model of the migrant city, a

5. Gregory Freeze, "The *Soslovie* (Estate) Paradigm and Russian Social History," *American Historical Review* 91 (February 1986): 24.

composite portrait based on the similarities of social configuration of the populations in nearly sixty urban centers. My profile is a statistical abstraction but one that finds confirmation in an impressionistic analysis of the evidence on migration and the laboring population in the expanding urban centers. Thus, my use of the term "Russian city" is more than a figure of speech: I seek to enlarge our understanding of social change in late imperial Russia by including the urban population as a whole. My model of the migrant city defines the social profile of the typical city and focuses attention on those urban areas that most closely conform to the pattern uncovered by statistical analysis.

My synthesis of late imperial urban history draws heavily on developments in particular cities in European Russia for which evidence is readily available. But these individual urban histories are significant here only to the extent that they are tied to the trends at work in the country at large. The efforts of the tsarist regime to regulate urban life through statutes and the positioning of administrative units and forces of order—police and army garrisons—made the state a pervasive presence in provincial cities and, to a lesser extent, in industrial settlements and district towns. The development of regional, national, and international markets that were serviced by waterways and rail lines leading to urban centers caused these towns to expand both economically and demographically. A print culture that included commercial newspapers encompassed a growing reading population in the cities and helped to give new meaning to urban life. Common forces were at work in all major urban centers. And at a basic level of intellectual discourse the idea of the city captured the imagination of influential townspeople, intellectuals, and officials.

In recent years a number of valuable studies have appeared on Russian urban history in the eighteenth and nineteenth centuries.[6] Most have focused on the growth of individual cities. As urban biographies, they offer the clarity of well-defined borders and a precise center of historical events. The questions they address are inspired partly by the principal issues of Russian historiography, partly by the conceptual perspectives suggested by urban history. They have enriched our knowledge of the complexity and diversity of prerevolutionary Russian social history, which—thanks to these and other studies—has begun to emerge from beneath what Michael

6. Particularly noteworthy among these studies are Michael Hamm, ed., *The City in Late Imperial Russia* (Bloomington, Ind., 1986); Joseph Bradley, *Muzhik and Muscovite: Urbanization in Late Imperial Russia* (Berkeley, 1985); Robert Thurston, *Liberal City, Conservative State: Moscow and Russia's Urban Crisis, 1906–1914* (New York, 1987); James Bater, *St. Petersburg: Industrialization and Change* (London, 1976); J. Michael Hittle, *The Service City: State and Townsmen in Russia, 1600–1800* (Cambridge, Mass., 1979).

Confino calls the "long shadow of the October Revolution."[7] The limitation of these studies, inherent in their approach, is their particularism. If my synthesis of Russian urban history is to prove of value, its contribution will probably be at the middle level of historical generalization, where Russian urban history occupies a place of importance equal to that of rural history and where the city is an essential feature in our understanding of Russia's unique historical experience.

7. Michael Confino, *Issues and Nonissues in Russian Social History and Historiography,* Kennan Institute occasional paper no. 165 (Washington, D.C., 1983), 7.

1

Facade Cities and Fugitive Populations

In the mid nineteenth century Russian cities were located on the fringes of European civilization. Occasional neoclassical building facades and formal street plans told of imperial ambitions to impose a Western model of the city on townspeople, most of whom lived in log cabins along muddy, smelly alleys. The shortcomings of tsarist city plans provided one visible measure of the disparity between the ideal and the real city. Throughout this history of Russian urbanism the various idealized visions of the West offer an important perspective on the contradictions and conflicts attendant on rapid urbanization in Russia, where the life of the urban population was a far cry from the plans laid for the city by various urban elites. These plans make clear the European origins of the efforts to control and guide urban development.

Europe was a potent cultural invention that suggested measures of progress (by invidious comparison) by which to judge conditions in Russian cities and to devise plans of action. This device, never openly acknowledged as such, operated elsewhere too. The bacteriologist Paul Koch, called in 1892 to witness the misery and filth of the Hamburg slums, where a cholera epidemic had broken out, summed up for the press his disgust by proclaiming: "Gentlemen, I forget that I am in Europe!"[1] His concern for public health turned a geographical expression into a con-

1. Cited in Richard Evans, *Death in Hamburg: Society and Politics in the Cholera Years* (New York, 1985), 303.

demnation of the neglect of the urban poor. In a similar sense, tsarist officials and educated Russians in the mid century possessed cultural maps on which they located the border separating civilized Europe and backward Asia within their own country. Its location fluctuated and so too did their sense of urgency to push that border eastward. Catherine II's urban policies resembled a sort of cultural crusade to bring civilization to her empire. Although Nicholas I's reign was a period of relative inaction, it carried forth Catherine's policies and proved to be a time of preparation for another wave of urban reform.

In the tsarist law code a juridical statute gave precise definition to official "cities," no matter what their size, by granting municipal government to their inhabitants. Almost all these official cities were provincial and district centers of tsarist administration because the well-ordered state that Catherine the Great and her successors sought presupposed the collaboration of townspeople in matters of imperial interests. An imposing array of duties and responsibilities were placed on townspeople in these "service cities" by a state that, as J. Michael Hittle reminds us, had great need of their assistance.[2] The empire's efforts to create orderly cities extended throughout European Russia. These efforts constituted a coherent urban strategy that left its mark on the landscape of the city and the activities of the townspeople.

But Russian urbanism also took other forms in those years—as later— and these forms escaped the control of tsarist officials. Behind the facade of imperial might bureaucratic agents of the state coped poorly with the multiple tasks that had been assigned to them, and townspeople conducted their affairs in a manner best calculated to shelter their private lives from public view. The institutional power of Nicholas I's state could ensure the submission of the population, but it could not impose its ideals of public behavior and social practices in municipal and economic affairs on the inhabitants. Resistance to the state largely took the form of passivity and inaction, a practice that I refer to as "fugitive." The conduct of urban daily life escaped tsarist control to such an extent that a few "enlightened bureaucrats" perceived it as a condemnation of Nicholaevan autocracy. The inadequacies of Nicholas's reign appeared in many areas, and the real city that was depicted in the bureaucratic inspections of the 1840s and 1850s contributed to the sense of crisis that was so pervasive among reformers at the beginning of Alexander II's reign. In the decades that followed, the

---

2. J. Michael Hittle, *The Service City: State and Townsmen in Russia, 1600–1800* (Cambridge, Mass., 1979), 240.

fugitive practices of the townspeople became an integral part of the life of urban migrants.

This study of Russian urbanism is in part the history of the visions and plans that sought to mold a city that would be worthy, in one way or another, of belonging to the Western world. However, it is also an inquiry into the practices of the urban population. These practices would shape a very different city, a city of migrants.

Cities in the Imperial Style

Although overly ambitious, Catherine II's plans for Russian cities set the framework for urbanism in the following half century. She assumed, as Robert Jones makes clear, that rigorous planning and Western architectural models would turn backward Russian towns into "centers of civilization."[3] Her extravagant rhetorical flourishes proclaimed that cities could be made—or remade—according to ideals that were adopted from the West. Her model exerted an abiding attraction among educated Russians for the nineteenth century. She prophesied that the "glories" (znamenitosti) of the architectural and street plan for one town would attract new inhabitants, and that the entire region would acquire a new life and take on a new appearance."[4] In this imperial rendering of the theme of city versus countryside, social progress followed automatically from the implementation of a rational urban plan.

As best we can assess them, the consequences of Catherine's plans in the Russian provinces were unspectacular but substantial. Administrative offices spread to provincial and district centers; garrisons gathered in the central town of each military district; archbishoprics and bishoprics brought the presence of high church dignitaries and the periodic practice of great public ceremonies into urban public life; architectural monuments glorified patriotic achievements; the facades of public and private buildings in town centers imitated the Palladian and baroque styles, albeit in plaster, of the great cities of the West. These elements of imperial urbanism were part of the panoply of autocratic power, a power that used the material and human resources of the empire to construct outposts of a peculiarly autocratic vision of civilization.

3. Robert Jones, *Provincial Development in Russia: Catherine II and Jacob Sievers* (New Brunswick, N.J., 1984), 97–98.
4. Quoted in I. I. Ditiatin, "Russkii doreformennyi gorod," in *Stat'i po istorii russkogo prava*, by I. I. Ditiatin (St. Petersburg, 1895), 14.

From this imperial perspective the city became synonymous with public order, and urban public space became the visual manifestation of this ideal. The official policy of "public orderliness" (*blagoustroistvo*) gave an autocratic character to public functions. The general supervision of urban affairs lay in the hands of provincial governors, who had the responsibility to ensure that "publicly useful measures" encouraged the "improvement in the well-being" of the townspeople who were placed under their "protection."[5] By Nicholas I's time municipal institutions had become part of the authoritarian ordering of the Russian city. For example, the governor of Vladimir province explained in the early 1840s that municipal rule had to be introduced in the new textile center of Ivanovo "for the strict enforcement of order and submission" among the town's fifteen thousand workers, who, "more than others, [are] prone to disorder."[6] The governor was little concerned with self-rule; rather, he focused on the expansion of the urban police force and the creation of municipal institutions through which the state would exercise direct control over the turbulent laboring populations of the settlement.

The visible manifestations of tsarist urbanism were embodied in city plans and in the regulations governing urban construction and public activities. The responsibilities of governors—and of the police—extended to the "orderliness and cleanliness of the streets, squares, and markets," the good condition of public buildings, street paving, and the enforcement of "the approved [city] plan and rules for building facades."[7] Architecture was to be the symbolic representation of public order, and St. Petersburg was the superlative embodiment of this urban vision. In the solemn eighteenth-century language of His Majesty's Imperial Building Commission, the architecture of St. Petersburg was to convey "a dignified appearance and grandeur [*paradnost'*]."[8] This directive was subsequently implemented using a variety of architectural styles; the last stage came in the 1840s when the railroad intruded on the capital's public space. Again following the model provided by Western Europe, the tsarist authorities hid the railroad station behind a neo-Renaissance facade. Unlike the West, however, the Petersburg version of facade planning was inserted within the larger polit-

5. Ibid., 22.

6. Quoted in P. G. Ryndziunskii, *Gorodskoe grazhdanstvo v doreformennoi Rossii* (Moscow, 1958), 498.

7. Ibid., 23.

8. Iu. Egorov, "Zastroika Peterburga," in *Istoriia russkogo iskusstva*, ed. I. Grabar (Moscow, 1962), vol. 1, pt. 1, 49; see also V. V. Kirillov, "Russkii gorod epokhi barokko (kul'turnyi i esteticheskii aspekt)," *Russkii gorod*, ed. V. Ianin (Moscow, 1983), 6:127–62.

ical ᵣroject of tsarist urbanism throughout the empire and was the center-piece of this policy.

Although the planned development of St. Petersburg was the model for the provinces, this model usually appeared in a diluted form. In new cities in frontier areas on the fringes of the empire tsarist urban objectives and plans succeeded, at least in appearance, in creating the ideal city. In recently settled areas, such as the southern Ukraine, towns like Ekaterinoslav, Potemkin's "Athens of southern Russia," retained its urban character in the mid nineteenth century "thanks solely to its importance as the major administrative point in the province," at least in the opinion of the town leaders.[9] The array of administrative offices was extensive in border cities such as Astrakhan, whose town elders listed with some pride the following governmental entities: "the port authority and admiralty of the Caspian fleet, Customs, the Salt Administration, the Committee for the Transportation of State Supplies, the Commission on Fisheries, the Military Administration of the Astrakhan Cossacks, and provincial educational institutions such as the gymnasium [and] the boys' and girls' district schools."[10] In the imperial urban vision state functions merged with the social order: symmetrical, harmonious building facades fronted on streets laid out with geometrical precision, usually radiating out from central squares, where troops from the garrison paraded and around which were located the imperial administrative buildings, the Orthodox cathedral, and the central market place. Whether on the borders or in the hinterland, these cities were frontier posts of autocratic power and European civilization.

Frequently, however, the plan of a particular city remained a paper project that was filed away with the elaborate documentation required by the ministry. Established towns, whose central areas were filled with older buildings and narrow, often tortuous streets, defied the ambitious planners and were never completely remade in the imperial style. The reconstruction of streets and reordering of building facades entailed enormous capital expenditures, to which neither the state nor the municipalities consented unless forced to do so by exceptional circumstances. Fires proved a useful tool of urban renewal: Moscow was substantially rebuilt following the

9. Ministerstvo vnutrennikh del, "Ekaterinoslavskaia guberniia," in *Ekonomicheskoe sostoianie gorodskikh poselenii evropeiskoi Rossii v 1861–1862 g.*, (St. Petersburg, 1863), 1: 4–6; these summaries of urban economic conditions were part of reports compiled by committees of local notables in 1862 in response to the request by the Ministry of Internal Affairs for information that would be used to consider municipal reform.

10. "Soobrazhenie," Tsentral'nyi gosudarstvennyi istoricheskii arkhiv [abbreviated TsGIA], *fond* [abbreviated f.] 1287, *opis'* [abbreviated op.] 37 (1862), *delo* [abbreviated d.] 2131, 10–11; these "Considerations" contain the complete reports of the committees discussed in n. 9.

devastating fire of 1812. The Moscow Building Commission received specific orders to be "guided by the plan of 1775 and carefully to ensure that all the streets and sidestreets preserve their legal dimensions."[11] The destruction of Kostroma by fire in 1773 was so complete that this old Volga trading town reemerged in the following decades in the new imperial style, an outpost of orderly, baroque city planning, standing as Catherine had intended like a "beacon of civilization" on the bluffs overlooking the river.

When not aided by natural catastrophes, the plans lost much of their force. Their implementation confronted urban poverty and the unwillingness of municipal officials to undertake any measures outside the narrow economic interests and needs of town traders and manufacturers. They had substantial justification for their lack of cooperation. One state report of 1853 warned that "expenses for upkeep and construction of public buildings" were impoverishing town budgets.[12] As required by the state, the municipality of Nizhny Novgorod devoted 10 percent of its total yearly funds to keep the six hundred oil street lamps functioning ten months of the year (and then only eighteen nights a month). Neither paving nor lighting existed in the city outskirts.[13] In these conditions public buildings, whose upkeep was a municipal responsibility, often fell into disrepair, and streets conceived on a grand scale became grandiose eyesores. Plaster fell off imitation granite walls, revealing the plain bricks beneath; in rainy weather mud rendered unpaved central squares and streets virtually impassable.

In these circumstances imperial urbanism depended on the broad authority that was granted to provincial governors both by custom and by statute. When inspired to do so, they could make the implementation of the city plan a matter of great urgency. The governor-general of the Kharkov region, S. A. Kokoshkin, an official cut to the authoritarian model so favored by Nicholas I, assumed his position in the early 1850s after a long military career. On his arrival Kharkov was a city with an expanding economy and a rapidly growing population. Its city plan, approved in 1837, had remained a dead letter until that time. Kokoshkin used his authority to rapidly construct several monumental public buildings. He kept within the letter of the law by setting out on street inspections but went far beyond the spirit of the law when he ordered wooden shanties in the town center to be torn down regardless of the fate of the inhabitants. Brick buildings with suitable classical facades appeared, and, in the place of the shanties, here and

11. I. Grabar, "Arkhitektura Moskvy," in *Istoriia russkogo iskusstva*, vol. 8, pt. 1, 188.
12. "Doklad," TsGIA, f. 869, op. 1, d. 308, 2.
13. "Soobrazhenie," TsGIA, f. 1287, op. 37, d. 264, 1–2.

there even sidewalks were constructed. Kokoshkin exiled the mayor for daring to oppose his plan to construct a new trading center, but even the governor's powers had limits.[14] The mayor became a hero to the townspeople and the number of brick buildings remained relatively few. Most important, Kharkov's expansion beyond the central area was creating a new city that Kokoshkin's imperial plan and political authority were powerless to contain.

By mid century the strict ordering given to buildings, streets, and urban space in general was doomed because the success of such plans depended on social stability and demographic stagnation. The imperial planners envisioned an urban world of order, not growth. Louis Mumford, an unsympathetic critic of all baroque planners, suggests that the spirit of such work excluded a sense of time, which proved to be detrimental to their ideal of "uniformity and standardization."[15] In the Russian plans this frame of mind led to town limits appearing on official city maps two-and-a-half miles apart as a rule. The Russian planners took little heed of local conditions or future expansion.[16] Outside the town centers the use of urban space was largely in the hands of the townspeople. When the population remained stable, enforcement posed few problems, but any rapid influx of migrants or expansion of business overwhelmed the meager resources for enforcing the regulations, and the regulations ceased to have any meaning.

In the mid nineteenth century most provincial capitals remained small, but here and there rapid population growth was already occurring. The capitals set the pace: Moscow had grown by 50 percent in the previous quarter century. A few other towns such as Saratov and Odessa expanded even more rapidly.[17] A trip in the 1840s from the center of Moscow to the newer wards quickly left behind the well-ordered city center to reach, in the words of one contemporary writer, "the area of simple, ideal existence—no paving, nothing resembling luxurious urban living, no trading enterprise. The little houses are entirely made of wood, one-story, and built according to the rules of free [i.e., unplanned] architecture."[18] The same conditions

---

14. D. Bagalei and D. Miller, *Istoriia goroda Khar'kova za 250 let ego sushchestvovaniia* (Kharkov, 1912), 2:50–51, 284–85.

15. Louis Mumford, *The Culture of Cities* (New York, 1938), 104, 127.

16. Robert Jones, "Urban Planning and the Development of Provincial Towns in Russia, 1762–1796," in *The Eighteenth Century in Russia*, ed. J. G. Garrard (Oxford, 1973), 325; the plans, it should be noted, were compiled largely by provincial and local authorities, who followed "generally accepted and representative concepts" laid down by the St. Petersburg Commission. See R. M. Gariaev, "Iz istorii pereplanirovki russkikh gorodov," *Istoriia SSSR* (November–December 1986):146.

17. Population figures are found in Thomas Fedor, *Patterns of Urban Growth in the Russian Empire during the Nineteenth Century* (Chicago, 1975), 183–202.

18. I. T. Kokorev, *Moskva sorokovykh godov* (Moscow, 1958), 176–77.

were evident wherever urban populations had begun to swell because of migration. The resulting jumble of houses, gardens, and streets, which "nowhere take the direct businesslike direction," turned Moscow into a vast "suburb or village," in the opinion of one Westerner. Unable except in the very center of the city to find "an assembly of human dwellings pressed closely together," he concluded that "Moscow is not a city."[19] His bewilderment provides a useful perspective from which to evaluate the state's urban plans. These plans relied on Western architectural models and imposed little coherence on the layout of Russian towns. Yet the depiction of Moscow as a "big village" is a disparaging exaggeration, drawn as it was (as in the above testimony) from the scornful views of outsiders, both officials and foreigners, for whom the life of the lower orders was alien and exotic. Urbanization in Russia bore little resemblance to preconceived notions of either Westerners or tsarist urban planners.

The maintenance of public order in the cities was in the hands of the tsarist police and the military. In mid century the state had not yet designated a special state agency to police urban centers. An edict of 1802 created a state police force, organized by district (uezd) units, that was responsible for both urban and rural areas. The state police were incorporated directly into the tsarist administration: they were subordinated to provincial governors but not to the municipalities. Nonetheless, municipalities had to rely on the district force to implement their statutes as well as to maintain public order, and they were obligated to fund the police assigned to their territory.[20]

The presence of two internal military forces, the Corps of Internal Guard and the gendarmerie, identified particular provincial cities as tsarist outposts. The Internal Guard, numbering nearly 150,000 soldiers in the 1840s, was distributed among eleven regional command centers and charged with "putting down acts of insubordination and riotous behavior." Peasant revolts were the unstated but obvious target of this internal army. The gendarmerie was small and active principally in surveillance, although it also operated a small cavalry force.[21] Despite the existence of these two internal forces, disorders among the urban population did not loom large in tsarist concerns. With the major exceptions of St. Petersburg and Moscow,

19. J. G. Kohl, *Russia—St. Petersburg and the Interior of the Empire* (London, 1844), 213.

20. E. Anychin, *Istoricheskii obzor razvitiia administrativno-politseiskikh uchrezhdenii v Rossii* (St. Petersburg, 1872), 224–25.

21. John Keep, *Soldiers of the Tsar: Army and Society in Russia, 1462–1874* (Oxford, 1985), 313–14.

policing the cities was an incidental affair within the broad tsarist concept of public order.

The police had originally received a somewhat paternalistic mandate toward the urban population. In her well-ordered city Catherine II conceived a universalistic role for her police: they would encourage the husband to "care for and protect his wife, the wife to be faithful in love and obedience to her husband, the parent to be imperious [*vlastitelen*] toward [his or her] children, and children to be submissive toward [their] parents."[22] However, her Germanic sense of police paternalism failed in subsequent decades to set the tone of police supervision, which was increasingly drawn to administrative duties.

In the mid nineteenth century urban police were largely concerned with enforcing the facade regulations of the city plans and looking out for their own livelihood. Their responsibilities were as broad and as ill-defined as those of the governors. They were charged with ensuring that all regulations on building construction, trade, and manufacturing were obeyed, that the streets were kept clean and passable, that temporary migrants possessed the proper documents, that army conscripts were called up when their time came, and so on. One physician serving in a provincial town recalled that the police enjoyed discretionary powers to enforce or neglect "a mass of various kinds of laws and regulations, unknown to almost everyone" and in doing so were able to hold the townspeople "in complete dependence."[23] His testimony, like that of many educated Russians in those years, was strongly colored by an abiding suspicion of all police action. For such witnesses autocratic rule and police power in the cities went hand in hand.

In mid century urban police forces were both small and poorly paid. They were woefully understaffed for the multitude of tasks that were assigned them. Understaffing was particularly acute in growing cities such as Kharkov, which had a population of nearly fifty thousand at mid century but a police force of only fifty men. Underadministered in this domain as in most others, the state continued to require that the urban population assume such petty police duties as that of night watchman. With the exception of the police chiefs (or captains in small towns) the police received miserly levels of pay. Because of their low salaries they often took advantage of their considerable powers to ensure themselves immediate personal profit. They used requests for temporary travel permits, navigation permits to boats on rivers and canals, the right to open taverns, and similar trans-

22. Ditiatin, "Russkii doreformennyi gorod," 15–16.
23. A. A. Sinitsyn, "Iz vospominanii starogo vracha," *Russkaia starina* 154 (June 1913): 498.

actions as occasions for accepting bribes. The physician previously cited observed that town traders and artisans, surrounded by administrative "unpleasantness that can trap them at every step," had the habit of "bribing everyone who shouts at them."[24]

As defined by police practices, public order in the cities was both capricious and selective. To critics of the tsarist system, it appeared to be yet another manifestation of that arbitrariness (proizvol) so characteristic of the autocratic regime. Nikolai Gogol included the town police chief among the inner circle of corrupt administrators in his play "The Inspector General"; the brutal policeman Derzhimorda ("the strangler," in a loose translation) belonged to the outer circle. In the more elegant language of the Voronezh municipal commission of 1862, the police "violate the urban peace and order that it is their duty to enforce."[25]

In these circumstances complaints about police behavior came from both tsarist authorities and municipal activists. Even the most zealous provincial officials could not overcome the inadequacies of the police. Similarly, municipalities objected not only to police abuses but also to insufficient policing of economic activities. The commerce of the port town of Rostov-on-Don was increasing rapidly in the mid 1800s, and its 1862 town commission judged its police work "far below the needs of the urban population and the business that they conduct."[26] Although state officials and civic leaders had differing priorities and assumptions about public order, they both agreed that the police were incapable of controlling the turbulent laboring population that was arriving in increasing numbers to search for work. Thus, limitations of tsarist urban planning were paralleled by the inadequacies in the ways the police enforced urban regulations.

Both the ambitious objective of creating public orderliness in the cities and the inadequacies of tsarist provincial institutions led the state to rely on the assistance of the urban population. Catherine II's Charter of Rights and Privileges Granted the Cities, issued in 1785, was conceived in a style similar to the city plans: "rights and privileges" were obligations placed on the urban electorate, designated the "city society," who were expected to participate actively in municipal affairs. Hittle's sanguine reading of this reform attributes the formation of a "new corporate basis for city society" to the charter.[27] Citizenship was determined by urban residence. The char-

24. Ibid., 498.
25. "Soobrazhenie," TsGIA, f. 1287, op. 37, d. 2146, 25.
26. Ibid., d. 2152, 212.
27. Hittle, The Service City, 228.

ter grouped the population into six separate categories (on the basis of estates, property, and occupation) for representation on the municipal council and included in the city society all propertied adult males over twenty-five, who were responsible for electing the mayor. However, the municipality fell directly under the authority of the tsarist provincial administration and its responsibilities were only those local tasks that the regime itself could not undertake, which included the regulation of commerce, building inspection, lodging garrisons, sanitation, and street paving.[28] The charter remained in effect until 1870, but the actual conduct of municipal affairs bore little resemblance to its regulations.

Until the period of the Great Reforms the role of municipalities in the urban communities was dominated by two related trends. On the one hand, the electorate, together with the pool of municipal leaders, shrank to minute proportions. On the other hand, the tsarist administration intervened increasingly in municipal affairs, undercutting the very notion of municipal autonomy and "privileges," both of which had been problematical from the start. Tsarist intervention was stimulated by the apathy of townsmen, who were discouraged by authoritarian practices from seeking to improve urban conditions. When local initiative received semiofficial sanction in the 1860s, civic activism quickly emerged in many cities. Until then municipal government operated primarily to fulfill, in the words of a nineteenth-century historian of municipal politics, "the specific demands, needs, and requirements emanating from state administrative institutions."[29] The failure of municipal governments to do so successfully created the crisis of mid-century urban rule.

The urban electorate that was to constitute the basis for corporate municipal life never came into existence. As a result, the city society itself atrophied, disappearing from municipal activities and leaving no at-large voting procedure. Of the six groups designated for representation, only three took any part at all in elections—the merchantry, the artisanry, and the petty bourgeoisie. Each sent representatives to the municipal councils in an apparently haphazard manner to fill the six seats specified in the charter. Other groups avoided participation altogether. Having no recognized place in municipal affairs, nobles and state bureaucrats boycotted elections (and also avoided municipal service), which had the effect of removing from urban affairs groups that some urban reformers of the 1860s would refer to wistfully as "the best and most honored members" of the urban

---

28. The provisions of the charter are examined in Hittle, *The Service City*, 220–29.
29. Ditiatin, "Russkii doreformennyi gorod," 23.

community.[30] At the other end of the social ladder peasants with legal urban residence refused to be registered in the city society. Representatives to town councils were chosen by meetings of the three urban estates, among whom only a handful of members bothered to participate. For example, when Yaroslavl chose a new council in 1842, only 100 of the 1,500 members of the town's bourgeoisie appeared at the elections.[31] An even smaller proportion of Moscow's merchants (120 out of 4,000) joined in elections in 1860.[32] Elections for mayor took place most often within the merchantry, the one estate society with some influence in town affairs. In 1840 the merchant elders in Kharkov invited members of the lower estates to join in choosing a new mayor but only twenty-four appeared.[33] The "well-ordered police state" of the Germanic monarchies of Central Europe relied on corporate and municipal collaboration in urban police affairs, but neither element was apparent in the autocratic state of Nicholas I.

The missing town citizenry had little reason to come forth in those years. Municipal affairs provided no inducement for civic endeavor because they consisted exclusively of obligations imposed by provincial administrators. The notion of a "self-governing community," which the reformers of the 1860s would glorify, had no place in the authoritarian political world of the preceding decades. One of these aspiring activists, examining the miserable state of public urban life on the eve of what he hoped would be a new era, complained bitterly that "the majority of the inhabitants of our cities have no consciousness of social needs," by which he meant public service. He provided, albeit disapprovingly, a key reason for their woeful failing when he added that they "consider these [public] affairs to be something completely alien to them that do not affect their personal interests, a burdensome pastime that takes them away from their own affairs."[34] Their urban world was a private, not public (obshchestvennyi), place. The civic duties that called for public participation were fulfilled in a chaotic, haphazard manner by tsarist fiat and private initiative. Imperial decrees regulated town affairs, and by this standard all municipalities managed their policies in an extralegal, if not illegal, manner.

Municipal politics made a mockery of Catherine's vision of city society,

30. "O dozvolenii dvorian," October 5, 1862, TsGIA, f. 1287, op. 37, d. 2004 (1859–65), 61.

31. Ryndziunskii, Gorodskoe grazhdanstvo, 406, table 50.

32. B. V. Zlatoustavskii, "Moskovskoe gorodskoe samoupravlenie v period reformy 60-kh godov XIX veka." (Kandidat dissertation, Moscow State University, 1953), 147.

33. Bagalei and Miller, Istoriia goroda Khar'kova 2:252.

34. "Mnenie Komissii naznachennoi Permskim gorodskim obshchestvom," TsGIA, f. 1287, op. 37, d. 2171, 5.

turning orderly procedures into a caricature of self-rule. In the absence of large numbers of voters, electoral methods bore no resemblance to free choice and majority rule. Either voters had to be rounded up without regard to proper electoral procedures or meetings turned into brawls between small groups seeking to dominate the elections. In either case elections were manipulated affairs. The reformist critic cited in the preceding paragraph painted a cruel portrait of the citizenry, "brought in almost by force," voting "as though they were carrying out a formality they could easily do without and that had been dreamed up only Heaven knows why."[35] The chaos was most apparent among the lower urban orders. The petty bourgeois society in Saratov appeared to one inspector in 1842 to be in a state of "complete disorder" where "the most important affairs" were in the hands of a few individuals.[36] Throughout the country tsarist provincial administrators and emissaries from St. Petersburg noted that only a small number of townspeople carried out the provisions of the charter, and these people did so reluctantly.

Municipal leaders came primarily from the merchant estate, the members of which were most visible and therefore most vulnerable to tsarist pressures to participate in public service. For merchants municipal office appears to have been an onerous duty that was avoided by whatever means possible. One governor from central Russia noted in 1842 that "the lack of benefits from service" leads merchants to "decline election to office . . . in almost all cities.[37] In theory some public service was obligatory, but the facade of regulations hid another world of devious private stratagems to subvert the rules. One merchant wrote that municipal service was a "trap" for his colleagues, who judged it "extremely unpleasant and dangerous" and were prepared "to pay up in order not to be elected to any sort of duties." A sufficient bribe would ensure that "a person with power could bypass all laws and regulations so that [he] would not be disturbed and would not be called to serve."[38] Merchants of the lower ranks (the second and third guilds) lacked the wealth and influence necessary to buy favors and seem to have provided the bulk of the recruits for town offices.

One consequence of this distortion of the ideal of public service was the use of municipal office for private profit. The incidence of corruption in

35. Ibid., 6.
36. "Po obozreniiu Saratova," TsGIA, f. 1287, op. 39 (1843), d. 78, 93.
37. "Po otchetam i zapiskam nachal'nikov gubernii o nedostatkakh nyneishnego ustroistva," ibid., op. 37, d. 120, 8.
38. N. Vishniakov, *Svedeniia o kupecheskom rode Vishniakovykh* (Moscow, 1911) 3:93; a history of Kharkov recounts a similar situation; see Bagalei and Miller, *Istoriia goroda Khar'kova*, 2:255.

urban administration was notorious; for example, it was the key satirical element in Gogol's play *The Inspector General,* which Nicholas I himself applauded. From the perspective of reluctant public servants the opportunities for personal profit through corruption were the only tangible reward for their onerous duty. Venality and favoritism were widespread, reflecting the private interests of officials and their "families" of supporters and protectors. Although trading fees and property taxes were insignificant affairs from the point of view of outsiders, they represented important economic considerations to local traders, artisans, and manufacturers.

The tenacity and skill of petty officials in manipulating these responsibilities were impressive to judge by the reports of the inspectors sent by the Ministry of Internal Affairs in the early 1840s. For example, by controlling fees on stalls for traders in the Tambov city market, the municipality favored local traders at the expense of peasants seeking to penetrate the urban commercial network. The inspector complained that the peasants "suffered real oppression at the hands of these middlemen" and added that the higher prices on produce "made the townspeople suffer as well." The governor sought to equalize the fees, and the police chief "tried several times to stop the abusive action of the middlemen and to establish order at the market." Both failed, however, because they were blocked by the skillful actions of the mayor and his backers. According to the inspector the mayor, who was a local miller, proved his unfitness for his position by diverting a stream running through town in order to provide water for his mill. His spirit of enterprise left "a swamp to form where the river previously ran."[39] Such actions were commonplace. Saratov's tax on commerce was set by the traders themselves, who, according to another inspector, declared "very low prices on their products" when fixing the tax rate.[40]

Property taxes, the principal source of municipal revenues, became a focal point of conflict. Tsarist officials demanded that municipalities pay various obligatory expenses, which necessitated higher tax rates, but propertied townspeople sought to keep tax rates at the lowest possible level. To avoid bitter conflict, municipalities sought as their "sole aim . . . to collect as quickly and as painlessly as possible the maximum amount of money. They consider all means to this end to be acceptable."[41] The inspectors, who brought to these affairs their "enlightened" sense of order and rational method, were deeply offended by the officials' *proizvol;* for their part they appeared intruders and trouble-makers to the protective family circles of

39. TsGIA, f. 1287, op. 39 (1843), d. 43, 58–61.
40. Ibid., d. 78, 159.
41. Ibid., d. 72, 103.

the municipal officials. The gulf between these two groups was as great as the disparity between the orderly city plans and the run-down, sprawling appearance of most towns, the grandiose vision of the civilizing city and the reality of the poor townspeople.

The gap between municipal duties and municipal deeds originated not only in the absence of "civic consciousness" but also in the prevalent perception among private interests in the towns that they received no benefits from their burdensome tax assessments. The need to fulfill obligatory tsarist tasks pushed municipal revenues up by 50 percent between 1840 and 1853.[42] Complaints by the townspeople that their taxes were excessively burdensome cannot be dismissed as self-serving. Ministry inspectors recognized the validity of excessive taxation. The Voronezh property tax, raised to 2 percent to cover growing expenses, exceeded the means of so many townspeople that "municipal officials went without their salaries for several months."[43] Once the state-imposed expenses for police, billeting troops, maintaining official buildings, and so on, were covered, very little was left over for the needs of the towns themselves. Street lighting and paving existed only in town centers, if at all. Bridges consisted of little more than logs. One tsarist inspector reported that in Tambov the bridges were so hazardous that they constituted a peril to travelers: carriages fall into the river or mud and there are "so many drowned horses [that] they are impossible to count."[44] Even allowing for some exaggeration, his lurid picture appears to have captured the condition of public services in provincial centers. Only in the capitals was there extensive paving and gas lighting along the streets. When residents of the capitals or Western visitors ventured outside St. Petersburg and Moscow, they quickly concluded that they were beyond the pale of European modernity. In terms of public life they certainly were.

Lacking both the means and the incentives to deal with urban needs, the municipalities operated primarily as inferior branches of state administration. Looking back on the prereform years, a Petersburg mayor observed that municipal officials "for many decades were free from responsibility," and, as a result, "they had long since acquired the habit of waiting for initiative and aid from the state administration, whose supervision and approval preceded every step in the activities of municipal government."[45]

---

42. "Obzor svedeniia," ibid., f. 869, op. 1 (1858), d. 262, 1.
43. TsGIA, f. 1287, op. 39, d. 65, 77.
44. Ibid., d. 43, 65–66.
45. M. M. Stasiulevich, *Desiat' let Sanktpeterburgskogo obshchestvennogo upravleniia* (St. Petersburg, 1884), v.

This situation was compatible with the authoritarian style of many tsarist officials, who were accustomed to assuming all important initiatives and who suspected insubordination in the initiatives of lower-ranking officials and citizens. In the mid 1870s P. P. Durnovo, the governor of Moscow province, deeply regretted the passing of the time when the Moscow municipality was "completely subordinated to the provincial authorities, who supervised all [of the municipality's] actions and without whose permission [the municipality] had no right to either lower or raise municipal expenses." To him effective urban public administration required that municipal officials should be "obligated to carry out unquestioningly all orders from the provincial administration."[46]

The disorder of Russian municipal rule had deeper roots in the privatization of urban life in the prereform period. An official report on Moscow municipal activities pointed to "the multitude of ancient customs and institutions that bring profits and privileges to various estates and that hide illegal actions and violations by city officials" and "block state authorities at every step."[47] In other words, a clandestine network of local officials functioned in the shadow of, and as a sort of mirror image of, tsarist authoritarianism and rationalist public order. Its purpose was to serve economic interests but these interests cannot be defined solely as "merchant" interests because the wealthy members of that estate zealously avoided any entanglement in town affairs. Merchant factions might occasionally compete for control of municipal institutions because profits were a reward for ingenious political stratagems. Family circles flourished in this environment. They provided valuable protection from higher powers and created a privatized context within which public affairs were transformed into private interests.

The Fugitive Urban Society

Tsarist policies to turn the city into the image of state power had their parallel in the social sphere in the decrees regulating rank and privileges among urban estates. The influence of tsarist officialdom, the respect accorded the hereditary nobility, and the wealth of the few first-guild merchants ensured that these groups would be preeminent within mid-century urban society. The pattern of urban social relations in the mid nineteenth century bears out Gregory Freeze's argument that in those years the "sos-

46. "Vsepoddaneishii otchet," TsGIA, f. 1281, op. 7, d. 82 (1875), 19.
47. Quoted in Zlatoustavskii, "Moskovskoe gorodskoe samoupravlenie," 107.

lovie system" had reached its peak of "group identity" and "social cohesion."[48]

Public life in the provincial capitals provided a stage for the display of uniforms and medals, the visual marks of standing within the small urban elite. The dignity and privileges associated with the merchantry (and the far smaller group of professionals who were recognized as "honorary citizens") were the autocratic model of productive, orderly, and loyal townspeople. Although the state's efforts to impose a well-defined, coherent, and stable hierarchy of power and prestige were somewhat successful, the state could not regulate the lives of the poor townspeople, much less the migrants who were beginning to swell the populations of various cities. The analogy between the state's social scheme and the tsarist urban political order can be carried one step further. In both cases the superficial appearance of compliance hid an extraordinary degree of disarray and disregard for both legal norms and state-imposed regulations. The social history of nineteenth-century Russian urbanism encompasses both a caste-like hierarchical order and disorder.

A social profile of the mid-century Russian city must rely largely on official reports, which attempted to take account of urban activities within the context of tsarist regulations on residence, estate membership, and so on. The apparent precision of the information in these reports is misleading: too often they offered the fallacious precision of Chichikov's "dead souls." Police reports contributed to the appearance of social order by providing precise figures for individual estates and total population in each town. They constitute the sole measure of urban population trends until the imperial census of 1897. At best these police reports are crude approximations, but their demographic data are useful in suggesting the modest level of mid-century urbanization. Only three cities had populations of over one hundred thousand (St. Petersburg, Moscow, and Odessa) and only fifty (of the six hundred urban areas officially classified as cities) were over twenty thousand.[49] Because almost all of the towns in the latter group were provincial capitals one can conclude that in the preindustrial era city size was largely a function of proximity to tsarist administrative activities, on which much of the population depended directly or indirectly for their livelihood. With respect to population size as well as other characteristics, then, the Russian city of that time was a tsarist outpost.

Official reports included figures for both "permanent" residents, en-

48. Gregory Freeze, "The *Soslovie* (Estate) Paradigm and Russian Social History," *American Historical Review* 91 (February 1986):24.

49. Ryndziunskii, *Gorodskoe grazhdanstvo*, 369, table 43.

rolled in the proper corporate organization ("society") of their estate, and the "temporary" residents, primarily peasants but also townspeople of the lower orders (artisans and the petty bourgeoisie) who were born outside the town limits. The mobility of the lower orders in the cities defied accurate police supervision. Moscow's passport office registered 142,000 temporary residents in 1859, nearly two-thirds of whom were peasants.[50] Most temporary residents were *otkhodniki*, migrants seeking short-term jobs. In 1859 *otkhodniki* made up over one-fourth of the total recorded population of Moscow, and by the 1870s they increased to nearly two-thirds of the city's inhabitants. The apparent precision of these police reports, however, did not signify that the entire population was properly registered. Occasional official complaints tell another story of missing "souls" who lived beyond the pale of tsarist regulations.

Black Sea ports, in growing need of stevedores for loading grain shipments, constituted a vast area of meager surveillance. The lure of work created a chaotic labor market where, even in conditions of serfdom, extralegal migration often occurred. Odessa police reported capturing 4,500 "fugitives" between 1849 and 1852, but one may assume that many more went undiscovered. The police prefect (*gradonachal'nik*) of Taganrog, on the sea of Azov, complained about the poor work of his police in this area. He was aware that illegal migration was a problem of large dimensions but unimpressed by the figures supplied by his police, whose "catch" (*ulov*) of unregistered migrants was far too low in his judgment. His solution was to request more police.[51] I assume that other areas such as Moscow and St. Petersburg had a similar hidden migrant society. In Moscow one uncontrolled migrant community existed thanks to the ingenuity of the Fedoseevtsy, an Old Believer group whose bonds were forged over generations of persecution. They cared for needy, undocumented brethren by making use of the "dead souls" that Nikolai Gogol found so intriguing. Purchasing the documents of dead petty bourgeois Muscovites, they transferred the names to their own fugitives, who automatically enrolled in that estate corporation.[52] Thus, ingenuity combined with venality and insufficient staffing to create another hidden dimension to the supposedly orderly cities of statutes and plans.

The motive for the risky violation of police regulations was uniformly

50. B. N. Kazantsev, *Rabochie Moskvy i Moskovskoi gubernii v seredine XIX veka* (Moscow, 1976), 61.

51. Ryndziunskii, *Gorodskoe grazhdanstvo*, 357–58.

52. P. G. Ryndziunskii, *Utverzhdenie kapitalizma v Rossii, 1850–1880* (Moscow, 1978), 472–74.

similar: the desperate search for work on the part of the mass of poor laborers, both urban and rural. Urban impoverishment was general throughout European Russia, although it was probably most acute in the cities and towns in the Pale of Settlement. During Nicholas I's reign the contraction of the boundaries of the Pale and the restrictions placed on Jewish employment in rural areas put enormous pressures on the urban labor market and led Jewish townspeople to avoid registration by all possible means. Official documentation meant fees and taxes, and to avoid making these payments an unknown number of Jewish families preferred legal nonexistence.

The absurdities of the police regulations were apparent to observers outside the Jewish community. When census time came, apartments and houses were missing their Jewish residents, whose presence the police conveniently overlooked in return for suitable bribes. Birth records in the 1850s reveal a sudden fall in Jewish births after a thirty-kopek registration fee was introduced. As a result of this fee, in Vilna almost twice as many Jews officially died in the following years as were born. One tsarist official commented ironically that "if, God forbid, this [trend] should continue, in 1875 Vilna will have no Jews." On a more serious note another official complained in 1861 that "it is no less difficult to ascertain the number of Jews today than in the time of King David."[53]

In these conditions the legal precision of legally defined urban estates and functions bore little resemblance to social reality. In the opinion of one historian the lowest merchants' guild appeared large only because so many traders falsified their figures of working capital to meet the criterion for admission. Merchant honors were not what mattered; rather, they were making a desperate effort to spare their sons twenty-five years of military service, which was not imposed on merchants. When this law was changed in the 1860s, the sudden fall in merchant membership suggested to one historian that perhaps two hundred thousand individuals had paid their merchant fees solely for this purpose.[54]

Among the lower orders the petty bourgeoisie (the approximate translation of the Russian term *meshchanstvo*) acquired a reputation among educated Russians for servility and obscurantism; its members were thought to be the epitome of all that defied the hopes of educated Russians for a civilized city that would be a beacon of Western culture. In the opinion of one critic of the autocratic system the petty bourgeoisie was the refuge

53. Quoted in Michael Stanislawski, *Tsar Nicholas I and the Jews: The Transformation of Jewish Society in Russia, 1825–1855* (Philadelphia, 1983), 161–62.
54. I. I. Ditiatin, *Ustroistvo i upravlenie gorodov Rossii* (Iaroslavl, 1877), 2:228–29.

of retired soldiers, beggars, bankrupt merchants, and all others "for whom there was no assigned place in that cursed caste society [v zakoldovannom soslovnom gosudarstve].[55] The disdain he showed for this estate was shared by tsarist administrators, who were empowered to apply to them "all the restrictions on mobility from place to place that applied to peasants."[56] The members of the petty bourgeoisie, which also included those who belonged to the smaller artisan estate, constituted about one-half of the population of provincial towns, and the "typical" townsperson of mid-century Russia was from this estate.

The salient characteristics of the petty bourgeoisie were the constant struggle with poverty and the desperate search for work. In certain respects it closely resembled the peasantry. Its members, placed in a semiservile status in terms of taxes, conscription, and passport requirements, took whatever trades or employment they could find to keep body and soul together, including working as farm laborers. Unlike the enserfed peasantry, its members might hope to escape by economic enterprise or state service, but in reality these opportunities were open to very few. Their lives were given over to work, and from the perspective of their practices the city was a work place, a pattern that was reinforced later by the massive influx of peasant migrants. The readiness of the members of the petty bourgeoisie to move in search of work was obvious to the urban leaders, who repeatedly cited the official figures of migration out of their towns to illustrate the impoverishment of their populations. The city commission of the upper-Volga town of Tver noted that in 1862 over one thousand petty bourgeois residents took out passports, which permitted absences of six months to a year. This massive departure, they explained laconically, was "indispensable even though the petty bourgeois [migrants] earn no more than thirty rubles a year" because "the petty bourgeois [residents] here live in extreme poverty and cannot even pay their taxes."[57]

Despite their appearance of castelike rigidity, estate regulations did not define precise limits to the activities of these lowly townspeople. The efforts of the state to isolate the artisanry as a separate corporate unit proved futile. The restrictions failed to control handicraft operations or to ensure proper employment to artisans. When a state inspector visited the town of Tula, he found such "absurd" variations in the registered number of guild

55. S. V. Bakrushin, Maloletnie nishchie i brodiagi v Moskve: Istoricheskii ocherk (Moscow, 1913), 17.

56. Ryndziunskii, Gorodskoe grazhdanstvo, 23.

57. Ministerstvo vnutrennikh del, "Tverskaia guberniia," in Ekonomicheskoe sostoianie 2:4–5.

masters from one year to the next (variations of over 100 percent) that he concluded that a "conspiracy [*zlonamerenie*] to hide the truth" must exist.[58] In less moralistic terms his findings suggest that urban artisans functioned in large measure outside the purview of the legal corporations. This phenomenon was most evident in the cities of the Pale. In Minsk the president of the artisan society complained that "affairs are such that any Jew hardly knowing his business calls himself a master, taking on work and apprentices." Adopting the official tone of a tsarist official, he warned that "disorder is spreading, for no one trusts anyone else."[59] Thus, tsarist efforts to construct their cities on the foundation of public orderliness could not overcome the human obstacles put in their way by the working population.

Poverty was the overriding concern of the petty bourgeoisie, and tsarist regulations could not contain their struggle for livelihood. Estate regulations on artisan activities were largely irrelevant. Many handicrafts were operated by "temporary artisans," that is, people from other estates. Few hereditary guild members actually practiced a trade. Three-fourths of the 12,600 artisans registered in the corporate society of St. Petersburg worked "as a rule in domestic service, as guards, errand boys, dispatch boys, etc."[60] In the quieter provincial centers any work at hand constituted the daily life of the urban poor.

In these circumstances the official barrier separating rural and urban estates dissolved at the level of daily life. Peasants sought employment legally and illegally in the city, competing as traders as well as laborers, and poor townspeople sought work in the fields on either private land around towns or estates. The reports from the 1862 urban commissions frequently noted the importance of rural labor as a source of livelihood for urban workers. The tsarist administration itself recognized the vital role that cultivated lands around provincial towns played in sustaining the urban population. The city of Saratov had an abundance of surrounding farm land, and the poor townspeople turned to agricultural work by choice because in the words of one observer, they judged their legal right to trade and artisanry a "burden" and valued land as their best income.[61] In other, less fortunate urban centers, members of the petty bourgeoisie relied even

58. "Po revizii," TsGIA, f. 1287, op. 39 (1845), d. 72, 39–40.

59. Cited in A. F. Vishnevskii, "Sotsial'no-ekonomicheskoe razvitie gorodov Belorussii v period krizisa feodal'izma" (Kandidat dissertation, State University of Minsk, 1973), 67.

60. K. A. Pazhitnov, *Problema remeslennykh tsekhov v zakonodatel'stve russkogo absoliutizma* (Moscow, 1952), 125–26.

61. I. A. Gan, *O nastoiashchem byte meshchan Saratovskoi gubernii* (St. Petersburg, 1860), 27.

more heavily on farming. In the opinion in 1842 of the minister of finance, without access to city land, "they would die from hunger."[62]

Poverty was only one explanation that the authorities used to explain the existence of the fugitive urban community. Outsiders who ventured into the provinces or even into the poorer neighborhoods of the major cities claimed to be overwhelmed by the stench (*zlovonie*) and the squalor (*griazn'*) that assailed their senses in streets and courtyards. Encouraged by the contemporary medical theory of "miasma," officials and observers easily associated these peculiar and repugnant qualities of poor townspeople with the prevalence among the population of infectious diseases. St. Petersburg itself, whose official death rate in those years was forty-seven per thousand, had the reputation of being one of the most unhealthy cities of Europe.[63] Most frightening to contemporaries were the cholera epidemics, the first of which occurred in 1830–31, the second in 1848. These epidemics struck the urban areas with special virulence, attacking, in the words of an English physician, "the lower classes of people, the ill-fed, ill-clothed, living in low and damp houses."[64] This description, which was drawn from his observations in Moscow, fit any of the mid-century towns.

The differences in social standing between the well-to-do and the poor townspeople appeared not only in official discrimination between privileged and unprivileged but also in a cultural language of disorder, disease, and misery that located the urban poor beyond the limits of Western urban civilization. These townspeople were absent from urban public life, without voice in municipal elections, and beyond the borders of the meager print culture of these towns. Urban disorder and poverty were important indicators of backwardness to educated Russian contemporaries, who judged their cities by Western cultural standards. Their awareness of the squalor and stench of the living conditions of the urban poor was typical of contemporary Western thought on the danger posed by urbanization.[65] Their manner of explaining these dismaying conditions, however, was peculiarly Russian. Heeding Western comments and their own admiration for Western civilization, they concluded that conditions among the urban population in their country were so inferior to those in the West that these places ought not—except for formal police and administrative reasons—to be labeled cities. One tsarist report of the early 1860s examining the statutes

62. Cited in Ditiatin, *Ustroistvo*, 340.

63. *Statisticheskii ezhegodnik Sanktpeterburga* (St. Petersburg, 1888), 130.

64. F. B. Hawkins, *History of the Epidemic Spasmodic Cholera of Russia* (London, 1831), 215.

65. See Alain Corbin, *The Foul and the Fragrant* (Cambridge, Mass., 1986), esp. chap. 9.

governing the artisans in the country concluded that "in our country cities are distinguished from villages purely by formal, official differences."[66] This oft-quoted judgment, which was intended to spur reforms for urban development, used the image of the village both to criticize facade planning and to lament the level of urban life in the empire.

Although the association of towns with villages proved a tenacious rhetorical device among educated Russians, it ignored the practices that made mid-century towns distinctly urban places on the country's social map. Urban life contained its peculiar type of misery. The pervasive instability of everyday life permeated economic and social relations. One Russian author of the 1840s, seeking to give his fiction a suitably realistic tone, plunges his readers into the world of the laboring population in his hometown, Saratov. In his grim inversion of estate privileges poverty is "hereditary." The tale centers on a petty bourgeois family living in "the poorest section of town filled with little houses, hovels, and cabins scattered here and there" in an atmosphere of "stench and foul gases." Their cottage, which resembles a decrepit log cabin, houses the father, an unskilled laborer working as a stevedore at the port, the mother, who finds summer work in the truck gardens, and six children. Their furnishings consist of a stove, benches, and wooden chairs. The family's story turns into a tragedy when the father drowns while working at the port, and, shortly thereafter, the mother and five children die in the cholera epidemic. At the end of the story the one surviving son confronts a future as bleak as the one his parents faced before him.[67] This author's imaginary city is a timeless place of labor; property, privileges, and estate honors belong to another world.

From this perspective the best the city could offer was a slight measure of personal security, embodied in personal possessions and property. Vissarion Belinsky captured the tangible immediacy of this private world when he wrote of his native Moscow that "the dream of every Muscovite is to have his own house, even if it is only one with three windows [i.e., the poorest dwelling]. It may be poor, but it is his own, and with a courtyard he may be able to raise chickens and even a calf. But the most important thing is that under this little house is a cellar—what more could he wish for?"[68] Belinsky's picture fits any town in European Russia. For the townspeople this dream embodied the essence of their idealized city. They rele-

66. Quoted in P. G. Ryndziunskii, *Krest'ianskaia promyshlennost' v poreformennoi Rossii* (Moscow, 1966), 70.

67. S. A. Makashin, "Nasledstvennaia bednost'," in *Rasskazy o starom Saratove*, by S. A. Makashin (Saratov, 1937), 165–79.

68. V. Belinskii, "Peterburg i Moskva," in *Fiziologiia Peterburga* (St. Petersburg, 1845), 1:40–41.

gated grandiose palaces and public orderliness to the domain of state power and privilege. The satisfaction of immediate needs and a modest level of private wealth were the limits of their hopes for the future.

The ownership of a hut or cottage represented an element of stability but was beyond the means of about half the urban population. The official records of housing, which were compiled for tax purposes, suggest that even those who owned a humble dwelling were privileged. In the early 1860s the city of Saratov counted six thousand houses for a population of about sixty-five thousand. Of these six thousand houses, one-third were too poor to be included in the tax roles.[69] The remaining four thousand housed the town's relatively well-to-do traders, manufacturers, and privileged townspeople. Below the house owners was a laboring population with so few abiding ties to the orderly society of estates that they formed a separate, fugitive city. This picture fits one characterization of petty bourgeois society in Shuia, a textile town in northern Russia: its "very poor" petty bourgeois population lived in families of "five to seven members," most of whom were "without their own home."[70]

The prevalence of such conditions, however, did not turn these areas into large villages masquerading as towns; the lives of these townspeople were focused on their own private concerns and local affairs. In mid century the outer limits of the urban world of the lower classes followed the contours of the neighborhood; in the neighborhoods the figures of authority were the parish priest and the police. Activities there revolved around the market, the tavern, the church, and the public bath (which by mid century had become accessible to the common people).[71] The carnival gatherings of holidays (gulian'ia) offered simple but tangible images of other lives both within and beyond the city.

By comparison with the countryside literacy was relatively high in the city. Lacking direct data, our conclusions depend on estimates based on the 1897 census. By these calculations probably half of the men and one-fourth of the women in mid-century towns could read and write.[72] Although literacy levels were far below those of Western cities, literacy had a definite place in the functional and liturgical practices of Russian townspeople. For

69. Ministerstvo vnutrennikh del, "Saratovskaia guberniia," in Ekonomicheskoe sostoianie 2:4.

70. Cited in B. N. Vasil'ev, "Formirovanie fabrichno-zavodskogo proletariata tsentral'nogo promyshlennogo raiona Rossii, 1820–1890" (Doctoral dissertation, Novocherkassk Pedagogical Institute, 1972), 1:161–62.

71. M. G. Rabinovich, Ocherki etnografii russkogo feodal'nogo goroda: Gorozhane, ikh obshchestvennyi i domashnii byt (Moscow, 1978), 131–32.

72. B. N. Mironov, "Gramotnost' v Rossii, 1797–1917 gg.," Istoriia SSSR (July–August 1983):149.

all but the small group of officials and intellectuals print culture consisted of the practical affairs of commerce and the spiritual matters of faith. The need for education could not be met by the state's network of district elementary schools, which consisted of only one or two small schools in the provincial capitals. Rather, education was achieved informally through a network of schools that owed nothing to the regime. For example, although the district school in the Volga town of Rybinsk taught only a handful of boys, almost all the town's merchant and petty bourgeois adult men were literate.[73] Presumably, their skills were acquired through informal instruction by priests or, more often, deacons in the so-called free schools, which taught reading, the prayers, the Psalter, numeracy, and writing.[74] Literacy was useful in urban commerce and reassuring to the faithful. Its role in city life did not extend beyond the narrow horizons of work and Christian dogma, or so we may presume, for example, from Gorky's portrait of his grandfather, who was born in the 1820s or 1830s. Although lettered in the Orthodox prayers, the old man appeared to Gorky to be incapable of even understanding their meaning.[75] No penny press existed in the mid century to provide townspeople with lurid stories of urban adventures, tragic or comic. Chapbooks on religious themes remained the predominant reading besides the Bible. In this respect urban practices bore some resemblance to those of the villages, where far fewer adults (perhaps one in ten) were literate. But the readiness of townspeople to create their own system of instruction, which was indicated by their higher literacy rates, was a special mark of the city. Town dwellers developed what one sociologist has termed a "scriptural economy," adapting learning to their own perceived needs and daily lives without regard to either the state's criteria of public education or the standards of enlightenment propounded by the "thick journals" of the intellectuals.[76]

The criteria by which one might define what was uniquely urban in the practices and conditions that were prevalent in mid-century Russian towns are varied and complex. Facile references to administrative decrees on civic duties only repeat the wishful thinking of the tsarist administrators; equally simplistic references to towns as "villages" make an invidious comparison between Russia and a somewhat idealized West, which is also mis-

73. Ryndziunskii, *Gorodskoe grazhdanstvo*, 405.

74. Rabinovich, *Ocherki etnografii russkogo feodal'nogo goroda*, 274.

75. Maxim Gorky, *Autobiography*, trans. I. Schneider (New York, 1949), esp. 11–22, 69–73.

76. The concept of distinct "scriptural economies" is contrasted to the general category of "culture" in M. de Certeau, *The Practices of Everyday Life*, trans. Steven Rendall (Berkeley, 1984), 131–33.

placed. Both standards are based on the experience and perceptions of an elite for whom the fugitive city of the mid century was an alien territory. Although we should not accept either of these elite views of the Russian city in their entirety, neither should we reject them out of hand. The preoccupation of intellectuals and administrators with Western models set a standard for urban cultural and civic development, and their own activities helped to spread these ideals. St. Petersburg and Moscow provided a refuge for people like Belinsky, and in small ways the provincial capitals felt the influence of the national capitals.

Similarly, one should not ignore the impact of tsarist activities and investments on urban life because both brought the power and resources of the autocracy to the urbanism of facade planning. For example, the state's capital investments in transportation were a key part of the commercial life of the urban population. These expansionist policies operated within strict limits. Nicholas's finance minister, Count Kankrin, had serious reservations regarding the disruptive social impact of railroads, warning at one point of the dangers of increasing "the mobility of an already insufficiently settled population" and thereby undermining the "indispensable social hierarchy."[77] His argument was intended to restrain state spending, but also revealed his awareness that social stability and economic development were incompatible objectives.

State policies and Western models were still feeble in the face of obstacles that in some respects resembled those that characterize so-called Third World cities in the twentieth century. Private capital was in short supply, and the skills associated with industrial enterprise were rare. Labor was overabundant, which led to endemic underemployment among the urban workforce. The life of the laboring population was extremely insecure. Also, the meager educational system contributed to the creation of many formidable cultural barriers. These conditions confounded tsarist efforts to impose its rigid estate system on urban society. Industriousness and enterprise were present, but they were constrained by the instability and insecurity of daily life. Work of whatever sort, wherever it might be located, found many ready laborers, who accepted employment at a pittance. The need for minimal literacy was met by the services of clerics in free schools (or by the Jewish elders among the Yiddish-speaking population in the Pale). Traditional religious beliefs, mixed with popular superstition, held sway over the fugitive population; deference to the powerful and

---

77. Cited in A. M. Solov'eva, *Zheleznodorozhnyi transport vo vtoroi polovine XIX veka* (Moscow, 1975), 39.

wealthy was the rule. "Squalor" and "stench" marked recognizable barriers, as effective as estate regulations on rank and honor in separating the laboring population from the elite.

Although urban misery was ever-present in mid century, the city was not a static world of unrelieved despair. The movement of migrants from village to town and from city to city pointed to the potential opportunities that the urban labor market presented. The economic historian Olga Crisp has emphasized the importance of the role, despite serfdom and state mercantilist regulations, of enterprise and innovation in the mid-century Russian economy.[78] Her observation applies particularly to urban Russia. The mobility of the population was becoming increasingly important to the economic livelihood of the country's urban centers and in certain areas had created an established network. The 1862 commission in the upper Volga city of Yaroslavl noted that "as many or more townspeople leave for work elsewhere as there are migrants arriving, and almost all who leave know what [occupations] are needed in one or another part of Russia." One-tenth of the town's adult men had obtained travel documents the previous year.[79] A similar trend was apparent among the province's peasants, who were already making a name for themselves as innkeepers in St. Petersburg and Moscow. The regularity in the moves of the fugitive population suggests that ambition as well as desperation were responsible for the migration. Although limited in scope, economic expansion was causing cities to grow.

Commerce was the principal motor of economic life in urban areas, and to the end of the century it remained the sector that was most responsible for the expansion of the Russian urban economy. Its importance was apparent in the findings of the first tsarist survey of urban conditions, which was launched in the early 1840s. One inspector in the upper Volga region calculated that in the town of Yaroslavl "local manufacturing and 'local handicrafts' account for only one-tenth of the income of the residents." His dubious efforts at statistical precision aside, his findings suggest that regional commerce was crucial to the economic livelihood of the city.[80] In 1857 a correspondent for the Imperial Geographical Society noted that in Orel "most city dwellers engage in petty trade, buying up from peasants farm goods and rural handicraft products for sale at a small profit to the

78. Olga Crisp, *Studies in Russian Economic History* (London, 1976), esp. 70–72, 92–95.

79. Ministerstvo vnutrennikh del, "Iaroslavskaia guberniia," in *Ekonomicheskoe sostoianie* 2:6–7.

80. Ryndziunskii, *Gorodskoe grazhdanstvo*, 228, table 18.

local inhabitants."[81] However, competition was keen with peasant traders, who, if one can believe the bitter report of the Briansk commission of 1862, were "wealthier than third-guild merchants."[82] This complaint hints at the substantial rewards open to enterprising traders, for whom estate regulations were apparently largely irrelevant.

Although small-scale trade and manufacturing provided work for most urban inhabitants, the expansion of urban economic activity depended above all on regional and national opportunities. By mid century urban leaders were already thinking of their towns in the context of the potential national transportation network, which if inaccessible to their traders, condemned their economic affairs to stagnation. The 1862 reports on urban economic conditions repeatedly lamented inadequate transportation links to national markets. This factor was the explanation the Voronezh commission used to explain their town's miserable level of trade despite the area's richness "in grain products and, generally, in agricultural production." The report noted that the Moscow road, "begun thirty years ago, is still not completed," and the town's exclusion from the "proposed network of railroads" promises "unfortunate effects on the future."[83] The Voronezh commission's perception of economic needs was clearly changing, and at the heart of their vision of the future was the necessity to forge links between the city and larger markets in their country and beyond its borders.

In mid century the routes to the distant emporiums were the country's waterways. A growing network of canals provided key connections among rivers and with bordering seas. The sole important rail line in operation in the early 1860s was the Moscow-Petersburg railroad. Railroad construction represented a major capital investment, one that the state could ill afford, particularly at a time when it was already engaged in important investments in water transportation. The major south-to-north shipping route in Russia passed from the Volga through a series of canals and locks to St. Petersburg. An earlier waterway through Tver had become obsolete and inadequate for commercial needs. Count Kankrin financed a new route, the Mariinsky system, which linked Rybinsk on the Volga with the Neva below Lake Ladoga. This system was capable of accommodating deep-water barges.[84] Even though it quickly proved insufficient, when it opened in

---

81. Quoted in Rabinovich, *Ocherki etnografii russkogo feodal'nogo goroda*, 40.

82. "Soobrazhenie," TsGIA, f. 1287, op. 37 (1863), d. 1267, 121.

83. Ministerstvo vnutrennikh del, "Voronezhskaia guberniia," in *Ekonomicheskoe sostoianie* 1:4.

84. F. M. Listengurt, "Rol' ekonomichesko-geograficheskogo polozheniia v istoricheskom razvitii gorodov Iaroslavlia, Kalinina i Rybinska" (Kandidat dissertation, Moscow Pedagogical Institute, 1960), 115–20.

1852 it represented a substantial incentive to commerce and opened new opportunities in bulk trade to ambitious traders.

The new trends in urban commercial activity were apparent principally in a few towns along the southern seaports and the Volga river. By mid century the grain trade in these places was beginning to take on a magnitude that promised a great future to the urban business elite. The enthusiastic tone of the 1862 Saratov commission's report cannot be explained simply as boosterism; the report claimed that "everyone trades here who has the money to pay the fee for a market stall or for a boat or who has strong arms and some rubles to spend." The authors, aware of a basic change in economic relations, explained that this trade was not the product of periodical local fairs, whose revenues "over the past twenty years" had been "diminishing regularly."[85] Rather, Europe was the key factor in the increased grain trade. The market for agricultural produce was spreading far beyond the confines of urban Europe. It reached as far as the traders in cities such as Saratov and held out the lure of commercial operations and profits that were far beyond their previous experience. In ports such as Odessa major Western grain firms had already founded their own offices; further inland Russian dealers assumed the role of middlemen for this international market. On a note of capitalist modernity Saratov's town leaders claimed in 1862 that their city was entering "the ranks of those cities that constitute the links in a vast network uniting all the important manufacturing areas in a European-wide trade network."

The basis of this economy was grain, which was brought in from the surrounding hinterlands in winter and milled in the town's fifty flour mills or stored in over three hundred grain warehouses, then either shipped upstream to the capitals or, more commonly, south to the Sea of Azov.[86] Saratov's scale of trade was exceptional among inland cities in those years, but the expansion of national trade was already notable. The best indicator of this trend is the turnover of goods at the yearly fair in Nizhny Novgorod, whose total revenues in 1862 exceeded one hundred million rubles, a record level and over four million rubles greater than the previous year.[87] The economies of cities scattered over European Russia were on the verge of rapid expansion and diversification, and the principal force for this

85. Ministerstvo vnutrennikh del, "Saratovskaia guberniia," in *Ekonomicheskoe sostoianie* 2:6, 8.

86. Ibid., 4–6.

87. Ministerstvo vnutrennikh del, "Nizhegorodskaia guberniia," in *Ekonomicheskoe sostoianie* 1:5.

event was commercial exchange such as that moving up and down the Volga.

Trade still came to most towns on a seasonal basis; in the summertime it brought traders, boatmen, and laborers in great numbers throughout the river network. Key transshipment points such as Rybinsk on the upper Volga were for a few months transformed by the arrival of so many boats that, as the town's 1862 commission claimed, the river is "almost entirely covered with ships from one side to the other, and at times it is possible without much trouble to cross the Volga as though across a bridge." A small town of eleven thousand permanent inhabitants, its population swelled each year with the arrival of forty thousand migrants, principally seasonal dock workers but also merchants. Traders and shippers conducted their affairs in the local taverns, not in the new commodity exchange building. The laborers were not provided any facilities for living by the town, so they formed a fugitive port city of their own.[88] Observers did not recognize that these temporary urban dwellers and their activities belonged to an urban way of life. The summertime presence of these workers had none of the permanence that was attached to the corporate city; rather, it resembled the encampments of nomads gathered briefly before dispersing again across the steppes.

Largely missing from mid-century Russian urban economic activity were industry and a factory labor force. A few industrial settlements that resembled European textile towns had begun to emerge in Moscow province, where over half of the country's textile factory workers lived. In Vladimir province, northeast of Moscow, the new factory settlement of Ivanovo Voznesensk had forty-five textile factories in 1850, and nearby Shuia possessed seventeen factories and 4,300 workers.[89] These centers, which were important to the early process of industrialization, were exceptional among the empire's towns. At this time (as later) commerce, not industry, was the most powerful motor in reshaping economic relations and the social dynamics of Russian urban expansion.

By mid century the ranks of merchants had grown; enrollment in this estate was a business necessity as well as a mark of standing within the community. A few entrepreneurs in Moscow and elsewhere had succeeded in amassing fortunes in the textile industry, creating family dynasties (for example, the Krestovnikov, Guchkov, Khludov, and Morozov families)

---

88. Ministerstvo vnutrennikh del, "Iaroslavskaia guberniia," in *Ekonomicheskoe sostoianie*, 2:34–35.
89. Vasil'ev, "Formirovanie," 280, table 32; see also Ministerstvo vnutrennikh del, "Vladimirskaia guberniia," in *Ekonomicheskoe sostoianie* 1:64–66.

whose rise to wealth is emblematic of Russia's early capitalist class. Alfred Rieber suggests that they were not representative of the merchant class, which in those years remained "trapped in traditional patterns of behavior."[90] His judgment makes "tradition" a form of invidious comparison between Russian merchants and Western bourgeois and reiterates the social stereotype of the Russian merchant that was shared by Russian nobles and intellectuals. One may better understand trading and manufacturing practices by examining the economic and social constraints and obstacles that confronted the protoindustrialists.

The condemnation of the merchant represented a manner of judging the shortcomings of the mid-century city that implicitly took a Western and elitist perspective. The memoirs of the Moscow nobleman V. Golitsyn stressed the barriers dividing Muscovites. His most abiding image of the prereform era was one of the "isolation" of the noble and merchant elite and their disdain for the "lower" ranks of the petty bourgeoisie and the artisans. Speaking from his perspective as a nobleman, he explained that the estates were divided by "mutual distrust, diffidence, a certain envy of one another, and fear of compromising oneself by familiar relations with people from another estate."[91] A similar judgment appeared in literary form from Vissarion Belinsky, who suggested that the most appropriate image of the Moscow merchant was a house with a walled courtyard "similar to a fortress, ready to withstand a long siege." Behind those walls "family solidarity [semeistvo]" mattered most. "Nowhere," he concluded, "is the city visible."[92] Looking for a literary and civic society, he judged the mid-century Russian city by Western standards of urbanism.

Social barriers were perhaps less impenetrable, but no less perceptible, among the lesser urban ranks. Although estate rank meant little in everyday urban life among the laboring population, it retained the full force of tsarist statute and constituted a formidable barrier to legal advancement in society. The admission into Moscow's petty bourgeois corporate society of six thousand peasants in a fifteen-year period in the mid century suggests that even this lowly estate was attractive to peasants.[93] Similarly, a small measure of status and economic security was accessible to the few townspeople who were successful in entering the state bureaucracy. In those years the principal importance of urban public schools appeared to be as

90. Alfred Rieber, *Merchants and Entrepreneurs in Imperial Russia* (Chapel Hill, N.C., 1982), 24.

91. V. Golitsyn, "Moskva v semidesiatykh godakh," *Golos minuvshego* (May–December 1919):119–20.

92. Belinskii, "Peterburg i Moskva," 45.

93. Zlatoustavskii, *Moskovskoe gorodskoe samouprovlenie*, 147.

paths into state service. One correspondent for the Imperial Geographical Society remarked, somewhat disdainfully, that "a certain group of townspeople put their children in schools because the boys from these schools sometimes become clerks in state offices and thereby receive without examination the lowest administrative rank."[94] Social exclusiveness operated even within the schools. The two Voronezh district schools catered to two distinct publics. In one, the sons of merchants and petty bourgeois predominated in a student body of forty-seven; in the other, one-half of the sixteen pupils were sons of state bureaucrats.[95] The small number of youth enrolled in these schools was typical for most district schools. It reminds us that the opportunities for advancement were insignificant and that any expectations for an escape from the poverty and insecurity that were typical of urban life were largely illusory.

The idea of another city of equality of conditions and opportunity only existed in the dreams—or nightmares—of a few visionary Russians such as Belinsky. The potential impact of the expansion of schooling and of business interests on social rank was profoundly unsettling. This prospect filled one observer with dismay. A participant in the urban survey of 1862 in his Belorussian town of Mogilev, he prepared a separate report that warned of dire consequences if conditions in the Russian city became such that "wealth and education give greater rights than [official] privilege. Presently, we see many merchants and petty bourgeois who enjoy greater advantages and esteem from society than nobles. We see nobles placed in the midst of poor petty bourgeois and other ranks; [the nobles are] in no way superior to them and [they are] denied any honors."[96] His fears of the subversive influence of "wealth and education" were in large measure a projection of the Western trend toward a democratic society (a term not used in his essay but arguably one that was very much on his mind) in which estate ranks would no longer segregate privileged from unprivileged townspeople. The presence of déclassé nobles living among the urban "rabble" was deeply offensive to conservatives, for whom the social disorder and administrative chaos evident in the towns of the empire represented isolated failings of a valid autocratic system.

This inconsistency, however, was an affair of great importance to critics

---

94. Cited in Rabinovich, *Ocherki etnografii russkogo feodal'nogo goroda*, 280.
95. "Obozreniia obshchestvennogo khoziaistva goroda Voronezha," TsGIA, f. 1287, op. 39, d. 65, 62–63.
96. "Mnenie," TsGIA, f. 1287, op. 37, d. 1262, 60; excerpts were included in the Ministry of Interior's compilation of provincial reports: Ministerstvo vnutrennikh del, *Materialy otnosiashcheisia do novogo obshchestvennogo ustroistva v gorodakh imperii* (St. Petersburg, 1877), 1:42–43.

of the old order such as the inspectors from the Urban Affairs Section of the Ministery of the Interior. The vision of the idealized city implicit in their reports assumed that municipal governance and urban economic expansion, if undertaken by men of talent and reason (regardless of rank), would make the Russian city the center of progress in the country. While shifting the criteria of public orderliness from the implementation of facade planning to the provision of extensive urban services, they also turned the specter of the mingling of ranks into a call for reform. These critics were certainly not aware of the full extent of economic growth and social upheaval that lay ahead. They understood urbanism in terms of culture and public service, but economic expansion was creating a very different pattern of urban relations. The history of Russian urbanism in the last half of the nineteenth century is a story of conflicting urban ideals and the social and economic transformation of urban life.

2

Railroads, Merchants, and Migrant Cities

In the decades following the Great Reforms the Russian city expanded beyond the activities of tsarist administrators, the civilizing pretensions of Petersburg's neoclassical facades and geometrical spatial order, and the economic leadership of a few wealthy merchants. The differences between the provincial towns and the capitals gradually dwindled. In the latter half of the century the expansion of commerce and manufacturing and the influx of migrants into certain towns enormously enlarged the sphere of economic operations and the diversity of the population. Urban growth appeared to be less and less a product of state activity and increasingly a social creation, the work of an industrious, mobile population that was adapting economic and social practices to their needs and to the opportunities of town life.

Models for a new-style urbanism emerged from industry, science, and technology as well as from new Western concepts of the civilized city. Russian imperial urban plans became anachronistic when the public embodiment of progress took the forms of the steam engine and the municipal sewage system. The promoters of the latter, striving for a Russian variety of the sanitized city, were a part of the civil society that was emerging around municipal government (a subject I discuss in the next chapter); the supporters of technological progress came from new groups of entrepreneurs and professionals. This modernistic image took concrete form in national exhibitions of science and industry, a latter-day capitalist rendering of the imperial urban plans. This version of the city beautiful had little in common with the lives of the petty artisans, traders, and manufacturers and was far removed from the world of migrant laborers. The gap was readily visible to the visitors to Moscow's All-Russian Industrial Exhibition of 1882 who cared to view the city's notorious labor market and slums of Khitrovka. Russian urban economic development was crucial to the transformation, both idealized and real, of the Russian city.

In historical perspective the conjuncture of commercial and manufacturing activity and urban growth in Russia closely fits the trends usually grouped under the labels of industrialization and urbanization. Machine technology, the intensification of the market economy, and capitalist enterprise were all present in late-century urban areas of Russia, whose rate of population expansion rivaled that of another borderland of the Western world, the United States.

In Russia, however, these trends evolved in a manner that was significantly different than in the United States or other Western lands. First, economic historians generally agree that the industrial revolution did not come to Russia before the mid nineteenth century and perhaps arrived decades later.[1] For this reason the economic foundations of Russian urbanization were shaped, much more than in the West, by the era of industrialization. Second, the expansion of manufacturing activity in Russia coincided with a rapid intensification of market relations. Previously, these two phenomena had been far more limited in their scope and intensity than in the West, where the so-called commercial revolution of the sixteenth, seventeenth, and eighteenth centuries had deeply penetrated the national and local economies. Olga Crisp has concluded that in the last half of the nineteenth century "the most significant aspect of the [economic] development in Russia was the erosion of the self-sufficiency of peasant households and the growth of a money economy." The characteristic pattern of Western economic growth in modern times was not repeated in Russia, where "the development of a market was part of the process of industrialization.[2] This belated commercialization placed some towns at the center of national and international markets, while others with little access to markets became "backwaters" in the overall pattern of economic exchange in the late century and in the eyes of their inhabitants. Thus, the creation of the new railroad network fixed the economic fate of towns throughout

1. See P. G. Ryndziunskii, *Utverzhdenie kapitalizma v Rossii, 1850–1880* (Moscow, 1978), esp. 185–228.

2. Olga Crisp, "Labor and Industrialization in Russia," The Cambridge Economic History of Europe (Cambridge, 1978), vol. 7, pt. 2, 350.

the country. It represented the harbinger of progress to its proponents and the pathway to the city for urban migrants.

Railway Journeys and Urban Travelers

By the 1860s business interests in Russia's trading towns spoke of the railroad as an instrument of salvation. The extensive canal-and-river system remained hostage to the forces of nature, but access to rail lines meant freedom from these constraints and for the towns located away from the waterways a chance at last to compete in national and even international markets. The town leaders of Feodosia, in mid century still a minor seaport on the Sea of Azov, wrote in 1861 that the "fate" of their city "depends on whether or not it will be linked by railroad with the interior provinces of Russia."[3] The grain trade was the prize they sought; they assumed its rewards would benefit the entire town population. The railroad appeared to be the key to both personal profit and town prosperity. An appeal to the Russian state was implicit in their statement; a rail line would only reach them with the encouragement and approval of the government.

An awareness of the importance of this revolutionary new means of transportation to the country's economy and to urban growth came gradually to the tsarist government. The Main Society of Russian Railroads, formed in 1857, looked to railroads "to facilitate foreign exports and to assure transportation for internal production," but it lacked a concrete plan of action and proved incapable of negotiating successful contracts with Western entrepreneurs.[4] What was missing in the Main Society, in addition to effective action, was strong backing from the government, which was still unpersuaded of the necessity for rapid railroad construction. A forceful and persuasive argument in favor of railroads came in an 1863 report to the imperial cabinet from the minister of state domains, A. Zelenoi. Its subject was "the mapping [*nachertanie*] of a network of railroads in Russia." He argued that railroad transportation was the path to progress: "The number of rail lines has become a sort of measure by which one may judge in the most accurate way the wealth of a country, the level of its manufacturing and trade activity, even its civilization." He judged that the

---

3. Ministerstvo vnutrennikh del. "Tavricheskaia guberniia," in *Ekonomicheskoe sostoianie gorodskikh poselenii evropeiskoi Rossii v 1861–1862 g.* (St. Petersburg, 1863), 2: 24–25.

4. Quoted in A. M. Solov'eva. *Zheleznodorozhnyi transport vo vtoroi polovine XIX veka* (Moscow, 1975), 66.

new form of transportation was "indispensable not only for the expansion of internal manufacturing and trade in Russia and a more correct and equitable distribution of prices on basic consumer goods but also for the lowering of these prices through more rapid, convenient, and inexpensive distribution of the workforce at those points in the country where the greatest need exists."[5] These developments implied a profound transformation of urban centers. His emphasis on consumer prices, manpower, and production amounted to an economic plan for the capitalist development of Russia.

Zelenoi made urbanization an integral part of economic growth. His proposed network of lines included "all the most populous and manufacturing cities of Russia" as well as towns "located on the navigable rivers," thus linking railroads with "the steamship lines for passengers and commercial goods." Certain urban centers would become transshipment points for the movement of agricultural products from the south and southeast of the country to seaports; northern cities, "often in need of agricultural produce," would be served by "the shortest lines" to grain-growing regions. Zelenoi's plan incorporated considerations of internal order as well; it ensured that rail lines would reach the "greatest number of provincial capitals."[6]

Government approval of this network of railroads remade the economic map of the country. From the mid 1860s the state's concessionary policy of railroad construction became an effective means of promoting the rapid emergence in European Russia of a nexus of key rail lines that were owned and operated by private companies that were subsidized by the state through low-interest loans.[7] Construction proceeded rapidly, with as much if not more profiteering by railroad entrepreneurs as in the United States. By the mid 1870s the basic network emerged, covering a total distance of nearly twelve thousand miles.

The importance of these rail lines to the towns along their path cannot be exaggerated. A certain number of urban areas experienced a transportation and marketing revolution. Moscow became the center of a radial grid of lines opening access to markets and facilitating the influx of agricultural produce and labor throughout central and northern Russia. From north to south and east to west the central regions were linked to seaports and the

5. "O nachertanii seti zheleznykh dorog v Rossii," Tsentral'nyi gosudarstvennyi istoricheskii arkhiv (abbreviated TsGIA), f. 207, op. 3, d. 162 (1861–64), 86–87.

6. Ibid., 138–40.

7. A meticulous, detailed account of state railroad policy may be found in I. S. Bliokh, *Vliianie zheleznykh dorog na ekonomicheskoe sostoianie Rossii* (St. Petersburg, 1878), vol. 1.

West. The southern ports of Odessa and Nikolaev on the Black Sea and Taganrog on the Sea of Azov could tap the produce of the Central Black-earth region through Kharkov. Voronezh became a gathering point for grain to be shipped to the southern port of Rostov-on-Don.

Other major lines cut across the principal river systems to carry goods between eastern and western lands. Rail lines competed with the Volga waterways by offering service from northwestern Russia to the regions around Tsaritsyn, Saratov, Samara, and Kazan, a territory that quickly became one of the principal suppliers of marketed grain in the country. The central area received access to the Baltic port of Riga via Orel and Smolensk, and commerce through Kiev reached into the German and Austro-Hungarian empires through Brest. Somewhat later, the Donets line extended across the southern steppes, where high-grade coal and iron ore deposits were located, to lay the foundations for the Ukrainian metallurgical industry. Despite ostensible state controls, the introduction of rail transport occurred in conditions as chaotic as anywhere in the West. Reports in the 1860s and 1870s of remarkably slow, erratic, and often dangerous rail travel added an aura of adventure to travelers' tales and provoked official investigations of incompetent and corrupt management. The spread of railroads opened a new dimension of public life that mingled power and profits, mobility and opportunity in ways never before experienced by Russian townspeople.

Medium-sized and small towns that had once existed largely as administrative centers or as transshipment points between land and waterways found within a few years vast markets for the purchase and sale of agricultural produce and manufactured goods. By the late 1870s railroads occupied the central place in transportation, a fact that drastically altered the practices of Russia's large-scale urban traders. The possibilities for economic opportunity expanded in tandem with railroad construction into promising territories. In a petition similar to many others sent to tsarist authorities, Samara's municipal elite begged at the end of the 1870s for the government to extend the rail lines from their city toward the northeast, where they claimed to behold visions of yet another "new granary" for the empire—and profits for Samara's grain wholesalers. They based their forecast on fact, not fantasy: the new line to the southeast through grain lands to the city of Orenburg, near the Urals, was already carrying twice as much freight as projected in the original plans.[8] Their eagerness to include still more agricultural territory within the scope of their trading activity was an

---

8. "Reviziia senatora Shamshina," TsGIA, f. 1391, op. 1, d. 23 (1880), 12–13.

affair of entrepreneurial ambition. It placed their city at the hub of a regional commercial economy.

This new perspective on the position of cities in the Russian economy entailed not only calculations of profit and freight movement but also estimates of the economic importance of railroads to towns whose economic livelihood was coming to depend on distant markets. Urban commercial and municipal leaders involved in railroad affairs were prepared to deal with rail companies either directly on their own or indirectly through the state. Rumors that wealthy Berdichev citizens had paid an enormous bribe to bring the Kiev-Brest rail line to their town (far off the most direct route the tracks could have taken) might have resulted from anti-Semitism. But they received credence because of the widely understood value of the railroad to any town's economic livelihood.[9] When the Southeastern Railroad company threatened to move its headquarters from Kiev unless it received municipal land for new buildings, the municipality gave in with scarcely a fight.[10]

Administrative reports from the provinces increasingly reflected the importance of railroads to urban growth and to the new economic practices of enterprising townspeople. In turn, new priorities that arose from the economic interests of the state and the population made some impression on the ponderous machinery of tsarist policy-making. Appeals from urban leaders and municipalities for greater access to rail transport, which in mid century had little discernible impact, often received a favorable reply from state officials in later years. In the 1870s governors' reports began to take account of urban economic needs for the first time. An investigation into railroad mismanagement, a serious concern by the late 1870s, appeared necessary to the state not only in response to the complaints of the army but also to satisfy "the interests of entire communities" that were suffering from the inefficiency and chaos that accompanied these early years of Russia's iron age.[11]

The Baranov commission, appointed to study and rectify these problems, set the issue of rail transportation in the context of national growth and the "numerous interests of the country," including the "interests of entire localities."[12] Its definition of national interest took the form of a sort of balance sheet of the country's productive wealth that was opened by rail-

9. *Novoe vremia*, 14 December 1899.

10. Michael Hamm, "The Emergence of Modern Kiev," in *The City in Late Imperial Russia*, ed. M. Hamm (Bloomington, Ind., 1985), 86.

11. V. V. Salov, *Istoricheskii ocherk uchrezhdeniia Komissii dlia issledovaniia zheleznodorozhnogo dela v Rossii* (St. Petersburg, 1909), 6–8.

12. Ibid., 9.

road transportation. In the territories of European Russia that were served by the various rail lines the commission established precise estimates of economic resources, which were expressed as the total agricultural surplus and the value of manufacturing production to which the railroads provided access.[13] The prospects of commercial growth contained in its statistical tables set urban economic activities in the new context of commerce and productivity. Although the report had little short-term effect on policies, it revealed that the tsarist administration was aware that railroads were having a nationwide impact. In the 1870s the state had begun to use freight rates as a device to influence internal commerce, but only in the 1890s did it implement a policy of satisfying "urban needs" for cheap bread through lowered short-haul rates on grain to northern cities.[14] Beyond these measures the Baranov commission's vision of productivity under state guidance had no apparent consequences. The state remained a remote presence in the reordering of commercial activities that was being sparked by rail transportation.

Although far less spectacular, the expansion of water transport during these decades also strengthened the ties among urban economies and enlarged the field of activities of migrant laborers and traders. Animal and human motor power was replaced by steam technology on rivers and canals. As on land, the consequences were increased speed for transportation and lowered costs, which together were sufficient to make river transport competitive with—when it was not complementary to—railroad transport. The number of steam boats on Russia's waterways grew from one hundred in 1850 to five hundred in 1866 and reached three thousand in 1898.[15] The water and rail systems became the channels through which goods poured into and out of key urban centers. Maps prepared by the Ministry of Transportation at the end of the century presented a vivid schematic picture of the flow of raw materials across Russia by rail and water. The Volga remained the most important commercial waterway, accounting in the 1890s for one-half of all water transportation. The paths of water and rail transport marked out by the mapmakers pinpointed certain transport hubs, such as Minsk in the west and Samara in the east, that were vital to

13. These tables appeared throughout *Trudy vysochaishei uchrezhdennoi Komissii dlia issledovaniia zheleznodorozhnogo dela v Rossii* (St. Petersburg, 1879), vol. 2, pt. 1, 84–104; pt. 2, 134–39, 154–77.

14. A. L. Shaulov, *Zheleznodorozhnaia tarifnaia politika tsarizma v 60–90 godakh XIX veka* (Kandidat dissertation, Rostov-on-Don University, 1977), 121; see also T. M. Kitanina, *Khlebnaia torgovlia Rossii, 1875–1914 gg.* (Leningrad, 1978), 181–82.

15. Ministerstvo putei soobshcheniia, *Aperçu statistique des chemins de fer et des voies navigables de la Russie* (St. Petersburg, 1900), 112.

regional, national, and even international trade.[16] By implication, such schematic renderings of transportation suggested how important marketing had become in the economic affairs of Russia's townspeople. In old port cities and new rail centers the population was increasingly involved in trade; the economies of these places were largely dependent on the income earned from occupations that involved the transshipment of goods.

The transportation revolution diminished the cultural isolation of provincial towns. It brought the capitals and their far-flung commercial hinterlands into close contact and offered more opportunities than ever before for city and countryside to collaborate. The iron rail was a lifeline for rapidly growing urban centers scattered across European Russia. Moscow in many ways was exemplary of the new city emerging in these conditions: its railroad stations were the funnels through which poured goods and people. In a somewhat idealized form it symbolized the new Russia of the late nineteenth century. In the literary imagery of Anton Chekhov the railroad passing near the cherry orchard was an inevitable victor over the gentle ways of landlords and dreamers; it brought the town to the countryside and turned the orchard into a suburban housing development. Rail transportation was crucial to the emergence of the new city. It expanded grain trade, increased the availability of foodstuffs in urban areas, quickened commercial growth, and intensified the movement of migrants into and through certain cities.

The rail lines brought new economic activities to towns in agricultural areas, both by opening up rapid bulk trade with grain growers and by providing access to national and foreign markets. Through the last half of the century the impact of the railroads gradually grew in scope and intensity. In a report written in 1907 local officials from the Volga city of Simbirsk recalled a somber, distant past before the time in the 1890s when "with the completion of the Moscow-Kazan railroad Simbirsk became directly connected with the entire railroad network and with the most distant parts of Russia." Their new town history was a story of commerce because the arrival of the railroad meant that the "grain trade particularly increased."[17] We know little of the provincial grain traders, many of whom were acting as agents for foreign commercial firms and who followed the rail lines in search of grain for European markets (which accounted for 60

16. The most grandiose of these visual renderings of Russia's new commercial activities was provided by the mapmakers who were charged with illustrating the volume on transportation that was prepared for the Russian pavilion at the 1900 Paris world's fair; see "Dvizhenie tovarov po zheleznym i vnutrennim vodnym putiam evropeiskoi Rossii," in Ministerstvo putei soobschcheniia, *Aperçu statistique*, endpages. (See figure 4.)

17. "Statisticheskie svedeniia po gorodam," TsGIA, f. 1290, op. 5, d. 240 (1907–9), 15.

percent of rail grain shipments in 1889).[18] Rail connections increased the dependence of Simbirsk's economy on outsiders at the same time that these connections opened new markets. The city's businessmen adjusted their trading practices to fit the new conditions of the railroad era.

In many ways the transportation revolution determined the evolution of the urban economy in the last half of the nineteenth century. Invariably, reports on economic conditions in individual towns and cities referred to the railroad in explaining the fate of the author's local economy. Whether accurate or not, traders, shippers, manufacturers, and even those whose world was limited to a local market believed that their success or failure depended on the presence—or absence—of the railroad. The reason why the town of Kaluga, located south of Moscow, had "lost significance as a central trade point for its region" appeared clear to city officials in 1907. The province's rail line to Moscow had undermined local business because it allowed the rural counties to "obtain all their goods directly from major centers."[19] The assumption that the urban economy was dependent on transportation appeared in a report that same year from Chernigov, a city in the northern Ukraine. "The absence of a broad-gauge rail line and any suitable means of transportation," the authors noted, was the cause of "poor trade and manufacturing affairs."[20] Whether accurate or not, the centrality of the railroad in observers' explanations of the economic condition of their towns suggests how crucial rail links to the outside world had become to urban elites throughout Russia.

Where rail connections had expanded and intensified, local assessments of urban affairs sounded a note of general well-being. So great were the opportunities created by the railroad in Minsk, which was located in a poor region of western Russia, that the city was "tranformed from an ordinary provincial town into a fairly strong commercial center," at least in the opinion of one traveler in the 1880s.[21] A quarter of a century before, the Minsk town fathers, in reply to a query from the Ministry of Internal Affairs, had noted glumly that "Minsk is insignificant in trading and manufacturing relations, less important than certain district towns."[22] The new Minsk was created by the railroad. It was located on the main line between the northern Ukraine and the Baltic, and its operations required supplies

18. V. A. Zolotov, *Khlebnyi eksport Rossii cherez Chernogo i Azovskogo morei v 60–90 godakh XIX veka* (Rostov-on-Don, 1966), 40.
19. "Statisticheskie svedeniia," TsGIA, f. 1290, op. 5, d. 234 (1907), 143.
20. Ibid., 272.
21. A. P. Subbotin, *V cherte evreiskoi osedlosti* (St. Petersburg, 1888), 1:8.
22. Ministerstvo vnutrennikh del, "Minskaia guberniia," in *Ekonomicheskoe sostoianie* 1:4.

and labor. "The shipment of grain provides work for very many," and "work is constantly available for suppliers, contractors, people supplying ties, firewood, etc." As a result, the town's population had doubled in the previous quarter century, "developing so quickly" that in the author's opinion its dynamism was comparable "only to [that of] new cities and a few of the railroad junctions in other regions."[23] This new city was the outcome of a commercial boom, the demand for labor, and a population explosion: its rapid transformation was attributable largely to the railroad.

The railroad was redrawing the map of urban Russia in the last decades of the century. A few cities exerted a power of attraction far beyond their borders, drawing in trade, manufacturing, and labor to expand their economic activities. This shift was apparent to the governor of Saratov province, who in 1897 observed that thanks to its newly developed rail connections and expanded river transport, Tsaritsyn was becoming "the trade center" for a vast southeastern territory.[24] Many thousands of migrant laborers were lured to such cities by an awareness of economic opportunity; although their labor was indispensable to transport and commerce in this new city, it also appeared to be threatening to high officials. That same year the governor warned the minister of internal affairs of the dangers posed to Tsaritsyn by "migrant laborers, generally undisciplined and extremely inclined to drunkenness and disorder."[25] His fears of social unrest were as important to his views of the city as were his visions of vast trading hinterlands.

The impact of the railroads was tangible in economic activities and the dynamics of urban growth. The shifting pattern of trade made itself felt by the 1880s at the yearly national fair at Nizhny Novgorod. In the opinion of a Soviet historian the decline of the fair, which began that decade, was primarily the result of "the development of railroad lines," which permitted manufacturers "to send their goods directly to the place of demand."[26] The speed with which these changes occurred was by contemporary standards extraordinary, particularly in those rural areas where the appearance of the railroad signaled the sudden creation of new towns. This aspect of urbanization was most apparent in the central Ukraine. The Ekaterinoslav railroad, running from the Donets coalfields in the east to the Dnepr river at Ekaterinoslav and, from there, to the Krivoi Rog iron ore fields, began

23. Subbotin, *V cherte evreiskoi osedlosti*, 9–10.

24. "Vsepoddanneishii otchet Saratovskogo gubernatora za 1897," TsGIA, f. 1282, op. 3 (1898), d. 300, 23–24.

25. Ibid., 21–22.

26. V. Ia. Laverychev, *Krupnaia burzhuaziia v poreformennoi Rossii, 1861–1900* (Moscow, 1974), 19.

full operations in the middle of the 1880s. Industrial settlements grew along its line in areas where cattle had recently grazed; the town of Ekaterinoslav, once an administrative town with virtually no economic activity, became a major industrial center with large metallurgical plants and a new community of traders, many of whom were Jews from the Pale of Settlement. This mingling of populations, which exacerbated ethnic tensions and quickly led to anti-Semitic riots, was a direct outcome of urban migration along the rail line.

The railroads also made food supplies available to town populations with greater regularity and more abundance than ever before. The opportunity to hold down urban food costs was politically important as a means to curtail economic hardship and social unrest among the urban laboring population. Thus, it is not surprising that in the early 1890s the state ceased using transport rates to subsidize grain growers in the distant southeastern territories and instead adopted a policy that was intentionally calculated to lower charges on short hauls. The move was a direct benefit to urban populations in European Russia, whose food shipments traveled relatively short distances.[27] This policy, coupled with increased grain marketing and the transportation revolution, kept the urban cost of living down despite rapid population growth and ensured, even in the famine year of 1891–92, that townspeople had adequate food supplies. These conditions served the needs of employers, who were eager to keep wages low, and reassured tsarist officials, who were anxious to avoid food riots. They also helped to make these cities a magnet for migrants. The railroad became the lifeline of Russia's cities.

The regularization and expansion of shipments along rail lines and waterways were paralleled by increased passenger travel by rail. The custom of the temporary migration of labor (*otkhodnichestvo*) turned into mass migration under the pressure of rural hardship, the lure of urban labor markets, and the availability of train travel. Distant destinations became accessible, even if the conditions of travel appeared intolerable to well-to-do Russians, who were accustomed to comfort. As the rail network grew, the number of Russians traveling by train increased even more rapidly. The old roads continued to attract many laborers, especially those whose destinations were the new southern and eastern grain fields. But urban migrants by the last decade of the century were largely train travelers.

The migrants' passage from village to city occurred in the cheap third-class coaches, where wooden benches accommodated an indiscriminate mix-

27. Quoted in Kitanina, *Khlebnaia torgovlia*, 191.

ing of social ranks. One traveler judged it "a barbarous means of trans-
porting laborers," which was done "in crowded, dirty, dark coaches."[28]
Disdained by Russians of privilege and rank, third class was a "democratic"
place where estates and wealth had little meaning (hence it was welcomed
by the repentant aristocratic hero of Leo Tolstoi's novel *Resurrection*). It
attracted four-fifths of all passengers throughout the late nineteenth
century.[29] According to official statistics, on average passengers traveled
relatively short distances—eighty miles at the end of the century—but
their numbers grew rapidly. The railroads transported twenty-four million
passengers a year in the first years of the 1870s; by 1897 (after a significant
fare reduction in 1894) they transported seventy-five million.[30]

The transition to mechanized travel was made less abrupt by both the
notoriously slow pace of Russian trains and the moderate distances that
passengers traveled. Still, the cumulative effects of growing numbers of
travelers, regularized rail service, and the social promiscuity of travel in the
popular third class created a collective experience that had a subversive
social and psychological impact on the way that the lower classes, urban and
rural, might view the Russia of estates, ranks, and order. The railroad also
created among Russian travelers a new sense of space and time and a new
measure of speed to compete with a man's pace or a winter sleigh. Traveling
from town to town enhanced the notion of an urban Russia identifiable to
passengers as their own destination points. In the opinion of a German
historian the cultural novelty of a rail journey was to bring departure and
arrival points into "immediate vicinity," thereby transforming the "traveling space" perceived by travelers into small, continuous temporal
moments.[31] Although the subjective meaning that Russian travelers gave
to their experience is still poorly understood, by the end of the century a
rail journey had become a notable part of the cultural imagery and social
relations of the urban population.

The impact of the railroad on personal mobility was most visible in the
Central Industrial region of the north, where from the railroad's inception
the scale of passenger movement was greater than elsewhere. A railroad
commission in the late 1870s reported that along the northern lines "di-

28. A. P. Subbotin, *Volga i Volgari: Putevye ocherki* (St. Petersburg, 1894), 7.

29. Such was already the case in southern Russia in the 1870s, as reported in Komissiia
dlia issledovaniia zheleznodorozhnykh del, *Passazhirnoe dvizhenie: Doklad Khar'kovskoi
podkomissii* (St. Petersburg, 1880), 3; figures for the entire network at the end of the century
are in Maksim Kovalevsky, ed., *La Russie à la fin du 19e siècle* (Paris, 1900), 861–62.

30. *Aperçu statistique*, 27.

31. The comment, directed to the impact of rail travel in mid-nineteenth-century Europe,
appears even more apt to a country as large as Russia. See Wolfgang Schivelbusch, *The
Railway Journal*, trans. Anselm Hollo (Oxford, 1980), 44.

rectly adjoining centers of manufacturing, a great mass (up to one hundred thousand on the Nizhny Novgorod line) of laborers and craftsmen work in factories in Moscow and the Moscow area." These passengers are "for the most part peasants from . . . the provinces closest to Moscow, to whom the third-class ticket is not a big expense and who very rarely travel on foot."[32] The scale of this movement reached such proportions that the smaller towns around Moscow such as Serpukhov, through which migrants had previously passed "around the time of holidays and for summer work," saw trade "fall severely" when these laborers turned to the two nearby rail lines to carry them to and from the great metropolis.[33] The city and the countryside were drawn much closer together for these migrants. The railroad brought a form of modernity into the ordinary experience of the masses of urban laborers from the countryside; it made the move from village life to city existence more rapid than ever before and created a unique transitional experience between rural and urban residence. The intensification of contact between the village and the city was perhaps the most profound human consequence of railroad journeys on Russian urbanism.

Railroad transport and passenger movement changed the very organization of urban space. They were the principal forces freeing urban growth from state tutelage. In the 1860s and 1870s imperial urban plans ceased to be effective guides to urbanization; their disappearance met with little resistance even though civic-minded reformers objected to the destructive effects of the railroad on urban order. One Soviet historian observed with obvious regret that "the location of railroad stations and railroad lines in a city often took place without regard to established urban plans for development." Land speculation and "a sharp reduction in state supervision of private building" rendered planning obsolete and inoperable.[34] Visions of the utopian city did not disappear from Russian cultural life, but the new forces of urbanization profoundly shaped the configuration of urban models in the late nineteenth century. The railroad station both symbolized and embodied the new urbanism in Russian cities; it did so to the same extent that it did in another continental-sized state, the United States.

The effects of the railroad were particularly dramatic in Russian urban areas because railroad engineers and topographers largely replaced the state in giving shape to the city. Their decisions on the location of rail lines (even

---

32. Komissiia dlia issledovaniia zheleznodorozhnykh del, *Doklad iugo-vostochnoi podkomissii ob usloviiakh perevozki passazhirov* (St. Petersburg, 1880), 43.

33. "Statisticheskie svedeniia," TsGIA, f. 1290, op. 5, d. 195 (1903), 139.

34. M. Il' in and E. Borisova, "Arkhitektura," in *Istoriia russkogo iskusstva*, ed. I. Grabar (Moscow, 1962), vol. 9, pt. 2, 258.

though subject to political supervision and, perhaps now and then, bribery) had an immediate effect on nearby towns. "The location of the station," concludes a Soviet historian, "determined the further construction of urban areas and produced a concentration of industrial enterprises there." The presence of a station distant from the old center of urban economic life shifted commercial and industrial activities toward the outlying station, creating at times a second town. Even when the stations were nearby, the effect was to "emphasize the contrast between town center and out-skirts."[35]

In Moscow the presence of the railroad terminals of several major rail-road lines produced a city "with a completely new appearance" in the eyes of a contemporary observer in the 1870s. "All the areas around the sta-tions, which were constructed on the outskirts of town, acquired new build-ings, and endless rows of two-story wooden buildings were constructed to house railroad employees and travelers."[36] The Khitrovka area, by the 1870s one of the most notorious of Russian urban slums, first appeared as a labor market for migrants, many of whom arrived in Moscow at the nearby train stations. The chaotic urbanization that the railroad brought about made no provision for city plans and public orderliness. If there was any order at all, it was the work of the railroad entrepreneurs and the architects who were responsible for the new railroad stations, the focal point of the new city.

Although distances between cities were increasingly measured in the amount of time it took to travel on the railroad, travel within towns still proceeded at the slow pace of horse and foot power. As in the West, horse-drawn trams were the first improvements in urban transport; by the end of the century they had spread to all major towns and most provincial capitals. Moving scarcely faster than a pedestrian (three miles per hour was the average speed of horse-drawn trams in Moscow), they mostly attracted townspeople of modest means, from clerks to washerwomen; neither the wealthy elements nor the poor laborers used them. Moscow's trams carried forty-five million passengers in 1895, and over two-thirds traveled in first class, where passengers could distance themselves visibly from the less fortunate.[37] By the turn of the century only a few municipalities had undertaken the construction of electric streetcar lines. The tsarist state intentionally brought them to Nizhny Novgorod in 1896 to exemplify

35. Ibid.
36. Ibid., 260.
37. "Moskovskie konno-zheleznye dorogi," in *Sbornik statei po voprosam otnosia-shchikhsia k zhizni russkikh gorodakh* 5 (1897):50–51.

(together with the national exposition) the spread of industrial progress to provincial cities.[38] Critics blamed short-sighted municipal leaders for the supposed lag throughout Russia in streetcar construction. However, a more general and persuasive reason was inadequate municipal budgets, which were held down by state-imposed expenditures and by the resistance of the mercantilist town elites to higher property taxes.

The lack of cheap urban transportation meant that the neighborhood remained the spatial center of most townspeople's lives, and as a rule housing for workers had to be located within reasonable walking distance from their workplace.[39]

For townspeople of some means horse-drawn cabs remained the quick means about town. The numbers of such cabs swelled each winter to provide sleigh rides down the snowy or icy streets. Many of the drivers were seasonal workers who worked their fields in the growing season and earned supplementary income as teamsters and cabbies in the winter months. Their numbers and visibility reinforced the impression of many observers that peasants were everywhere in the city. The increased movement of people into and within the city heightened the need for cabbies, who were a visible sign of old Russia juxtaposed alongside the new railroad stations. At the end of the century a newspaper correspondent from the western town of Viazma, a "rather large trading city located at the junction of three rail lines," hinted at his dislike of villagers when he warned of the dangers that Viazma's cabbies posed to the townspeople. "There exists no surveillance of cabbies," he complained, "the majority of whom are crude, coarse, and obey no rules while driving."[40] To many observers the cabbies' undisciplined habits and uncomfortable vehicles were an unavoidable relic of backward city life. According to a journalist in Kiev gynecologists warned their patients never to take a cab.[41] Thus, those Russians who envisaged orderliness, civility, and efficiency as their ideal of urbanism had one more reason to believe that progress had scarcely touched their cities.

The Merchant City

By tsarist statute and public expectation the economic and social leadership of urban society belonged to the merchant estate. Legal rights and

38. Information on urban public transportation appears in the 1904 survey of Russian towns. See *Goroda Rossii v 1904 g.* (St. Petersburg, 1907).

39. One geographer's graphic concept of this typical "journey" in St. Petersburg of the 1860s is found in James Bater, *St. Petersburg: Industrialization and Change* (London, 1976), 123–39.

40. *Moskovskii listok*, 23 January 1899.

41. *Kiev v 80-kh godakh: Vospominaniia starozhila* (Kiev, 1910), 10.

obligations had been ascribed to this estate since Peter the Great's time, and these regulations underwent only slight modification in Alexander II's reign. As in the past, all trade and manufacturing above a specific level of capitalization belonged to the merchants in the first or second guilds (the difference between these two guilds depended essentially on income). In the opinion of some contemporary observers as well as that of certain historians, the permanence of the merchant estate's legal preeminence in economic affairs contributed to an attitude of social conservatism. Alfred Rieber, in his very thoughtful study of the nineteenth-century merchant estate, argues that in the late 1800s "the bulk" of these traders and manufacturers remained firmly attached to "the old ways." In reaching this conclusion, however, he suggests that the model of social modernity for Russia's middle classes could only have been "the classical bourgeoisie in nineteenth-century Europe." In his judgment successful Russian entrepreneurial activity in that period was eccentric and exceptional.[42] One might object to Rieber's conclusion on the grounds that the socioeconomic evolution of Russia's urban propertied classes was embedded in a cultural context unlike that of Western Europe. Rieber's evaluation of the merchant estate, and other evaluations like it, reveal the extent to which images of the West inform our assessments of Russia's social history. However, such images do not make clear the changes in either the role or the identity of urban traders and manufacturers in the postreform years.

The records of the number of "merchants" (both individuals and, in a very small proportion, joint-stock enterprises) tell a precise but misleading story. By 1898 there were 6,500 first-guild merchants and 138,000 second-guild merchants in the entire country. Many of these individuals had become merchants solely to meet legal requirements for economic activity, remaining at the same time enrolled in their estate of origin (as permitted by the reforms of the 1860s). In Moscow, arguably the city with the greatest entrepreneurial opportunities, over half of the merchants had combined estate titles. For over 20 percent this meant that merchants were also "trading peasants."[43]

Apparently, by the end of the century merchant status was largely irrelevant as a mark of social standing. In 1899 the great majority of enterprising Russians abandoned their membership in the merchant estate when the opportunity to do so arose. The 1898 revision of trading and manufacturing regulations permitted people from any estate to purchase

42. Alfred Rieber, *Merchants and Entrepreneurs in Imperial Russia* (Chapel Hill, N.C., 1982), xxiv, 83–88, 33–35.
43. Ibid., 89, table 3.1.

business certificates without enrolling in the merchant estate. The following year the number of second-guild merchants suddenly fell to thirty-
eight thousand, and the number of first-guild merchants shrank to four
thousand.[44] The continued visibility of a few conservative merchant families obscured what one might call a flight from merchant identity.

Nonetheless, images of the traditionalist merchant remained pervasive
in popular and political discussions of Russia's present and future society.
They emerged in debates over the primacy of the nobility, whose supposed
paternalistic care of their laborers was contrasted to the cruelty and crude-
ness of "merchant values." These images were echoed by foreign entrepreneurs in Russia, especially Germans, who disdained their "backward"
Russian competitors. They also emerged in contemporary literary and popular writings, including Ostrovsky's plays and the stories of Maxim Gorky,
where the merchant and the petty bourgeois (meshchanin) were equated
with the philistine. Writers for the new penny press often used the merchant stereotype to illustrate the confusion of urban social roles that was
created by new wealth in the hands of those unfit for preeminence. By the
end of the century the old-fashioned merchant appeared primarily in the
guise of either a comical character or a "provincial merchant," who was
damned by one observer for his "feeble initiative" and "ancestral" economic operations.[45]

The tenacity of this stereotypical portrait drawn from the Russian past
suggests more than a nostalgia for an imagined patriarchal past or a dramatized moral confrontation between the forces of progress and backwardness. The conduct of urban entrepreneurs drew heavily on past experience
in confronting difficult economic conditons. The studies of the economic
historian Fred Carstensen reveal that there were many substantial reasons—financial, technological, and cultural—for Russian businessmen to
be cautious about innovation and to avoid risk-taking, even in circumstances when substantial profits rewarded successful entrepreneurial
daring.[46]

The paths of new economic activity moved in predictable and visible
directions across the urban landscape of the country. Those cities with

44. A. Bokhanov, "Rossiiskoe kupechestvo v kontse XIX–nachale XX veka," Istoriia SSSR
(June-August 1985):107.
45. O.F., "Nashe russkoe kupechestvo," Moskovskii listok, 6 April 1899.
46. See Fred Carstensen, American Enterprise in Foreign Markets: Singer and Interna-
tional Harvester in Imperial Russia (Chapel Hill, N.C., 1984), esp. 101; see also Gregory
Guroff and Fred Carstensen, eds., Entrepreneurship in Imperial Russia and the Soviet Union
(Princeton, 1983), esp. the essay by Thomas Owen, "Entrepreneurship and the Structure of
Enterprise in Russia, 1800–1880," 59–83.

access to agricultural markets and manufacturing opportunities became centers of enterprise, investment, and employment; by contrast those towns isolated from the new economy appeared backward and stagnant. In the public eye Moscow epitomized the former; the latter retained the pejorative title "provincial" and included places like Gorky's fictional creation, "the little town of Okurov," which was a bitter, satirical portrait based on the author's personal experience in exile in a Kazan district town. In these places life seemed to have stopped.

Two traits of the urban economic expansion are of particular importance to Russian urbanization in the late ninteenth century. The first characteristic is the remarkably rapid rise of trade in agricultural produce that moved through the commercial and transportation networks of certain cities. In part this trade fed the urban population, but to a far greater extent it was part of the export market for Russian farm products. The activities associated with these commercial affairs turned an increasing number of urban centers into transshipment points. The sales from agricultural marketing in these cities stimulated the internal market for goods, increasing the demand for essential consumer goods, which were produced in part by the urban manufacturing economy. Although these cities began to thrive on the basis of agricultural trade, they did so at the price of dependence on the vagaries of the Russian harvest. The close links between urban economic well-being and agriculture became a source of concern for tsarist administrators. In 1891 the Moscow provincial governor noted that urban trade suffered that year because "the bad harvest in the grain-growing regions" had "significantly curtailed the buying power of the population."[47] Although the city had established its distinct and vital role in national economic development, it drew its material wealth largely from the countryside.

The second important characteristic of the urban economy was the multiplication of the number of occupations that were necessary to sustain and enrich urban life. These trades filled the city with a multitude of petty enterprises and laborers—the cabbies already mentioned being among the most visible—whose availability varied with the seasons, the state of the urban economy, and the level of rural hardship.

The urban entrepreneurs and traders who made their livelihood in these new or expanded sectors remain for the most part a scarcely visible segment of the urban population. The most successful left their mark on Russian public life, playing out roles not unlike those of the captains of industry in the United States who moved into the cultural world to become great

47. "Vsepoddanneishii otchet," TsGIA, f. 1284, op. 223, d. 152 (1892), 8.

patrons of the arts. One such successful industrialist, Savva Mamontov, turned from railroad building to the support of artists and musicians. These activities earned him a condescending accolade from an aristocratic acquaintance: "Merchant, kulak, petty tyrant, and to the fullest extent a self-starter. . . . [Savva Mamontov is] handsomely gifted with mind and talent."[48] The great majority of Russia's men of affairs could not possibly fit this mold. The traces of their presence are to be found only in the practices that marked their ventures, which most often were modest and liable to failure. These traces are most easily discernible in the domain of trade.

In the early postreform period the rhythm of the annual fairs still set the pattern of urban trade. These gatherings were ephemeral affairs. A few, however, operated at an intense level of activity. Of the total of sixty-five hundred fairs in the 1860s that one Soviet historian counted, thirty-three produced over one million rubles in transactions.[49] The most illustrious and lucrative fair was the one held each summer along the banks of the Volga in Nizhny Novgorod. In scale and variety it dwarfed all other fairs; its growth through Alexander II's reign suggests the relative unimportance of year-round urban trading at this time. In the early 1860s its business activity entered a period of remarkable prosperity, reaching an average of 116 million rubles by the end of the decade and rising to its greatest level of 243 million rubles in 1881 (in the late 1840s yearly turnover had amounted to only forty-seven million rubles).[50] Its operations changed during those years in response to industrialization; textiles became the major commodity, and the ease of telegraphic communication made sales increasingly a matter of quick agreements that linked trade representatives and owners at the fair with their enterprises.[51] But the great days of that fair were passing. Business would never again reach the 1881 level; by the early 1890s the average yearly turnover was down to 150 million rubles. The same decline occurred at the major Ukrainian fair at Poltava.

These fairs scarcely disrupted the daily routine of life in the city because the fair's sellers, clients, and products appeared and disappeared within a few days or weeks. Urban traders traveled regularly about the country to conduct their business whenever and wherever a major fair was held. Their

---

48. *Khudozhnik ushedshei Rossii* (New York, 1955), 39.
49. P. I. Liashchenko, *Istoriia narodnogo khoziaistva* (Moscow, 1948), 1:483.
50. "Ekonomicheskoe znachenie Nizhnego Novgoroda," in *Sbornik statei po voprosam* (1896), 3:225.
51. An excellent general history of the evolution of the fair in the nineteenth century is found in Anne L. Fitzpatrick, "The Nizhnii Novgorod Fair, 1840–1890" (Ph.D. diss., University of Virginia, 1980), esp. chap. 2.

residence was located in one or another town; their economic activity was as itinerant and sporadic as the fairs themselves. Despite the growth of the Nizhny fair through the 1870s, this manner of organizing urban economic activity offered fewer opportunities in commercial affairs than year-round business. To those Russians who were persuaded that the economic future belonged to technology and the productive city, the fair symbolized the peculiar customs and narrow horizons that they associated with the stereotypical Russian merchant.

The regularization of trade required a place of central operations. For the bulk of traders this place was a provincial urban center. Warehouses provided a regular supply of wholesale goods; prices increasingly were set by weekly and daily trading; the distribution of goods occurred along the rail lines at urban centers where stores could meet the demand for goods thanks to the telegraph and rail transport. Moscow was the hub of this new network and the epitome of the Russian mercantile city; it was most closely linked to the national market and it was the home of some of the greatest trading houses. Its advantages included its location in the major manufacturing region of the country, its access to most major rail lines, and its proximity to major markets—including its own booming population. In the early twentieth century the statistical office of the Moscow municipality noted a fact of economic life in the previous decades, namely, that Moscow was "the most important center of manufacturing and trade [in the country]. Therefore, the prices on all manufactured goods are set by Moscow, not only for the Nizhny fair but also for the East."[52] Trade had become a regularized business, and the practices of the Russian traders involved in the national market differed greatly from the personalized, ephemeral routine of the traditional merchant.

Trade in agricultural produce constituted the single most important sector in the new Russian urban economy. By the 1880s the movement of marketed grain, both by rail and water, involved a network of wholesale and transportation firms with links to towns and cities throughout the grain-growing regions and into the northern urban centers that were dependent on food imports from the south and east. Shipments of grain to the international market (roughly half of the total by the 1880s) were in the control of major Western firms such as the French company of Louis Dreyfus; Russian middlemen, who were the links to the grain growers in the countryside, gathered around these foreign firms.

The dominance of large companies in the grain trade was most visible in

---

52. "Statisticheskie svedeniia," TsGIA, f. 1290, op. 5 (1910), d. 195, 10.

the Black Sea ports, through which passed one-third of Russia's grain exports. In the north, where the internal market was as important as foreign shipments, wholesale firms remained relatively small in size and were dispersed throughout the provincial urban centers. In all parts of Russia inequality between the buyers and the wholesale enterprises was a common characteristic. Because of the large volume of their purchases the major firms passed on to the "buyers" and "agents" (*ssypshchiki*) the task of gathering the surplus at small market points and sending it to the regional and national transport centers.[53] The profits, which were relatively small and dependent on commissions on purchases, represented the difference between ruin and prosperity for these traders.

Operating from international ports such as Odessa and regional centers such as Saratov, small operators fanned out into the countryside. Although written in the early twentieth century, a report from a town in Tambov province suggests that the origins of the pattern of urban commercial operations dated from several decades earlier. The author describes how "forty to fifty buyers, mostly from the petty bourgeoisie, of whom only a very few are well-to-do" worked with two or three employees, who earned on average fifteen to thirty rubles per month, to purchase crops, which were paid for with bank loans.[54] They conducted their affairs on a slim margin of security and were easy prey to ruin from sudden price movements of the commodities. They and outside traders gathered the produce for shipment to Russian or foreign markets. From one "grain-trade point" in Kazan province a local official reported that these middlemen "store their supplies in warehouses and send it to Rybinsk and St. Petersburg twice a year: in spring as soon as navigation opens and in the fall."[55]

The volatile grain market, the difficulty of obtaining bank credit, and the slim margin of profit lent an aura of petty profiteering and ruthless greed to the entire operation. The world of speculative trade in food products had little to attract the sympathy of either the *intelligent* or the tsarist official, each of whom for different reasons was prone to view trade and credit as parasitic. However, by the 1890s even provincial governors had to take note of what the Saratov governor termed the successful commercial operations of "very important firms" with "extensive trade" with Moscow and St. Petersburg.[56] All along the Volga such activities made trade in agricultural

53. A good survey of this increasingly complex commercial network is found in Kitanina, *Khlebnaia torgovlia*, 60–65.

54. "Statisticheskie svedeniia," TsGIA, f. 1290, op. 5 (1910), d. 243, 79–80.

55. Ibid.

56. "Vsepoddanneishii otchet," TsGIA, f. 1284, op. 223, d. 176 (1894), 14.

produce a source of wealth for some businessmen and employment for large numbers of laborers and employees.

In the late nineteenth century the dominance of agricultural trade in the urban economy was evident in the southern ports on the Azov and Black Sea, including Odessa, Taganrog, Nikolaev, Mariupol, Feodosia, and the river port of Rostov-on-Don. The traders of Feodosia, whose complaint to the state in 1861 I cited earlier, acquired rail communications with the eastern Ukraine. The sleepy naval port of Nikolaev, with neither railroad nor maritime commerce in the 1860s, became the principal outlet for grain from the southern Ukraine. By the 1870s all these cities possessed port facilities, all had extensive rail links with a productive agricultural hinterland (and several had good river transport as well), and all were the seat of large grain exporting companies, most of which were foreign owned. In Rostov-on-Don, for example, three firms controlled two-thirds of the grain exported in 1898. Odessa remained the center of operations of the major international grain companies in Russia. Between the late 1870s and the late 1890s the average yearly grain shipments from these ports doubled, amounting to over two-thirds of the country's total grain exports.[57]

The trading operations of the small concessionaires that worked for these companies depended not only on the harvest but also on accessible credit. A Soviet study has shown that funds came from "banks and other credit institutions, the [grain] exporters themselves, and railroad companies."[58] The speculative nature of these transactions was repugnant to Odessa's city prefect of the mid 1890s: he condemned what he called the compelling desire for "quick profit" among townspeople. His dislike of the city's mercantile character was strongly colored with anti-Semitism. It also revealed his own assumptions regarding urban public life: he blamed business for the absence of "normal civic consciousness."[59] Competition and profit-seeking determined the difference between wealth and poverty for Odessa's traders, but for the governor these activities represented moral defects.

The volatility of the export market, both in quantity and prices, reflected its dependence on harvests and on international grain markets. Exports of produce, not imports, set the pace of Odessa's economic activity. The ban

57. An excellent survey of this southern grain trade is Zolotov, *Khlebnyi eksport*, esp. 185–99.

58. Ibid., 227–28; the shortage of operating capital, which necessitated these loans, was one of the most debilitating obstacles confronting Russian enterprises, both large and small. See Fred Carstensen, "Numbers and Reality: A Critique of Foreign Investment Estimates in Tsarist Russia," in *La position internationale de la France: Aspects économiques et financiers (XIXe–XXe siècles)* (Paris, 1975), 281–82.

59. Cited in Frederick Skinner, "Odessa," in *The City in Late Imperial Russia*, ed. Michael Hamm (Bloomington, Ind., 1986), 228.

on grain exports in 1892, which followed the bad harvest and famine in northeastern Russia the previous year, brought hardship to business and labor in Odessa. The city prefect reported a sudden rise in "major bankruptcies" that was accompanied by a rash of fires in business premises to double the normal rate. His suspicion that arson was the cause—and insurance repayment the goal of desperate businessmen—appeared correct after a sudden decline in fires when he warned that arsonists would be tried by military court. The sudden loss of work by dockers and day laborers— the city prefect estimated that thirty thousand lost their jobs—led the authorities to provide municipal soup kitchens and public work for three thousand.[60] The municipality, seeking to ease the crisis of unemployment among white-collar workers, begged traders to show " 'the most elementary sense of moral responsibility' by retaining their employees."[61] The economic collapse that year represented only the most extreme example of Odessa's dependence on agricultural marketing. In the 1880s, from one year to the next the volume of exports oscillated as much as 50 percent, and prices varied by 10–20 percent.[62] In the period between the 1870s and 1900 the long-term trends were a gradual fall in grain prices and a remarkable expansion in the volume of grain exports.

Urban commercial operations expanded throughout the last decades of the nineteenth century. Moscow's role as a trade center arose as a result of its position in the national manufacturing and transportation network. The type and scale of its commercial operations reflected this growing activity and diversity of demand. By the late 1880s trading activity was becoming rationalized as a result of the "increased application of modern methods of credit and accounting in both mercantile and banking operations," which were replacing the "traditional habits of trade such as enormous markups on small inventory."[63] The clothing trade shifted toward the production and sale of ready-made items and one journalist wrote that "in the last ten to fifteen years" the production of these items had concentrated "in Moscow more than in any other city."[64] Salesmen began to span out from the major urban centers. In the judgment of a Kharkov reporter, by the 1890s traveling salesmen had undermined the trading activity of small shopkeep-

60. "Vsepoddanneishii otchet," TsGIA, f. 1284, op. 223, d. 180 (1892), 3.
61. Cited in Lewis Siegelbaum, "The Odessa Grain Trade: A Case Study in Urban Growth and Development in Tsarist Russia," *Journal of European Economic History* 9 (Spring 1980): 137.
62. Reports by the Odessa city prefect made specific mention of such oscillations from year to year. See TsGIA, f. 1284, op. 223, d. 116 (1887), 167 (1888), 156 (1889).
63. Thomas Gohstand, "The Shaping of Moscow," in *The City in Russian History*, ed. Michael Hamm (Lexington, Ky., 1976), 177.
64. *Moskovskii listok*, 18 July 1903.

ers and traders in the area. They "travel around to places in Russia where previously even the police had rarely appeared. . . . [They] carry with them the entire range of goods that rural traders offer and fill orders more cheaply. Also, they offer the same credit as the old general trader."[65] One consequence of this trend was that trading operations began to be concentrated in urban areas. The city and the countryside were becoming distinct economic spheres.

Agricultural marketing brought manufacturing as well as trading activities into urban economies. The processing of farm products gave a new industrial dimension to urban business. The first census of Kiev, conducted in 1874, found 10 percent of the active population in trade and transportation and 20 percent in manufacturing, and food processing was the principal manufacturing sector.[66] Twenty years later the provincial governor reported that the city had become "one of the major points for the grain trade . . . in the entire southern region." He also emphasized the emergence of the city's food processing industry, which produced sugar from the region's sugar beet crop and flour from the area's grain.[67] In these commercial and industrial enterprises the state obtained an important source of new tax revenues and the population found a major source of livelihood.

Industrial production was at the center of urban economic activity only in the older Urals manufacturing towns and in the industrial settlements of northern Russia and the Ukraine. Industrialization, although profoundly altering the country's economic development, remade the urban landscape only in these regions. Mechanized textile factories dominated the skyline of some new towns, but more frequently they created distinct factory communities on the outskirts of older cities. The shift to mechanization had a major impact in urban manufacturing centers. In these cities cottage industry did not have the same marginal advantage it had in rural areas, where it remained a major part of textile manufacturing until the turn of the century. By the early 1880s Moscow's cotton textile industry included fifty-nine enterprises with 11,500 workers, and its machine construction factories employed eight thousand workers; to the northeast the new textile plants of Ivanovo Voznesensk had 13,400 workers. The author of the most thorough study of industrialization in northern Russia estimates that by

65. Ibid., 26 January 1896.
66. Cited in "Zapiska Senatora A. Polovtsova o sostoianii obshchestvennogo upravleniia v gorodakh Kievskoi gubernii," in *Trudy komissii Kakhanova*, (St. Petersburg, 1884), vol. 2, pt. 2, 10–25. Michael Hamm offers detailed evidence of this trend in "Change and Continuity in Late Imperial Kiev," in *The City in Late Imperial Russia*, ed. Michael Hamm (Bloomington, Ind., 1986), 85.
67. "Vsepoddanneishii otchet," TsGIA, f. 1284, op. 223, d. 176 (1894), 14.

this time twenty-nine urban areas in this region had become centers of "major factory industry" where almost eight hundred enterprises operated with 170,000 workers. Cotton spinning factories contained twenty-five thousand power looms but also made use of twenty thousand hand looms, a good measure of the intermingling of handicraft and mechanization in and around urban manufacturing at that time.[68]

Observers reported that the new industrial settlements of the Ukraine resembled urban frontier communities. Areas that were once sparsely settled grazing and grain lands with a few administrative centers were transformed by the appearance of towns along railroad lines that linked coal and iron ore deposits. Important factories emerged around quiet provincial capitals such as Ekaterinoslav, Prince Potemkin's "Athens of southern Russia." In the 1880s this city reemerged as a Ukrainian Pittsburgh: iron foundries began operations, and the population jumped from thirty-two thousand to seventy thousand. In 1890 the provincial governor remarked that "several hundred new houses have been built [in Ekaterinoslav and] new markets have opened." In his opinion these boomtown conditions were the result of the "grandiose iron bridge" just completed over the Dnepr river, the three new iron mills, and the expanded coal mining in the region.[69] Writing later in the decade, the governor argued that the human impetus for the town's economic development came from a fever of speculation among "all the local inhabitants." With lyrical exaggeration he described a "trading and industrial class" that seeks out "risky enterprises in the hopes of great income—and these hopes often come true . . . ; yesterday's pauper is today's self-supporting individual, sometimes becomes a very wealthy man; land worth nothing today is sold almost on the city streets in anticipation of the construction of a factory or a railroad line."[70] Where industrial resources and business enterprise—foreign or Russian—met, the face of the city was transformed.

The presence of captains of industry was much less important for urban employment than the activities of small manufacturers. Conditions in the city of Kharkov, for example, were closer to the norm for towns with extensive manufacturing. In 1904 its statistical bureau reported that enterprises with between fifty and two hundred workers constituted the largest category of factory in the city, but workshops (*masterovye*) that employed

68. Vasil'ev, "Formirovanie fabrichno-zavodskogo proletariata tsentral'nogo promyshlennogo raiona Rossii, 1820–1890" (Doctoral dissertation, Novocherkassk Pedagogical Institute, 1972), 2:24, table 6.
69. "Vsepoddanneishii otchet," TsGIA, f. 1284, op. 223, d. 189 (1891), 3.
70. "Vsepoddanneishii otchet," TsGIA, f. 1282, op. 3, d. 255 (1899), 7–8.

between five and nine workers were an even more important source of jobs than factories. The total work force in manufacturing was considerably smaller than that in handicrafts (including master artisans and their workers and apprentices), which totaled 22,500, or one-tenth of the entire population of the city.[71] These quantitative measures of economic activity suggest the extent to which the Russian city remained the domain of small enterprise, even when the character of production gave a gloss of industrialization to the urban economy.[72]

Large-scale commercial enterprises and manufacturing operations were surrounded by what one historian, referring specifically to Moscow, has termed the "institutions of barter, haggle, and street vending."[73] Although these "institutions" retained all the color and exotic character of the pre-reform city, their pervasiveness and middle-class clientele made them an integral part of the new urban economy. The numbers and miserable conditions of the small traders and artisans, many classified by tsarist statute as petty bourgeois, provided tangible evidence of the isolation of wealthy entrepreneurs in the merchant town.

Most trade and handicraft businesses were extremely small in scale, especially in the western towns of the Pale of Settlement. Tiny shops abounded in towns such as Minsk, where there was one store for every twenty inhabitants (the norm for all Russian cities was one store for every one hundred to two hundred inhabitants). Competition in these cities was keen and profits small.[74] The city of Vilna, one of the largest in the Pale, had three times the number of artisans as distant Saratov even though the two cities were roughly the same size. One economist reported that too many small handicraft enterprises created "fierce competition [that] reduces pay for work to the lowest possible level."[75] Such conditions perpetuated and even increased the number of families living at subsistence levels.

71. Cited in D. Bagalei and D. Miller, *Istoriia goroda Khar'kova za 250 let ego sushchestvovaniia* (Khar'kov, 1912), 2:550–51.

72. This issue is the subject of a battle of correlation coefficients (based on urban employment statistics) between historical geographers. One side has concluded that a high relationship between urbanization and industrialization did not exist in late-nineteenth-century Russia, but this conclusion is contested by the other side. See Roger Thiede, "Urbanization and Industrialization in Pre-revolutionary Russia," *Professional Geographer* 25 (February 1973):16–21; Robert Lewis and Richard Rowland, "A Further Investigation of Urbanization and Industrialization in Pre-revolutionary Russia," *Professional Geographer* 26 (May 1974): 177–82.

73. Joseph Bradley, "Moscow: From Big Village to Metropolis," in *The City in Late Imperial Russia*, ed. Michael Hamm (Bloomington, Ind., 1986), 19.

74. Subbotin, *V cherte evreiskoi osedlosti*, 1:9–10.

75. R. M. Blank, *Rol' evreiskogo naseleniia v ekonomicheskoi zhizni Rossii* (St. Petersburg, 1908), 20–21.

In the opinion of one observer, over half of the population of Berdichev, one of the cities of refuge for Jews who were expelled from villages in the Pale, was living "from day to day."[76]

The impoverished artisans and traders were numerous throughout Russia and were dependent for survival on the commercial, manufacturing, and administrative fortunes of the new city. In St. Petersburg in the early 1890s the police prefect judged that only one-fourth of its artisans were "more or less prosperous economically."[77] It is unlikely that the level of wealth in any other city surpassed that of the capital. The poverty among the bulk of the sixteen thousand "hereditary guild artisans" of Moscow was such that it excluded over 90 percent of them from the right (which was defined by a minimum payment of tax on property) to participate in the artisan society's elections.[78] Little distinction existed between handicraft work and trade: artisans sold their own wares, and traders at times sold goods of their own making as well as those that they bought. Secondhand products were as salable as new ones. Some poor townspeople eked out a miserable income trading used items that had been passed on from hand to hand.[79] As in the mid 1800s, rural employment remained common for many of the urban poor. Farm labor was an attractive alternative where agricultural estates required hired hands, as in the Saratov region. In 1893 the Saratov governor commented on the decline in the number of artisans in his province, which was caused by a good harvest that made "field labor . . . more profitable than artisanal pursuits."[80]

Poor townspeople, even those with some skills, were forced by economic necessity to take whatever work was available. Artisans often moved in search of a better place of work; a survey of artisans in several provincial towns in the mid 1890s found that a large majority were born elsewhere. Owners usually employed one or two workers and one apprentice and operated on a very small scale. Their hours were long—twelve to thirteen were the average—and most did not even own their place of work.[81] This profile was probably typical of what we might loosely term the urban "underclass" of the Russian city at the end of the century.

76. Subbotin, V cherte evreiskoi osedlosti, 2:121–22.

77. "Vsepoddanneishi otchet," TsGIA, f. 1284, op. 223, d. 200 (1893), 33.

78. Moskovskii listok, 25 June 1892.

79. Two Soviet ethnographers explore this aspect of petty commerce in the town of Kaluga in the late nineteenth century in L. A. Anokhina and M. N. Shmeleva, Byt gorodskogo naseleniia srednei polosy RSFSR v proshlom i nastoiashchem (Moscow, 1977), 72.

80. "Vsepoddanneishii otchet," TsGIA, f. 1284, op. 223, d. 176 (1894), 46.

81. This survey, from which I extract data for only a sample of artisans from four towns (Aleksandrovsk, Voronezh, Nizhny Novgorod, and Kremenchug), was never published. The manuscripts are found in TsGIA, f. 1290, op. 5, d. 37 (1893).

As before, the hereditary estate divisions were virtually meaningless among these petty entrepreneurs. The Saratov Artisan Society, official organ of the hereditary artisan estate, numbered nine hundred masters in 1881 at a time when the municipality counted three thousand artisans, most of whom belonged to the category of "temporary artisan." As in earlier years, a large number of the "master artisans" of the society in fact came from other estates; half were from the petty bourgeoisie, almost 20 percent were peasant, and 3 percent belonged to the nobility.[82] In Moscow the famous Yaroslavl peasant tavern keepers were one visible reminder of the mobility (and regularity) of movement across estate borders.

One reason that the merchant city of Russia differed substantially from the Western capitalist model was that the Russian network of banks and credit institutions was inadequate and underfunded. Only in the 1860s did a statute appear offering "full freedom of operations in all Russia" to private banks. From that time on they were able to tap private capital funds that had previously had no regular outlet for investment.[83] Financial opportunities grew as the demand for credit expanded in the second half of the century. By 1875 there were over 350 private and municipal banks in Russia, and private reserves amounted to 1.5 billion rubles, twenty times the credit reserves fifteen years before.[84] This expansion proved excessive and risky in the unstable economic conditions of the 1870s. According to the provincial governor, in Kiev the commercial banks were "giving out easy but expensive credit," and bad loans and corruption suddenly brought "extemely tense conditions on the money market."[85] One might rephrase his bureaucratic view by suggesting that inexperience and a precarious urban economy led to the contraction of much-needed credit.

The situation became more threatening in the economic recession of the mid 1880s. Municipal banks were particularly hard hit because they operated with lower reserves and less security than the commercial banks. In the 1860s and 1870s over eighty municipalities had tried their hand at banking. The municipality of Tambov had benefited substantially from the operations of its bank, obtaining several million rubles yearly in profits. Municipal public services had expanded and local businesses had obtained relatively easy access to credit. But agriculture was the basis of the municipality's banking enterprise, and a poor harvest and lower grain prices in

82. "Otchet po revizii Saratovskogo remeslennogo upravleniia," TsGIA, f. 1391, op. 1 (1880–81), d. 145, 50–51.
83. I. I. Levin, *Aktsionernye kommercheskie banki v Rossii* (Petrograd, 1917), 1:20–21.
84. Liashchenko, *Istoriia narodnogo khoziaistva*, 2:108–9.
85. "Vsepoddanneishii otchet." TsGIA, f. 1284, op. 69, d. 435 (1877), 3.

1883 brought this golden age to an end. Bankruptcies spread and the bank's risky loans collapsed. Even the secret police paid attention; in his yearly report the provincial gendarme officer noted ominously that "the bank is rocking on its foundations [*shataetsia*] and has almost stopped making loans."[86] Many municipal banks folded in the 1880s as a result of the economic instability of their towns and rural hinterlands. For example, the Moscow provincial governor anticipated that nothing could save two banks in district towns because they had each lost over half of their small reserves and held very "questionable loans."[87] The instability of the municipal banks was both a cause and an effect of the fragility of the local economy.

The prosperous times in the 1890s proved a boom period for banking as well as for the economy as a whole. The commercial banks increased their provincial branches from 94 in 1893 to 274 in 1900.[88] By the 1890s a variety of other financial institutions such as credit societies were able to provide small loans to their customers. More numerous facilities and abundant funds created the possibility for more varied financial operations, including a modest boom on the stock market as companies sought public funding. A note of capitalist exuberance was evident in the comment of one banker that "almost all major cities and even small towns" participate in stock trading, some with their own stock exchanges and many more with "little stock exchanges" that are located in "almost all . . . provincial branches and bank offices."[89] The opportunities for speculative investment also included urban real estate. In some cities municipal officials and landlords worked together to promote land development and quick profits. One reporter for a Kharkov newspaper sounded a well-known Western theme when he complained of housing that was "built only to give a satisfactory return on invested capital, neglecting the basic needs and conveniences of the apartment dwellers."[90] Landlords and rentiers did not figure alongside the great manufacturers in the pantheon of civic leaders, but they represented an updated counterpart to the traditional merchant in the sense that they sought to find a safe place in the new urban economy.

The shortage of credit remained a serious problem for small-scale producers. Tula metalworking artisans complained in the mid 1890s that the "principal brake on production came from the complete absence of

86. Tsentral'nyi gosudarstvennyi arkhiv Okt'iabrskoi revoliutsii (TsGAOR), f. 102 (tret'e deloproizvodstvo), d. 89, chast' (chap.) 55 (1884), 5.

87. "Vsepoddanneishii otchet," TsGIA, f. 1284, op. 223, d. 219 (1890), 52–54.

88. I. F. Gindin, Gosudarstvennyi bank i ekonomicheskaia politika tsarskogo pravitel'stva, 1861–1892 (Moscow, 1960), 87.

89. Levin, Aktsionernye kommercheskie banki 1:263–64.

90. Quoted in Bagalei and Miller, Istoriia goroda Khar'kova 2:77.

credit."[91] Only in the 1890s did small credit institutions such as mutual credit societies and municipal pawn shops begin to serve petty traders and artisans. Only very small sums were loaned—nine rubles on an average—and demand far exceeded available loans. When it opened in 1891, Kharkov's municipal pawnshop exhausted its fifty thousand ruble loan credits in three months; it had to turn to the municipal bank to obtain a two hundred thousand ruble loan.[92]

The concentration of wealth in the hands of a very small urban mercantile and propertied elite that lived in the capitals and a few provincial cities was one of the most notable features of Russian urban growth in the postreform years. By one Russian geographer's count, in the early twentieth century nearly one-third of the officially designated cities (227 of 761) did not even produce one hundred thousand rubles yearly from trade and industry.[93] However, a relatively small number of towns presented their inhabitants with a wide range of economic opportunities and employment.

Thanks to the municipal statute of 1870 we possess an approximate profile of the distribution of propertied and commercial wealth in the cities. The male electorate was divided into three curiae according to taxes on trade, manufacturing, and taxed real estate. Each curia had to contribute an equal share of the total taxes, which divided the three curiae into groups whose members possessed about the same taxable wealth. The overall range in taxes was enormous. The minimal payments (which were primarily made by small artisans and traders) were twenty kopeks in Nizhny Novgorod's third curia in 1890; members of the second curia paid between twenty and two hundred rubles; the highest tax in the third curia that year (presumably the commercial and manufacturing leaders of the city) was seventeen hundred rubles.[94]

By this crude measure of taxed wealth the elite numbered only a handful. In Kiev in 1879 a total of 120 individuals (3 percent of the city's 4,200 enfranchised male residents) belonged to the first curia, among whom slightly over half were officially classified as merchants; even with the addition of the second curia, well-to-do Kievans totaled only 600. Kiev's third curia had twice as many merchants as the first two curiae combined, but they were intermingled with the more numerous petty bourgeois and

91. Quoted in *Moskovskii listok*, 7 January 1896.
92. Bagalei and Miller, *Istoriia goroda Khar'kova* 2:569–70.
93. V. P. Semenov-Tianshanskii, "Gorod i derevnia v evropeiskoi Rossii," *Zapiski po otdelu statistiki Imperatorskogo russkogo geograficheskogo obshchestva* 10 (1910):73–77.
94. N. N. Baidakov, "Vvedenie Gorodovogo polozheniia 1870 g. v Nizhnem Novgorode i vybory v 1870–90-kh gg.," *Uchenye zapiski Gor'kovskogo Gosudarstvennogo Universiteta, seriia gumanitarnykh nauk* 105 (1969):77.

"privileged" (noble) electors.[95] Urban economic growth during the 1870s and 1880s increased the isolation of the wealthy voters in the first two curiae as the middle ranks of the propertied and trading townspeople swelled. In Moscow in 1872, 2,400 voters belonged to the first and second curiae and 15,000 to the third; fifteen years later the numbers of voters in the first two curiae had shrunk to 1,600, and the third curia had grown to 18,000.[96] Although opportunities for small-scale enterprise abounded in cities such as Moscow, the path to substantial wealth was accessible only to a few.

The array of municipal electoral statistics, although they make no distinction between productive and nonproductive wealth, suggests more clearly than contemporary memoirs and official reports the limits to economic enterprise in what I term the merchant city. To the extent that this label is meaningful it refers not to one but to two spheres of urban economic activity. On the one hand, the typical occupations of propertied townspeople involved both "haggle and barter" urban trade and retail and wholesale commerce that was dependent largely on marketing agricultural produce. This world was one of risky affairs without substantial financial rewards, enterpreneurial glory, or technical sophistication. On the other hand, the captains of Russian trade and industry were a tiny social elite far above the masses of propertied townspeople. Presumably, they embodied a way of life that was respected and admired by the small-scale traders and manufacturers but that was largely unattainable both because of the constraints of the urban economy and the instability of commercial affairs. Thus, the term merchant city should be most closely identified with petty enterprise and a modest level of wealth.

To those who were repelled by the rough-hewn economic traits of the Russian city, the West offered beguiling models of sophisticated and successful enterprise. The English writer Samuel Smiles served up the most highly touted formula for middle class success in his book *Self-Help*. It turned the Protestant admonition that "God helps those who help themselves" into an ethical prescription that was suitable to the industrial age. Translated into Russian in 1866, it must have found a large audience, for it went through eight printings in the next fifteen years.[97]

In visual form a model for the ideal city of industry and science was

95. "Zapiska Senatora Polovtsova," vol. 2, pt. 1, 95, table 41.

96. E. A. Pavliuchenko, "Moskovskoe gorodskoe upravlenie v 70–80-kh godakh XIX veka" (Kandidat dissertation, Moscow State University, 1956), 49, 57.

97. The publishing record of the Russian editions of *Self-Help* is found in the "alphabetical service catalogue" (*sluzhebnyi alfavitnyi katalog*) of the Leningrad Saltykov-Shchedrin library.

ready at hand. From the time of the French Revolution, expositions had been used in Western Europe to bring artifacts of national progress to the public eye. Pride in the industrial economy and concern with the prestige of nations found their most spectacular visual forms in the many world's fairs that were held in Western Europe, starting with the London Exposition of 1851 and occurring frequently in subsequent decades. Taken in isolation, each exposition's individual displays and separate pavilions laid out the wares of manufacturers, the resources of nature, and the achievements of science and technology in the Western world. The enormous dimensions and planned activities of these fairs attracted millions of visitors to specially designed buildings, gardens, and walkways that the planners had turned into a sort of utopian city of the future. One anthropologist has argued that nineteenth-century world's fairs created "idealized consumer cities within their walls. They presented a sanitized view of the world with no poverty, no war, no social problems, and very little nature. World's fairs promulgated a whole view of life."[98] To the Russians who were attracted by the power and prestige of the industrialized nations and by the cultural and economic dynamism of Western cities, these grandiose events represented an encapsulated vision of Russia's path to progress.

Gradually the scope and contents of the Russian expositions took on the shape of miniature cities. Small-scale replicas of Western expositions, monumental in concept but constrained by a lack of vision of the future and by paltry funding, had appeared periodically in St. Petersburg and Moscow from the 1820s. They were attractive principally to manufacturers seeking to promote new products. Sponsored by either the St. Petersburg or the Moscow municipality with some support from the state (particularly the Ministry of Finance), the "expositions of manufacturing" resembled the great fairs in the West only in miniature. Decorated in palatial style and displaying a limited selection of luxury and industrial products, such public gatherings were intended for a small elite. The "luxury and glitter" of the 1861 exposition in St. Petersburg brought the somewhat wistful thought to one visitor that he might be in Paris or London. He reminded his readers and himself that "in Russia people also know how to live, there is a demand for refined, elegant [products], and there are those who can satisfy these needs."[99] Neither he nor the organizers of the exposition thought of its displays of manufacturing skills and wealth as a unified model of civic progress.

98. Burton Benedict, "The Anthropology of World's Fairs," in *The Anthropology of World's Fairs: San Francisco's Panama-Pacific International Exposition,* ed. Burton Benedict (Berkeley, 1983), 5.

99. M. Ia. Kittary, *Obozrenie vystavki 1861 goda* (St. Petersburg, 1862), 7.

Twenty years later, however, the Moscow exposition of 1882 assumed the trappings of a major national event and its grounds assumed the form of a minicity. For the first time, land on the outskirts of the city was set aside for a complex of buildings to house the displays. The exposition site was linked to the central city by special transportation—a horse-drawn carriage line—and a railroad spur that permitted passenger coaches from the main lines to reach the edge of the exposition. To emphasize its importance in Russian life the organizers gave the exposition the title "All-Russian Artistic-Manufacturing Exposition" and added agriculture to the fourteen fields they judged to be suitable for display. When completed, its array of buildings bore no resemblance to the pseudopalaces of the earlier Russian manufacturing fairs. Its central hall of metal and glass was an imitation of London's Crystal Palace.

Incongruities in tone between the modern and the traditional appeared to remind the visitors that the exposition represented an unusual event in Russian public life. The festivities on opening day mixed two Russian societies. The Russia of orders and titles was present in the persons of the metropolitan of Moscow, Grand Prince Vladimir Alexandrovich, and the Moscow governor-general. Merchant Russia was represented by the leaders of the Moscow stock exchange and merchant society and the minister of finance, for whom the exposition had a specifically economic purpose. The opening ceremonies included an orchestral performance for the elite that was followed by popular festivities (*gulian'e*) for the people. By the time the exposition closed at the end of the summer it had attracted an estimated one million visitors. It offered both an escape from and an alternative to the Moscow of taverns and slums, beggars and migrant laborers, factories and shanties.

The promise of a new city, hinted at rather than proclaimed openly, appeared repeatedly in the evaluations and reports of the fair. In part such documents reflected their authors' public or official positions, but they were also serious efforts to capture the meaning—if not the actual content—of the fair as a major public event. Three aspects of the fair suggested that it presented an idealized urban model. First, for the exhibitors it constituted a sort of giant store that "accurately represented" the achievements of Russian manufacturing and "acquainted the public" with the many items for sale.[100] In other words, the exposition was a marketplace. Second, the entire organization and disposition of the buildings, the displays (educa-

---

100. *Soobrazhenie Kievskogo vspomogatel'nogo komiteta po ustroistvu Vserossiiskoi vystavki* (Kiev, n.d.), 1.

tional and artistic as well as economic), and the orderly movement of people was an example of a collective endeavor that was intended to be on a par with the best attainments of the West. In the self-serving words of the final report: "The outstanding order reigning at the exposition makes Russia appear to be a fully European country, enlightened and well-ordered [blagoustroenno]."[101] The ephemeral city of the exposition brought the borders of Europe to the Russian merchant city.

Third, the very shortcomings of the exposition were noteworthy of the labors remaining to be undertaken. Although the objects on display typified the best Russia could create, in the judgment of one observer the Russian "public" appeared to be on a cultural level far below the exposition itself. He considered the viewers to be typical of "intellectually backward [Russians], who have inadequate means of communication, insufficient awareness [glasnost'], and little precise information about Russia."[102] Such language could easily have appeared in any educated Russian's description of the typical townsperson. For educated Russians, then, the idealized city of the exposition was not of one piece. The criteria of excellence established by those who constructed the exposition discredited the very population whom it was intended to instruct and enlighten. How could the city be the source of productivity and progress in the face of such obstacles? The organizers had few answers to that question.

The sense of a special urban vocation, embodied in a national exposition, appeared even more prominently in the next (and last) all-Russian fair, held in Nizhny Novgorod in 1896. The element of symbolic meaning was obvious to officials and observers, who pointedly commented on the fair's quest to demonstrate the spread of modernity from the capitals to the provinces, and from the core of Westernized Russia to a city located on the borderlands of Asia. A few cities, for example, Kazan and Ekaterinburg, had attempted ambitious expositions on their own in the intervening years, but only the Nizhny Novgorod event received the political patronage and public attention inevitably associated with a national event. For the occasion the city itself became exemplary, installing (at state expense) electric streetcar lines and street lighting. The lighting turned the city, in the words of an exuberant young newspaperman named Maxim Gorky, into "a hill of lights, as though it had been sprinkled with stars from heaven."[103]

101. B. P. Bezobrazov, ed., Otchet o Vserossiiskoi khudozhestvenno-promyshlennoi vystavki, 1882 g. (St. Petersburg, 1883), 6:7.
102. Ibid., 11.
103. Odesskie novosti, 11 June 1896.

The exposition itself was constructed on land at the junction of the Oka and Volga rivers not far from the site of the traditional annual trading fair. To underline its essential difference from the crowded, ramshackle buildings of the trade fair, it was laid out in a vast "garden city" that was twice the size of the Moscow exposition. Its main pavilions incorporated elements of the latest Western architectural style (labeled by Russians as "style moderne"). They displayed models of modern industry and technology, cultural and educational materials, exhibits of "progressive" municipalities, and even artifacts from the exotic Russian borderlands of Siberia and Central Asia. Nicholas II's much heralded visit to the exposition that summer brought the highest possible imprimatur to the efforts of the modernists (the most important of whom was Minister of Finance Sergei Witte) to make this artificial "city on a hill" the symbol of national economic and cultural progress. It constituted the major public event in Russia that year and attracted nearly one million visitors (despite complaints of poor rail connections and weeks of rain).

Like the Moscow exposition fourteen years before, the Nizhny Novgorod exposition proved an occasion for observers to assess the gap between the ideal and the real city, between technological progress and the old merchant ways. The decision of the organizers to locate the fair in a provincial town was a daring act because it broke with the assumption of the Westernizers that Russia beyond the capitals was uniformly backward, even "Asiatic." The organizers hoped to make clear to the country that European civilization, in its Russian variant, was moving eastward into Asia and that urban modernity had spread far beyond the borders of St. Petersburg and Moscow. The official guide claimed that provincial cities such as Nizhny Novgorod "have acquired 'meaning' as industrial and education centers in Russia."[104] In their judgment the traditional Nizhny Novgorod fair no longer typified urban economic practices, and the exposition, with the old fairgrounds nearby for contrast, proved the point.

The opinions of the visitors, for whom we have only the words of contemporary journalists and writers, may have been less sanguine. The perfection and glitter of the exhibits contrasted sharply with the poverty of the workers at the exposition; the modernity of the electric lights and street cars in the town did not penetrate the dirty, dark side streets. The exhibits were "extremely visible," one writer remarked sarcastically, "amidst our provincial order where nothing dims their contours" and where "the level of knowledge . . . stands at a point one hundred years behind that repre-

104. "Ustroistvo vystavki," in *Opisanie Vystavki*, ed. V. Kovalevsky (Moscow, 1896), 2.

sented" in the exposition.[105] His culturist view that modernity was a human quality that was largely defined by education and Western learning assigned the typical provincial townsperson to the ranks of the backward and benighted (summed up in the scornful Russian term *obyvatel'*). More tolerant social critics such as Maxim Gorky, however, took the economic meaning of the fair very seriously. To him the fair was a "fairy-tale" world of "miracles of technology" that served as "publicity" for manufacturers and that masked the "imperfections of human life."[106] Whether viewed from either the culturist or the technological perspective, the exposition city did not represent a tangible or attainable reality.

The duality of the merchant city in those decades emerges vividly in the visual ambiguity and critical judgments of the Nizhny Novgorod exposition. In one sense the contradictions of Russian urbanism emerged most clearly in the provinces because the livelihood of the expanding economies of provincial Russian towns depended heavily on trade with the countryside and on the harvests. The perfection of modern crafts and industrial machinery, which was the main attraction of the exposition, represented industrial modernity in cities such as St. Petersburg, but it was irrelevant in the lives of the small traders and manufacturers who made up the propertied business groups of the provincial urban centers.

Taken separately, the exhibits had the specific intent of promoting the products of those few entrepreneurs with the incentive, in the form of capital, markets, and skills, to adopt the most advanced industrial and technological tools. Taken altogether, however, the exposition served the larger goal of promoting a rational, productive ordering of public activities in a modern city. From the perspective of Russian urbanization in those years this vision was so unattainable that it was an urban utopia drawn to the measure of the Minister of Finance, Sergei Witte. Although urban economic practices had evolved far beyond those of the mid-century merchant estate and bore little resemblance to the government's formalistic estate regulations, they were also distant from the model of technology and science that the Westernizers proposed in the idealized city of the national exposition.

Urban Migrants
and Migrant Cities

Visitors to the Moscow Exposition of 1882 could quickly travel between the fairgrounds and the center of Moscow on a new tramway. If they chose,

105. N. Iakobson, *Chto takoi byla Nizhegorodskaia vystavka?* (St. Petersburg, 1897), 3.
106. *Odesskie novosti*, 21 June 1896.

they could pass through the notorious slum neighborhood of Khitrovka. The contrast between the fair's images of urban modernity and the misery of the Khitrovka dwellers illustrates another duality embedded in Russian urbanism in those decades: the slum had no place in the dreams of civic leaders, public-spirited intellectuals, and progressive entrepreneurs. It represented a grim reminder of the depths to which any townsperson could fall when misfortune struck. The deeper meaning of the slum, one that applied to all the growing urban centers of the country, lay in the presence of thousands of migrant laborers who congregated there seeking work. Their attire and mannerisms identified them as strangers in the city. Writing at the end of the century, one Moscow journalist identified the arrival each spring of this "enormous mass of laborers" as a sort of invasion. "They fill Khitrov square to overflowing, . . . and drink, eat, and even sleep right on the pavement."[107] The appearance of crowds of migrants in the city was a visual reminder that the country's urban growth was bringing the countryside to the city.

This trend troubled contemporaries and remains a perplexing issue confronting historians of Russian society in the late tsarist years. Did this migration constitute a sort of "peasantization" of the cities or, on the contrary, were many of the new arrivals rapidly adapting to urban culture? Was the expansion of the urban population an indication of the beginning of a profound process of integration of Russian society or did it mark a trend toward social turmoil that would further accentuate the division between "society" and "the people?" From the urban perspective the experience of the migrants has two historical dimensions: first, the practices of the new and temporary residents in Russia's urban areas; second, the perception of this event by outsiders—tsarist officials, municipal activists, intellectuals—with their own programs for urban development and their own appreciations of the place of the masses in urban society.[108]

The census of 1897 tells a dramatic tale of the rapid surge of the population of the country's cities. In absolute figures the urban population doubled in size in the last half of the nineteenth century, rising from 5.2 million in 1856 to 12.2 million in 1897.[109] We can appreciate the human

107. "Khitrovka i ee obyvateli," *Russkoe slovo*, 27 May 1897.
108. In the wide array of studies touching on migration two recent works that look closely at the experience of urban migrants are Robert Johnson, *Peasant and Proletarian: The Working Class of Moscow in the Late Nineteenth Century* (New Brunswick, N.J., 1979), and Joseph Bradley, *Muzhik and Muscovite: Urbanization in Late Imperial Russia* (Berkeley, 1985). A statistical study based largely on aggregate, provincial-level data is Barbara Anderson, *Internal Migration during Modernization in late Nineteenth-Century Russia* (Princeton, 1980).
109. These data are conveniently grouped in the appendix to Thomas Fedor, *Patterns of*

dimensions of the urban migration by noting three trends: the increase in city populations came largely from new settlers, it touched a relatively small number of urban areas, and it resulted as much or more from a rapid turnover of migrants as from permanent settlement in the city. First, settled townspeople were responsible for only a small part of urban growth; a decline of birth rates among this segment of urban dwellers is apparent in the last decades of the nineteenth century.[110] Thus, the impression of contemporary urban observers that they were undergoing an invasion of outsiders is more than a vivid figure of speech. In sheer numbers these strangers were overwhelming the native townspeople.

Second, the destination of most of the new urban dwellers was a limited number of cities scattered across European Russia. The spectacular expansion of the capitals is only the most vivid evidence of the bias the migrants showed in choosing their cities of temporary residence. Their choices played a decisive part in establishing Russia's pattern of urbanization. Unfortunately, only the all-Russian census of 1897 contains the demographic data we need to construct a profile of these cities; even this source gives reliable information only on migrants for cities with a population above twenty thousand.[111] With these limitations a statistical examination of the census results reveals the outlines of a cluster (or "family") of urban centers so strongly shaped by migration that I have labeled them "migrant cities." These towns constituted the locus of urban growth in the last half of the nineteenth century, and epitomized, both demographically and socially, the "new city" of late tsarist Russia.

The essential features of these new cities are apparent when we examine the urban centers in 1897 where over half the inhabitants were—in the language of the Central Statistical Committee—"born outside their place of residence." Nearly sixty migrant towns of over 15,000 population had emerged in European Russia by the end of the century (see table 1), and on average they had doubled in population since the 1860s. They ranged in size from Moscow, which grew from 350,000 to over one million between 1856 and 1897, to new industrial settlements like Ivanovo Voznesensk, which had expanded from a village of one thousand to a city of 54,000, and

Urban Growth in the Russian Empire during the Nineteenth Century (Chicago, 1975), 179–216.

110. M. B. Kurman, "Vosproizvodstvo naseleniia dorevoliutsionnogo krupnogo goroda (po primera Khar'kova)," in *Brachnost', rozhdaemost' i smertnost' v Rossii i v SSSR*, ed. A. G. Vishnevskii (Moscow, 1977), 239–40.

111. B. V. Tikhonov, *Pereselenie v Rossii vo vtoroi polovine XIX veka po materialam perepisi 1897 g. i pasportnoi statistiki* (Moscow, 1978), 54–55, table 7; the author discovered that in towns with populations of less than twenty thousand the census takers classified both those born in the city and those born in the surrounding district as urban "local born."

Table 1. *The Russian Urban Population in 1897: A Demographic Profile of Cities Above 15,000 Population*

	Total cities (N = 144)	Towns with 50% or more local born (N = 86)	Migrant towns (50% or more born elsewhere) (N = 58)	Cities of Central Indust. Region (N = 20)	Cities above 50,000 (N = 38)
Median population	28,000	27,000	47,000	30,000	74,000
Population by place of birth					
Local born	57%	68%	40%	51%	45%
Same province as city	19	13	27	25	23
Another province	24	19	33	24	32
Peasant estate	38	33	44	52	38
Of whom local born	39	49	25	38	25
Petty bourgeois	50	57	40	34	47
Of whom local born	67	75	55	67	59
Households with five or more members	41	49	26	27	28
Population below twenty years old	42	44	39	38	40
Literacy					
Peasant estate	36	34	39	40	39
Urban estates	46	42	52	57	50
Male population	52	51	53	53	52
Female population	48	49	47	47	48
Employment					
Personal service	19	18	20	15	20
Manufacturing	28	28	28	35	29
Trade	13	14	13	10	12
Self-supporting	46	42	52	55	50
Nonfamily living quarters housing over two members (*artel'*, etc.)	4	2	6	8	5

Source: Pervaia vseobshchaia perepis' naseleniia Rossiiskoi imperii (St. Petersburg, 1898–1905). Percentage of local born is, as indicated on p. 77, probably too high for towns of 15–20,000 population.

provincial commercial centers like Saratov, which grew from 61,000 to 137,000. The rapid growth of the migrant cities stood in sharp contrast to those towns in which in 1897 over one-half of the inhabitants were locally born. Typically, their populations had declined in the two decades before the census.

Although urban expansion had begun in some areas in the first half of the nineteenth century, it assumed nationwide proportions in the reform era. Kiev, whose experience was probably similar to that of many other migrant cities, reached a population of nearly one hundred thousand by 1874 (the year of its first comprehensive census). In that year only 28 percent of its inhabitants were born in the city. Similarly, nearly three-fourths of Moscow's population in 1882, when its first city census was held, were migrants (that is, born elsewhere), a proportion that was sustained in 1902 when the municipality conducted its second census. In simple demographic terms the migrant city is characterized by the predominance of outsiders.[112]

In the descriptions of observers the migrant invariably appeared in peasant garb. The 1897 census gave substance to these impressions when it reported that the typical migrant belonged to the peasant estate. The emphasis on the rural laborer, repeated often in contemporary literature and historical studies, is somewhat misleading, however, because it suggests that movement only occurred between town and countryside. The censuses reveal that a substantial proportion of migrants belonged to estates other than the peasantry. The migrant cities were a social magnet for the entire population. Among those who belonged to the urban and privileged estates of Kiev (petty bourgeois, merchant, noble) in 1874, at least half had moved to the city from elsewhere. This proportion appears to have remained relatively constant to the end of the century. Although not as detailed as the Kiev census, the 1897 census suggests that it held true for migrant towns throughout the country (see table 1). Privileged and unprivileged, relatively well-to-do merchants and poor traders and artisans, peasants and petty bourgeois were all engaged in the creation of migrant cities.

Third, the population was remarkably mobile. Migrants came and went from the migrant towns, as did townspeople. The apparent incremental character of urban growth is belied by data that indicate the moves of migrants within and between towns. Seasonal laborers (*otkhodniki*) were the most visible new arrivals who soon left for other destinations (in their

---

112. "Zapiska o sostoianii Kievskoi gubernii," in *Trudy komissii Kakhanova* (St. Petersburg, 1884), vol. 2, pt. 1, 10–25; on Moscow see also Anderson, *Internal Migration*, 93, table 4.3.

case, usually back to their villages). Bradley's careful study of the Moscow censuses of 1882 and 1902 shows that at the time of both censuses about one-fifth of the migrants had resided in Moscow for less than two years. In the ten-year period at the turn of the century that separated the two Petersburg city censuses, over half of the locally born dwellers had departed, a situation that James Bater refers to as "itinerant residence." By contrast, slightly over two-fifths of Moscow residents in 1882 and 1902 had lived there for over ten years, long enough perhaps to identify themselves as Muscovites.[113]

These figures tell us nothing about the subjective meaning of social mobility and stability to urban dwellers. They suggest, however, that we should pay less attention to the peasant as migrant and more attention to the conditions created by urban migration. In mid century urban commissions across the country reported the high rate of temporary migration of the lower urban estates in search of employment (see chapter 1). Decades later, the scale of this population movement had increased dramatically, and a familiar array of practices that linked at least some of the urban laboring population with the peasant migrants remained in existence. For all their shortcomings the census data reveal the extent to which these migrant cities were places that were occupied by and, in some areas, appropriated by a transitory population. The impression that the migrant cities were growing in an absolute sense is based in part on a statistical mirage: the increasing turnover of migrants. This mirage, however, seemed like a reality for contemporary observers. However short and transitory their stay in any one city, the migrants left a strong imprint on the social complexion of Russian urban areas.

Any inquiry into Russian nineteenth-century urbanization needs to pay close attention to the demographic peculiarities of the process, which can be gleaned through a statistical analysis of the 1897 census. Despite its imperfections, this census is the only source with which to construct a picture of the typical migrant city in European Russia.[114] When the numerical totals compiled by census takers for the populations of Russia's towns

113. James Bater, "Transience, Residential Persistence, and Mobility in Moscow and St. Petersburg, 1900–1910," *Slavic Review* 39 (June 1980):240–42; see also Robert Johnson, "Peasant Migration and the Russian Working Class: Moscow at the End of the Nineteenth Century," *Slavic Review* 35 (December 1976):659; Bradley, *Muzhik and Muscovite*, 137, table 2.

114. On the problems of the census see A. Kotelnikov, *Istoriia proizvodstva i razrabotki vseobshchei perepisi naseleniia 1897 g.* (St. Petersburg, 1907); Barbara Anderson's study of urban migration (*Internal Migration during Modernization*) groups census data primarily by provinces, a very different demographic perspective from the one that I have adopted.

(which must be restricted only to those of over twenty thousand inhabitants) are reduced to percent values, they can be used to identify the unique characteristics of the cities of high migration. The method known as "discriminant" analysis, explained in the appendix, identifies a cluster of social traits that are shared by all the migrant cities and, conversely, that are absent from the towns where a majority of the population is locally born. When statistically defined, these traits are historically meaningful and suggest the substantial outlines of the social profile of the migrant city (see appendix, table A-1).

The traits most strongly related to migrant cities fit a pattern one might intuitively have expected to find in a type of city inhabited largely by a transient population, namely: comparatively few large households (defined as those with over five members); a large percentage of adults of working age (twenty to forty years old); a relatively high level of people of the urban and peasant estates from distant regions (beyond the province in which the town was located); and a significant proportion of people living in communal (*artel'*) housing. In the abstract terms of statistical values this social profile contains the characteristics of a family of cities whose single outstanding human characteristic is adaptability to sustained labor. Migrants often supported a large, extended family, but it was left behind. Communal living was favored because of its low costs to the laborers, who, in addition to living expenses, had to pay taxes and, often, the expenses of a distant family out of their meager income. The migrants' hopes for employment focused on particular cities that were accessible by railroad, even if they were located far from home. Thus, labor and a way of life that was appropriate to long- or short-term urban employment appear to be the salient qualities that shaped the migrant cities. From the point of view of the incoming population these cities were primarily work places.

Observers of this transformation of the city attempted to make sense of the experience in terms that reflected their own understanding of Russia's social order and economic future. To tsarist provincial administrators and municipal leaders urban migration represented a phenomenon of growing political importance that challenged their sense of social and public order. Seasonal laborers were the most visible of the migrants, and their presence was profoundly disturbing to officials because to them these newcomers personified poverty and disorder. The "thousands of workers" whom a tsarist inspector found in the Volga port town of Samara in 1880 "waiting on the squares to find work" were living "on the edges of the river with only the sky as a roof." He noted that their situation was particularly terrible in bad weather: most were "terribly poor, not even owning a coat."[115] He was shocked at the indifference that the municipality displayed toward these migrants, not only because his sense of moral and patriarchal justice demanded that the authorities accept responsibility but also because he, as other officials, feared the presence of the urban mob.

The impersonality of the urban labor market meant that employment was at the mercy of economic cycles and the whim of employers or foremen. This impersonality and the conditions it produced seemed a new and threatening social problem to conservative Russians, and it was one to which tsarist social policies had no easy solution. What sense could the authorities make of situations such as the one reported by a gendarme officer in Rostov-on-Don in 1884, when, as a result of an economic recession, a "mass of local and migrant workers, without any occupation, roam the streets and fill the taverns"?[116] In the well-ordered estate society these unemployed, even if local workers, were out of place because they had no fixed abode. To tsarist authorities they were a public burden that had to be dealt with by the municipalities and the police. But they could not be contained, both because of their numbers—the reports invariably cited "thousands" or "tens of thousands" of migrants in these commercial centers—and because so many were temporarily uprooted.

The official status of most urban migrants was doubly uncertain. They were not living in their ascribed place of residence (which for the lower ranks, both urban or rural, was fixed as the place of birth and could only be moved with great difficulty) and were often in violation of the regulations on internal travel. In theory the passport system gave legal standing to temporary migration, but it attempted to draw a distinction between short-term travel, regulated by "certificates," and year-long absences requiring special passports. In practice migrants often appear to have dispensed with proper documentation. The challenge that urban migration posed to officials was not simply one of laborers lacking proper documentation. By the 1880s the rising tide of migrants was beyond the capacity of the police to take account of the new arrivals. Official reports continued to claim some awareness of the scope of violations, but they were unconvincingly precise in their descriptions of the problem. For example, Tsaritsyn's police asserted that of the ten thousand seasonal laborers who arrived during the 1887 navigation season, one-fourth lacked passports.[117] More revealing was

115. "Reviziia Senatora Shamshina," TsGIA, f. 1391, op. 1, d. 23, 4.

116. "Politicheskoe sostoianie Ekaterinoslavksoi gubernii," TsGAOR, f. 102, d. 59, ch. 27 (1885), 20.

117. "Otchet o sostoianii Saratovskoi gubernii," TsGIA, f. 1284, op. 223 (1888), d. 168, 18.

the admission of the Nizhny Novgorod governor at the end of the century that the "enormous influx of temporary inhabitants, most of whom belong to the lower classes and find lodging in flophouses, empty municipal lands, and on the piers," was so great that the police could not keep track of the "overflow."[118]

This flood of migration was not always considered to be inherently threatening to public order. In certain instances officials used their powers with some discretion, replacing the bureaucratic formalism of the tsarist state with a more flexible understanding of the condition of these newcomers. According to one investigation of the capital's "lower depths," the Petersburg police and justices of the peace collaborated in selective law enforcement among the "thousands" of passportless inhabitants whom they captured. They punished only those who were judged "harmful" and permitted the "harmless" ones to stay, even providing some with temporary residence permits until their passports reached them.[119] This relative flexibility—or laxness—operated within the context of state surveillance of the outsiders: the authorities judged whether they were fit or unfit for residence in the city. The arbitrariness of this process opened the door to bribe taking. There is an abundant record that bribes were taken and that in their own way they made the police accomplices in opening the city to the undocumented migrants. To the extent that this unofficial policy existed in other cities it represented a subtle means to ensure that the laboring population remained available to the urban economy and that it was also reminded of its menial place in urban society.

The human face of the newcomer was easily overlooked, both by the authorities and by the ordinary townspeople. Often the newcomers were greeted by ethnic or social prejudice. Hostility was clearest toward the Jewish migrants, who in the 1860s and 1870s began to move out of the western areas of the Pale of Settlement into the new and expanding towns of the central and eastern Ukraine. In 1880 Kiev's mayor asserted that "the city is overcrowded [perepolen] with people who lack the right to live here, . . . of whose existence the police know nothing."[120] He thought that the Jewish settlers were such a menace that, if they continued to pour into the city, they would "end the historical life of Kiev."[121]

The same view, expressed in similarly threatening language, came from

---

118. "Otchet o Nizhegorodskoi gubernii," TsGIA, f. 1282, op. 3 (1902), d. 545, 845.
119. V. Mikhnevich, Iazvy Peterburga (St. Petersburg, 1886), 55.
120. "Zapiska Senatora Polovtsova o Kievskoi gubernii," in Trudy komissii Kakhanova (St. Petersburg, 1884), vol. 2. pt. 2, 353.
121. Ibid., pt. 1, 53–54.

the Ekaterinoslav provincial governor a decade later. His fears centered on the influx of "migrants from many areas," who were moving to new industrial settlements in such numbers that there existed "no chance of registration of the population." His principal concern was what he termed the "Jewish invasion." "At first, one or two" Jews settled in places that he called "the most turbulent points," and they were quickly followed "by others even from other provinces."[122] He was particularly concerned about public order, but his preoccupation with Jewish migration echoes in a mild form the popular anti-Semitic prejudice that was becoming increasingly evident—and violent—in those years.

These threatening images of invasions and floods created an imaginary wall around the city, whose defenses were meager. The authorities recognized that there was a place—and a need—for the migrant worker but often seemed to classify him as a disreputable and immoral type. One governor wrote that the population of southern boomtowns consisted of a "mass of people who were unbelievably hungry for quick wealth."[123] The array of migrants included "various sorts of speculators and adventurists" alongside "large numbers of working people," who the Odessa police prefect claimed in 1873 were drawn to his city by its "great trade position."[124] According to Laura Engelstein contemporary medical discussions identified migrants as undesirables, blaming them for the diffusion of certain dangerous diseases. Some doctors, faced with an apparent epidemic of syphilis, speculated that the disease was spread by the male migrant and female prostitute (who was often assumed to be a migrant who had abandoned domestic service). The migrant's marginal position between townsperson and villager supposedly made him a prime candidate for "sexual license and the propagation of sexually defined disease."[125]

Another trait of the migrant as a threatening outsider was drunkenness. Warnings about its ominous role in the outbreak of urban riots revealed growing concern about the ill effects of vodka and a profound unease at the presence of transient workers on the fringes of urban life. In this view migrant practices were a combination of "indiscipline, drunkenness, and riotousness [buistvo]," terms that the Saratov provincial governor used in

122. "Otchet o sostoianii Ekaterinoslavskoi gubernii za 1895 g.," TsGIA, f. 1263, op. 2, d. 49 (1896), 10–12.
123. "Otchet o sostoianii Ekaterinoslavskoi gubernii za 1898 g.," TsGIA, f. 1282, op. 3 (1899), d. 3255, 7.
124. "Otchet gradonachal'nika," TsGIA, f. 1284, op. 69 (1874), d. 150, 10–11.
125. Laura Engelstein, "Morality and the Wooden Spoon: Russian Doctors View Syphilis, Social Class, and Sexual Behavior, 1890–1905," Representations, no. 14 (Spring 1986):181–83.

the mid 1890s to describe the laborers in Volga port cities.[126] The stereo-typical migrant was drunken, diseased, disorderly, and without legal papers. It is no surprise that many thought him to be a menace to public order.

Although we have many descriptions of migrants in the reports of tsarist officials, the migrants' experience is much more difficult to understand in their own terms. Historians have written extensively about the movement in recent centuries of populations from country to country and from countryside to city because these phenomena are some of the fundamental features of modernity and the emergence of industrial economies. These studies usually make commonsense assumptions about the economic motivation of migrants, who are most often portrayed as disadvantaged or impoverished peasants seeking refuge in the city. The experience of the Russian migrants, however, should be viewed in the context of their own cultural background.

Mobility, labor, and urban residence formed the central features of the migrants' collective and personal histories. With few firsthand accounts to counterbalance those of officials and educated observers, the historian who seeks to analyze urban migration from "within" must rely on fragmentary information that suggests rather than makes explicit the actors' views and behavior. The conclusions can only be tentative. Not surprisingly, historical studies explain the migrant experience from both an economic and a social perspective. One debate has centered on the polarities of peasant and worker and asks whether to place the migrant close to one or the other pole. Another line of inquiry has focused on the life cycle of the migrants in terms of their age, family, and social ties.[127] These approaches are complementary, not exclusive, and tend to emphasize narrowly defined dimensions of the migrants' experiences.

To move the issue of migration into the context of urbanization shifts the perspective from structure or process to social context. The central issue that I propose to address is the manner in which migrants occupied urban space for their own purposes, and used, in the words of the French writer Michel de Certeau, "spatial practices" to become, however briefly, a part of

126. "Otchet o sostoianii Saratovskoi gubernii," TsGIA, f. 1284, op. 223, d. 20 (1898), 21–22 (the specific context of his remarks was the thirty thousand seasonal workers in the port city of Tsaritsyn).

127. A recent study by P. G. Ryndziunskii gave new life to the Soviet investigation of this subject: see Krest'iane i gorod v kapitalisticheskoi Rossii vtoroi poloviny XIX veka (Moscow, 1983). In the West, Robert Johnson has undertaken a thorough examination of the problem in Peasant and Proletarian. The implications of migration for women and the family have been explored in Barbara Engel, "The Woman's Side: Male Out-Migration and the Family Economy in Kostroma Province," Slavic Review 45 (Summer 1986):257–71.

that alien urban territory where they chose to reside.[128] This approach assumes that even if these migrants were urban outsiders in terms of their cultural background, social bonds, and skills, they were nonetheless aware of their new surroundings and were capable of inventing behavioral skills to deal with the strangeness of the city.[129] The urban experience of the migrants represents a third approach to the problem of urban migration. It separates the migrants from both the communities they had left—and to which many were still bound and to which they would probably return— and the urban community to which they found themselves.

This separation bears some similarities to the cultural condition that the anthropologist Victor Turner has defined as a "liminal period."[130] Although it is usually associated with tribal rites of passage and symbolic rituals of departure and return to the group, the concept of the liminal period has been applied to other collective human experiences of dramatic separation and cultural discontinuity and provides a fruitful perspective on the experience of Russian migrants. In the context of Russian urbanization it appears particularly helpful in studying the condition of the temporary migrants, the *otkhodniki*, who were separated from their village and who worked in one or more urban centers during that time. As I noted before, the temporary migrants made the most forceful impression on observers, although we should keep in mind that migration also included other towns-people. In the case of the petty bourgeoisie the pattern of temporary migration strongly resembled that of the peasantry: it included separation from family, the move to distant centers in search of work, and periodic return to the place of birth and legal residence.

The issues pertinent to the concept of liminality are similar to those that are often addressed in other studies of migration: separation, companion-ship, status, cultural adaptation, and vulnerability. However, these issues assume a new meaning when the key problem is the emergence of new urban communities in migrant cities. The historical issues raised by the presence of the migrants focus on cultural discontinuity and its effect on the migrants' sense of identity.

The questions of who the migrants were and where they came from are

128. M. de Certeau, *The Practices of Everyday Life*, trans. Steven Rendall (Berkeley, 1984), 93.

129. In the lexicon of geographers this manner of making cultural sense of a geographical place is termed "enirvonmental perception" and entails the processes by which "people form images of other places" and "how these images influence decisions" (Peter Gould and Rodney White, *Mental Maps* [Baltimore, 1974], 17).

130. Victor Turner, *The Ritual Process: Structure and Anti-Structure* (Chicago, 1969), 94–97; see also A. van Gennep, *The Rites of Passage* (Chicago, 1972), 39, 177–78.

usually approached through the documentation that they were in theory required to obtain. As with so many other tsarist tabulations, however, these figures are only useful for comparative purposes. In the 1880s one *zemstvo* study of peasants who left their villages in search of work made every effort to avoid the appearance of an official inquiry but was still incomplete because the population feared unpleasantness with the police. One of the *zemstvo* workers noted that the reason the peasants feared the police was that "a majority [of the migrants] are without passports; they only have a travel certificate and some lack even that."[131] The figures on the issuance of passports, which the state required of both petty bourgeois and peasants when they moved, give only a very approximate notion of the scale and rate of growth of population movement, and they provide no indication of destination. These figures do, however, suggest an extraordinary surge of internal migration, which more than tripled between the 1860s and 1880s (reaching 3.5 million at the end of this period). Short-term certificates, which were in far greater demand than the passports, grew at a similar rate. By the last decade of the century they were issued at the rate of 177 per thousand population in the northern provinces, and 74 per thousand in the southern lands (the Ukraine, the blackearth region, and the middle Volga).[132] According to the Soviet historian P. G. Ryndziunskii, by the last years of the century the combined totals of all travel documents for nonblackearth and blackearth provinces had attained 450 per thousand.[133] The impact of this massive movement on the communities from which migrants departed (and to which they periodically returned in most cases) is a key and little explored issue in Russian social history.

The very existence of a city under these conditions seemed problematical in the late century. The educated elite used the term "village" to indicate their dismay at the pervasive presence of a population of rural origins in the city. But language and practice also revealed the importance of the sense of community that the migrants carried into the city from their places of birth. Once the most visible form of village migrant association, the cooperative work gang (*artel'*), dwindled in importance in the cities as the century came to a close, but it endured as a sort of semicommunal living and eating arrangement and provided an effective means for builders to organize construction gangs.[134]

131. Quoted in Ryndziunskii, *Krest'iane i gorod*, 92.
132. Boris Tikhonov, *Pereselenie v Rossii*, 211–12, tables 12 and 13.
133. Ryndziunskii, *Krest'iane i gorod*, 105–6 (including a discussion of the dangers of reading these statistical aggregates as if they told life histories).
134. Ibid., 119–20.

The ties of village or regional "fellowship" conveyed by the term *zemliak* were a powerful and enduring bond that was practiced and understood within urban migrant groups. Robert Johnson points out that migrants expected to establish themselves in their new place with the help of earlier arrivals from their home territory, who would aid them in finding work and a bed in which to sleep and who would offer companionship in an alien environment.[135] The *zemliachestvo* established the close ties that sociologists have found at work in other countries, ties that "establish a relationship between the migrant and the receiving community."[136] The migrants assisted in this manner were not likely to experience the anomie that urban sociologists once thought accompanied the shift from rural community to urban society. Still, the migrants' entrance into the *zemliachestvo*, as transient in its composition as was their own stay in the city, was an indication of their distance from both their villages and the urban communities surrounding them.

This state of social discontinuity of the urban migrants became integrated into their everyday practices. It appeared in the modest family ritual that marked the departure of a youth on his first trip, for example, the "small ceremony" of a father's prayers, blessing, and moral exhortation that marked one sixteen-year-old's day of departure for work as an apprentice in Moscow.[137] It emerged over a period of months or years in the changed appearance of the migrants: they were proud of their city clothes and manners, and on returning home the young women of the village singled them out from those they had left behind, at least if the observations of one village doctor on life in Kostroma province are typical.[138] Social discontinuity was also embodied in the gender isolation of the lives of the migrants. Boys and men left their families and entered a largely male community of laborers. We know little of the women migrants. Their conditions of work—most often they were domestic servants—largely determined their place in the city. Their remoteness from their homes was probably even greater than that of the men.[139]

However, the migrants brought with them, or quickly acquired, an array of practices that they could share with the urban laboring population.

135. Johnson, *Peasant and Proletarian*, 67–75.
136. C. Tilly and C. Brown, "On Uprooting, Kinship, and the Auspices of Migration," in *An Urban World*, ed. C. Tilly (Boston, 1973), 111.
137. S. I. Kanatchikov, *A Radical Worker in Tsarist Russia: The Autobiography of Semen Ivanovich Kanatchikov*, trans. and ed. Reginald Zelnik (Stanford, 1986), 6.
138. D. N. Zhbankov, *Bab'ia storona* (Kostroma, 1891), 15, 27.
139. The issue of gender among Moscow migrants is examined in Bradley, *Muzhik and Muscovite*, 134–38.

Vodka had a privileged place in their rituals of work and leisure. Collective fistfights brought men and boys from factories or neighborhoods together in a common and bloody form of leisure time activity. Neither of these bonds was unique to migrants. At neither end of the migrant's path were the social boundaries impenetrable. A large proportion of temporary migrants ultimately reestablished village residence; others found satisfying work and joined the ranks of the townspeople. The instability of employment that most migrants confronted represented a deeply unsettling element in their lives. Municipalities offered only occasional, short-term aid for the unemployed. The sudden loss of work meant a return home or, at its worst, a descent into the marginal life of beggars in the cities.

Home ties were a substantial obstacle to establishing urban residence. One Moscow-based artisan, bringing suit in court in the 1880s against his home community (*rodina*, presumably a village), argued that he had "no ties [*osedlosti*] whatsoever [to his community] and no place to return." Even so, he was still bound to pay an exorbitant sum to that community for his passport. He believed himself to be a Muscovite, but the records do not reveal whether the court agreed.[140] For reasons presumably of both financial interest and personal identity, he chose to consider himself a townsman who was being unjustly obstructed by greedy rural officials. These officials probably believed that they were defending their "closed corporate community," in Ben Eklof's words, and its fiscal needs.[141]

The marginality of the migrants was a temporary affair, and liminality was a problematic condition, one that perhaps best characterizes a period in the life of migrants. Even in these terms, however, the growing size of the migrant population through the last decades of the nineteenth century meant that this marginal group always constituted a substantial presence within migrant cities.

Was the migrants' experience accompanied by an awareness of separateness within the urban community? The evidence is meager but sufficiently compelling to give a tentative answer to the question. The discontinuity between the old home and the future place of reenty—whether a new city or the old community—was a function of the distance, real and perceived, separating the migrants from their places of origin and of the social borders of the urban community within which they found themselves. Factory employment was the goal of some urban migrants, but the data collected by Johnson reveal that in Moscow (and undoubtedly in other migrant towns as

140. Cited in Tikhonov, *Pereselenie*, 119.
141. Ben Eklof, *Russian Peasant Schools: Officialdom, Village Culture, and Popular Pedagogy 1861–1914* (Berkeley, 1986), 15–16.

well) only a small proportion (15 percent) of the migrants found factory employment.[142] The migrants in the city were not stationary, either in work or in residence (although the newly constructed outskirts tended to house a high proportion of migrants). They were physically inseparable from the city, but in most cases they were without a fixed place of residence. Their sense of transience made the city a place of passage, both literally for transitory migrants and figuratively for those living on the margins between the city and their distant home.

The separate identity of the migrant, as perceived by educated observers and perhaps by many of the migrants themselves, took on specific shape and color in Moscow's Khitrovka slum. With the help of journalists like Giliarovsky and publicists like Lev Tolstoi, Muscovites tended to view Khitrovka as a place so alien that it resembled "darkest Africa." To incoming laborers it was a refuge—a place of hire and perhaps a gathering point for comrades from home. In a literal sense it was a place of passage from which workers might leave for better quarters, go to other towns, or return to their home communities. Its tangible, harsh, yet ephemeral place in their lives suggests that what most marked the migrant identity in urban communities was not its "savagery," as authorities readily assumed, but its very marginality. It offered some hope of employment and security, but it also threatened hunger, cold, and even death to the unfortunate. The "lower depths" that Maxim Gorky imagined to be both the physical and moral abyss of the urban poor were close to, but not a part of, the migrant's existence. Khitrovka was both a "skid row" and a labor market, and these two aspects of its identity were easily confused by outsiders. To the migrants, crossing the imaginary line separating the two represented, perhaps even more than returning to their village or town empty-handed, the failure of their endeavor.

The new city of railroads, merchants, and migrants was both a physical place and a cultural creation. These three elements are key to the processes of urbanization of late imperial Russia; they also present three distinct faces of the image of Russian urbanism in those years. The economic dynamism that distinguished urban Russia from earlier times owed its existence in large measure to the pattern of economic exchange between city and countryside and to the facilities of transportation, both of which largely depended on the railroad. The economic hinterlands of the commercial centers expanded enormously, and the territory from which migrants could travel to seek urban employment also expanded. The new vistas of prosperity and

142. Johnson, *Peasant and Proletarian*, 34.

progress, which were given ideal form in the national expositions of Moscow and Nizhny Novgorod, emerged as much from this new urban economic life as from the flights of fancy of Westernized bureaucrats in the Ministry of Finance.

Although wealthy townspeople were a very small group within the city, their stereotypical embodiment—the merchant—enjoyed a place of prominence, whether derided or proclaimed a hero of Russian enterprise. His presence was inseparable from that of the other stereotypical member of the new city, the migrant. The migrants came from diverse origins, worked in many different occupations, and stayed in the city for various lengths of time, but they had a place there and an identity of their own. I argue that we should think of the migrants not only as protoworkers or transplanted peasants but also as urban outsiders. Their humble condition and poverty placed them among the urban poor, and their cultural condition between town and country and their transitory situation located them on the margins of the city. In taking the form of the migrant city Russian urbanism defied the very concept of the city as a place of settled townspeople.

3

Russian Municipal Reform and Urban Civil Society

The institutions of urban self-government in Russia acquired increasing importance in the last decades of the nineteenth century. New economic practices, expanding migrant communities, and conflicting perceptions of justice and private interests made the urban public arena a place of struggle for political influence and social control. Municipal autonomy raised fundamental questions of order and disorder, self-rule and discipline, and those questions were expressed in a language that ascribed exalted roles to the various actors. "State" and "society" made their voices heard in municipal government, and "society," which included tax-paying citizens and educated Russians, confronted the "people" in a well-defined but constantly expanding arena. Until mid century the city, in its principal architectural and institutional forms, represented the power of the imperial state. Although autocratic power remained a pervasive presence in later years, new actors and activities gave municipal government a separate and increasingly visible part to play in public affairs.

The reasons for the newfound importance of municipal government lie partly in new imperial policies and partly in the dynamic growth of the migrant city. The reforms of Alexander II's regime included the mobilization of public leaders, who were called on to take an active role in addressing social problems. Municipalities, together with regional assemblies (*zemstva*), had a designated place in the reformed autocracy. The spread of a protoliberal sense of public service and the pressures that increased economic activity created were as important as state initiatives in raising the issue of social needs. In this complex intermingling of the state, the public, and the private, areas of conflict and cooperation were not consistent and uniform. Provincial governors at times supported and at times opposed municipal policies and activists; business interests and educated, public-minded leaders agreed on some local priorities and fought bitterly over others. A small segment of the enfranchised voters honored and deferred to their "betters" in municipal elections; the large majority, however, proved indifferent to public affairs. Specialists with technical training such as statisticians and physicians offered authoritative opinions to the state and to municipalities on how to order and to sanitize, for the good of everyone, the urban areas occupied by the impoverished masses.

The meaning and implications of these developments become clear if we examine the political vocabulary in Russia at that time that was inspired by Western European liberalism. Political conditions in eighteenth-century France—and nineteenth-century Germany as well—bore a strong resemblance to late-nineteenth-century Russia (hence the popularity in Russia of the works of Alexis de Tocqueville, somber prophet of monarchical apocalypse, revolution, and democracy). Western European precedents were very much on the mind of Russians—some to decry the trends of the day, others to welcome them—and theories of power derived from the West European experience help to interpret the nature of the conflict and the manner in which some Russians perceived the issues.

Throughout the late nineteenth century political opposition to the autocracy was identified in public discussions not in institutional but in cultural terms. The chairman of the Council of Ministers, Peter Stolypin, used this language in a speech in 1907 that called for reform in order to end the "confrontations between public life and state life [*mezhdu obshchestvennosti i gosudarstvennosti*]."[1] His description of a sort of "dual power" recognized the success of an oppositional public (*obshchestvennost'*) in creating a separate political identity. In sense and derivation the use of this term (or the alternative term "society"—*obshchestvo*) resembles the German term *bürgerliche Gesellschaft* ("civil society"). Friedrich Hegel employed this term in his political writings to designate a key mediating force, based on economic interest, between the family and the state.[2] It was a vital concept in Hegel's theoretical endeavor to reconcile power and freedom in the modern state.

1. Quoted in Robert Thurston, *Liberal City, Conservative State: Moscow and Russia's Urban Crisis, 1906–1914* (New York, 1987), 184.
2. See Shlomo Avineri, *Hegel's Theory of the Modern State* (Cambridge, Mass., 1972), 141–47.

The theoretical and historical implications of civil society have been refined in a recent work by the German philosopher Jürgen Habermas. He has proposed the term "civil public sphere" (bürgerliche offentlichkeit, translated alternatively as "bourgeois public sphere") to identify that arena of independent public activity between the state and society that the bourgeoisie opened in the eighteenth century. In Habermas's interpretation of the emergence of political liberties the key factors are critical reasoning— found in literature—and autonomous action—found in commercial capitalism. The bourgeoisie uses these two factors to challenge the authority of the absolutist state.[3] Hegel's concept of civil society gives him a theoretical model to associate the rise of the bourgeoisie with the development of rational state power. Like Hegel's concept, Habermas's civil public sphere interprets the reordering of power in modern Western society in terms of social practice but places particular stress on two things: the accessibility of the public sphere to groups besides the bourgeoisie, and the public sphere's essential quality of the "publicity" of public affairs, that is, the emergence of public opinion in opposition to the absolutist state's monopoly of power. This manner of explaining the origins of a politically powerful public sphere minimizes the institutional and legalistic issues central to the liberal or Whiggish historical school.

Habermas's theory is germane to the study of Russian public life in the late nineteenth century. It suggests that opposition to absolutism arises in the opening of a public domain that is legitimated by rationalism, more or less rooted in pragmatic political practice and discourse, and defended by writers and politically active representatives of influential social groups— urban business groups, landed gentry—that are convinced of the legitimacy of their own public action. I use Habermas's theory to interpret the origins and development of the activities and rhetoric of Russian municipal affairs. These affairs were explicitly recognized as autonomous in the municipal reform of 1870; implicitly, they occupied a separate sphere from tsarist administration to the extent that they constituted distinct functions of urban public life.

The usefulness of Habermas's (and Hegel's) theory to the history of Russian urbanism lies particularly in its attention to political practice and participation. From the Russian political perspective in the late nineteenth

3. Jürgen Habermas, L'espace public: Archéologie de la publicité comme dimension de la société bourgeoise, trans. Marc de Launay (Paris, 1978), esp. chap. 3. The original title is Strukturwandel der Offentlichkeit: Untersuchungen zu einer Kategorie der bürgerlichen Gesellschaft (Darmstadt, 1962). I am indebted for this source to Benjamin Nathans, "Habermas's 'Public Sphere' in the Era of the French Revolution" (Unpublished paper, Dept. of History, Univ. of California, Berkeley, 1988).

century the West offered a reservoir of models of political action. The example of Western municipal liberties in itself tended to strengthen the significance of municipal activities to Russians of a liberal persuasion. Vocal *intelligenty* added their voices—either in chorus or in opposition—to commercial and manufacturing interests to define the proper content and role of municipal practices in a Russian civil public sphere. The practice of municipal power, when legitimated by a belief in its value and importance, enhanced the role of municipalities as political entities distinct from the state. The very intensification of municipal "small deeds," even though restricted largely to the migrant cities, gave the urban elite a sense of autonomous governance. This dimension to the story of nineteenth-century Russian urbanism encompasses both the institutions of municipal power and the practice of that power within the context of rapid economic development and the massive influx of migrants. It is also important to understand the limits to the arena of municipal activism, in terms of both power and participation. Civic activists, tsarist administrators, and townspeople differed widely in their attitude toward the municipal public sphere. The nature and origins of that diversity of views suggest the extent to which Russian urbanism acquired a meaningful political role in public life by the end of the century.

The State and the Municipalities

In the early years of Alexander II's reign the city assumed a special place in administrative as well as in public discussions of political reform. The Urban Affairs Section of the Ministry of Internal Affairs assigned a new role in public affairs to the country's towns, and it defined this role in ways that were fundamentally at variance with the Nicholaevan facade model. Provincial governors drew inspiration from the "spirit of the age" to urge the municipalities to undertake new initiatives. Outside town councils, voices spoke out from the once silent nobility, requesting a part in urban public service. The state's decision in 1858 to cease meddling in urban architectural affairs was symptomatic of the new mood. The decision ended the requirement that private buildings adhere to the model facades that were officially authorized by state agencies.[4] The city of this new age had to demonstrate its inspirational influence not by image but by deed, not through orderly town plans and neoclassical facades but through public service to promote worthy causes.

4. V. N. Ivanov, ed., *'Obraztsovye' proekty v zhiloi zastroike russkikh gorodov XVIII–XX vv.* (Moscow, 1961), 184.

The eagerness of certain Petersburg administrators in the ministry's Urban Affairs Section to reform and activate municipalities inspired them to take unprecedented initiatives. In the previous fifteen years they had conducted investigations into the problems of Russian urban life. This work had persuaded them that they possessed a clear sense of the role of the Russian city as a setting for constructive public activity. They realized that urbanism did not appear "by renaming a settlement a 'city,'" as they emphasized in a memorandum written in early 1860. Their understanding of the "character" of the city was multitiered and encompassed the urban economy as well as municipal policies and priorities. It incorporated a profile of the "real conditions of the urban population," which included commercial affairs, rural occupations, migration, availability of work, and property-holding. These factors in turn determined "local needs," on which was predicated the proper "form of self-rule [obshchestvennoe upravlenie]." Convinced that they were in a position to act on the problems confronting the Russian city, they prepared instructions that year for a nationwide survey of political and economic conditions in urban areas. The purpose of this survey was "to familiarize [the ministry] with the peculiarities of the cities" and to obtain "accurate indications of [their] real needs." For these "enlightened bureaucrats" cities contained a vast amount of essential information that special local commissions made up of "deputies of all urban estates" would collect and that the Urban Affairs Section would analyze and interpret.[5] Their goal was quick action on municipal reform. Their enthusiasm was not shared, however, by the Council of Ministers, which judged that emancipation and the reform of rural administration were highest priorities. In April 1860 it declared that the creation of the commissions was "premature."[6] Two years later it finally authorized the call to begin work on municipal reform.

The discussions on municipal affairs in these years offer intriguing insight into the expectations of tsarist reformers for local self-rule. These officials proposed a new definition of urbanism. The pressure behind municipal reform was clearly instrumental: it was motivated by a sense of crisis in local and provincial governance. In the judgment of an 1860 memo

5. Ministerstvo vnutrennikh del, Ekonomicheskoe sostoianie gorodskikh poselenii evropeiskoi Rossii v 1861–1862 g. (St. Petersburg, 1863), 1:v–vi. This introduction spells out the principles that inspired the 1860 initiatives taken by the Urban Affairs Section.

6. "O sostavlenii soobrazhenii otnositel'no uluchsheniia obshchestvennogo upravleniia v gorodakh," Tsentral'nyi gosudarstvennyi istoricheskii arkhiv (abbreviated TsGIA), f. 1287, op. 37, d. 2137, 124.

the cities would remain unable "to solve many current needs as long as municipal self-government remains in its current condition."[7]

In 1863 the local commissions submitted their "considerations" on economic, social, and administrative conditions in their cities. From these reports the urban affairs officials tendentiously drew the conclusion that "all [cities] unanimously explain the deficiencies of the existing order by their lack of autonomy [*samostoiatel'nost'*] in all major actions of urban welfare and economy."[8] The reformers were prepared to carve out a sphere of municipal action separate from the tsarist administration on the assumption that "public self-government" [*obshchestvennoe samoupravlenie*] was the solution to the decay of the cities, which they perceived to be emblematic of the decay of the country as a whole.

The role that the urban affairs officials assigned to municipal self-rule did not intentionally encompass the creation of a civil public sphere. In their estimation an urban elite was needed to accomplish certain tasks unworthy of the tsarist administration. Nikolai Miliutin, a key figure in the early discussions of the *zemstvo* reforms, emphasized in a memo written in 1863 the importance for the central government to "focus on the most notable state affairs." He believed that local bodies, which by implication included the municipalities, ought to concern themselves with "a wide range of local interests, mostly petty, that are unimportant to the central government but that represent real needs for the local population."[9] He failed to explain what might happen if the local institutions did not or could not cope with these needs. His view, which was one generally shared by reform bureaucrats, assumed that a revival of previously moribund local institutions on the basis of self-rule would result in a remarkable improvement in initiative and effectiveness.

Implicit in his reasoning was a second key assumption, namely, that the cities contained an abundance of human talent waiting for the opportunity to serve the public good. In his call in 1862 for the formation of the local urban commissions the minister of internal affairs, Count Valuev, included an appeal that was more than a rhetorical flourish for the participation of "the most experienced and outstanding people" from all estates.[10] In Miliutin's memorandum, cited earlier, such public-spirited citizens were char-

---

7. Ibid., 19.

8. *Materialy otnosiashcheisia do novogo obshchestvennogo ustroistva v gorodakh imperii* (St. Petersburg, 1877), 1:84.

9. TsGIA, f. 1275 (Sovet ministrov), d. 33, 105. Excerpts of this memorandum are cited in S. Frederick Starr, *The Politics of Decentralization and Self-Government in Russia, 1830–1870* (Cambridge, Mass., 1976), 250–52.

10. Ibid.

acterized no less grandiloquently as "the best and most educated people." They would find a "practical direction" for their idealism in opportunities for local reform (and presumably would not choose the alternative model of "new people" that was proposed that year by Nikolai Chernyshevsky in his novel *What Is To Be Done*).[11]

As in other periods of rapid reform, the Russian state relied as much on the sudden mobilization of committed, talented, and loyal subjects as on major institutional changes for the success of its measures. Like the models of technical ingenuity and social progress that had been singled out for emulation at the national expositions, the appeal for public support revealed the extent to which the reformers' plans idealized public life in the city. The experience of a century of municipal self-rule had taught the public to expect officials to dominate public life. But suddenly townspeople were to believe that local power lay in their hands. This dubious assumption informed much of the discussion of municipal reform. For example, it appeared in the "considerations" drawn up by the town leaders of Perm. After chastising their fellow townspeople for treating civic duties as a "formality that they could easily do without, dreamed up only God knows why," the authors promised that their "apathetic" and "disorderly" municipality would be transformed into a "free, self-governing community" if only arbitrary state intervention were eliminated.[12] Why and how, after decades of mediocre municipal leadership, men of extraordinary ability would suddenly emerge represented a dilemma that the reformers could not resolve.

One group had already laid claim to the title of "best people" in urban affairs. Between 1859 and 1860 numerous petitions reached St. Petersburg from provincial and district noble assemblies, backed at times by the governors, that called for special representation for the nobility in municipal dumas. The reformed St. Petersburg municipality of 1846 was their model. In St. Petersburg deputies representing personal nobles (largely state officials who had risen to a rank conferring on them the title of noble) and those representing hereditary nobles each had their own separate curia; hence they could potentially dominate the merchant estate, which was the sole active public force in most towns. In the province of Penza a delegation of landed nobles and bureaucrats presented their petition to the governor, whose supporting message to the capital explained that these groups could bring "real aid" to urban affairs thanks to "their education and proper

11. "O sostavlenii soobrazhenii otnositel'no uluchsheniia obshchestvennogo upravleniia v gorodakh," TsGIA, f. 1287, op. 37, d. 2137, 176.
12. "Mnenie o soobrazhenii," TsGIA, f. 1287, op. 37, d. 2171, 5.

knowledge of the laws."[13] Through their district assembly the members of the Moscow nobility petitioned to participate in the public affairs of their city. Count Stroganov, the governor of Moscow province, officially baptized the local nobility as the "best people" and added that they would end municipal "disorder [*rasstroistvo*]."[14] Odessa's nobles followed suit. Although the petitions adapted the nobility's political role to the reform spirit of the times, the legitimating principle behind this appeal for local leadership was the legal preeminence that the tsarist regime granted to the noble estate.

The reasons for the sudden outburst of noble interest in exercising municipal leadership are hidden beneath the rhetoric of the petitions. Perhaps the convocation of the consultative noble committees on serf emancipation and their subsequent dismay at the growing power of the state bureaucracy in controlling the decisions on emancipation inspired nobles to consider the potential benefits of occupying a dominant place in municipal affairs. The petitions came to a quick end—probably dampened by official disapproval—but the issue of a special place for nobles in the new self-governing municipalities remained in public view for several years. Although Minister of the Interior Valuev may have had his doubts, he heeded the tsar's favorable reception to the Moscow petition. In 1862 he approved a new Moscow statute that was modeled on the St. Petersburg statute. The next year Odessa also received a new municipal statute, which did not, however, recognize separate representation for nobles; rather, it created a new curia for large property owners who did not belong to the urban estates (primarily nobles).[15] In a few major cities the doors to urban civic activity were opened to the highest estate of the empire.

Although noble leadership might have seemed anachronistic to those familiar with Western European municipal rule in those years, in the 1860s some Russian nobles assumed an active part in urban affairs. In both Moscow and Odessa the mayoral position passed into the hands of aristocrats, presumably as a consequence of the reforms. Count Shcherbatov, Moscow's mayor from 1863 to 1869, conducted his affairs from the point of view of noblesse oblige, at least if we go by the spirit of his summary report to "urban society" at the end of his term. Wishing to be true to the new principle of "openness" (*glasnost'*), he presented Muscovites with a

13. These petitions are discussed in "O sostavlenii soobrazhenii otnositel'no uluchsheniia obshchestvennogo upravleniia v gorodakh," TsGIA, f. 1287, op. 37, d. 2137, 2–12.

14. TsGIA, f. 1287, op. 37, d. 2004 (1859–65), 38–39.

15. Frederick Skinner, "City Planning in Odessa" (Ph.D. diss., Princeton University, 1973), 210–13.

full account of the activities of the municipality that would enable them to make "a correct and dispassionate judgment [about] whether their chosen representatives carried out their duties."[16] One of his colleagues in the duma from the merchant estate, I. A. Liamin, proclaimed that same year the dawn of a new era of social brotherhood in municipal public life. In his opinion the "mutual distrust and alienation of estates" in previous decades had given way to the "rapprochement and union of the so-called upper urban classes." He attributed this situation to the new spirit of cooperation in the duma, where there now existed "a whole, strong, and integral society."[17] His flowery rhetoric suggests the existence, at least in his imagination, of a Muscovite version of civil society.

The reality of municipal life in the reform years is more prosaic and less benign than Liamin's description implies. First, the meager evidence we possess does not reveal an outpouring of civic ardor on the part of the newly empowered urban nobility. In St. Petersburg, where members of the urban nobility had received special electoral rights twenty years earlier, they proved even less zealous in voting than the merchants.[18] As was the case for the urban estates, only a handful of members of the nobility turned out to be civic-minded. Second, the municipal activities of even this small urban elite was narrowly confined by administrative demands and fiscal limitations. Shcherbatov's principal message to Moscow's "urban society" was the heavy burden of obligatory state expenditures—a doubling of funding for the municipal police, repairs on state buildings, etc.[19] When major projects were undertaken, they came about either because the duma accepted new taxes—the case in Moscow—or because the tsarist administration set a high priority on capital improvements in particular cities. For example, Odessa's municipality was able to launch a development program of street paving, lighting, water supply, and harbor improvements thanks to the encouragement and financial backing of the state.[20] In general, the deeds necessary to make the city the symbol of progress entailed both state support and new civic leadership.

In fact, the presence of nobles among the urban elite appeared to be

---

16. *Otchet Moskovskoi gorodskoi golovy Kniazia Shcherbatova o deiatel'nosti Moskovskoi gorodskoi dumy* (Moscow, 1869), 1.

17. Cited in B. V. Zlatoustavskii, "Moskovskoe gorodskoe samoupravlenie v period reformy 60-kh godov XIX v." (Kandidat dissertation, Moscow State University, 1953), 200–201.

18. I. I. Ditiatin, *Ustroistvo i upravlenie gorodov Rossii*, vol. 2, *Gorodskoe samoupravlenie* (Iaroslavl, 1877), 494.

19. *Otchet Kniazia Shcherbatova*, 9–12.

20. Frederick Skinner, "Trends in Planning Practices: The Building of Odessa," in *The City in Russian History*, ed. Michael Hamm (Lexington, Ky., 1976), 149–51.

incidental to the activation of civic initiative. Previously moribund municipalities became infused with the spirit of the reform period without any enlargement of their constituency. In Kharkov the city acquired the "appearance of self-government" owing to the encouragement of the new governor-general. The replacement of the Nikolaevan martinet by an activist administrator set the stage for the municipal duma to consider town schooling, gas lighting, a new railroad station, and much more. All these changes were made by the established merchant leaders, whose transformation seemed like "a miracle" to the townspeople.[21] All was not changed as if by magic, however. When the new mayor of the port city of Rostov-on-Don, chosen in 1862 by the unreformed duma, set an activist agenda of paving, municipal banking, and schooling, he encountered such disorder and indifference that he concluded that a spirit of "anarchy" reigned there.[22] Such conditions, whether exaggerated or not, suggested to urban activists that they had to form their own faction. They believed that they had been entrusted by default with leadership responsibilities; they also believed that they were endowed with the vision and dedication necessary to build a new city, both literally and figuratively. Although conceiving of a civic sphere of vast proportions and significance, municipal leaders found that their circle of supporters was small and their powers still circumscribed by the indifference or skepticism of townspeople. These unresolved problems were the result of decades of municipal inaction and provincial officials jealously defending tsarist prerogatives.

Under these circumstances it is not surprising that municipal leadership from the nobility made its most visible impact in public conflicts with the state. The reform period brought changes in power relations that transcended urban affairs, where questions of power, prestige, and ideology were acted out in a setting that was incidental to the underlying issues. When in 1865 the new mayor of Odessa, Count Aleksandr Stroganov, discovered what he believed to be deceitful action by the minister of finance in dealings with the municipality, he used a duma meeting to accuse the minister of "lying" and called for a public investigation. "There never has been such a speech in the entire existence of the duma," noted an enthusiastic duma member in his diary, "or in all Russia!" A courtly aristocrat could claim liberties of which townspeople had no experience. Unfortunately for Odessa and Stroganov, the tsar saw in Stroganov's speech an act

21. D. Bagalei and D. Miller, *Istoriia goroda Khar'kova za 250 let ego sushchestvovaniia* (Kharkov, 1912), 2:2.
22. A. M. Baikov, *Obzor deistvii Rostovskogo (na Donu) gorodskogo khoziaistvennogo upravleniia za 1863 g.* (Odessa, 1864), 2.

of defiance. The municipality lost the right to publish its duma proceedings, and Stroganov's career as mayor came to a quick end.[23]

In 1870 the same outcome ensued when the Slavophile mayor of Moscow, V. A. Cherkasskii, tried to turn his duma into the voice of the Russian people. He obtained from his deputies, among whom were several ardent Slavophile nobles like himself, approval of a motion that stressed the "mutual unshakable ties between the tsar and the people." The motion pointedly lauded the venerable medieval tradition of the gathering of the estates of the land, the *zemskii sobor*.[24] The tsar was not pleased because Cherkasskii was obviously trying to raise Moscow's duma to a national political role. In words that undoubtedly echoed Alexander II's disdain, Moscow's governor-general later denied the duma's "authority or competence" even to represent "all the inhabitants of Moscow, much less the entire Russian people."[25] His definition of the reformed autocracy left no room for an autonomous public sphere either in the municipalities or in the *zemstva*, the other forum for oppositional Russian nobles.

Despite these conflicts, the reform of 1870 still retained the municipal autonomy that the reform bureaucrats had defended a decade previously. The "golden words" of the municipal statute accorded a municipality the right to function "autonomously [*samostoiatel'no*] within the limits of the authority granted to it."[26] Although its language was somewhat ambiguous, this legislation recognized "public self-government" for the municipalities, something not accorded the *zemstva*. Perhaps the reason for the exceptional treatment of the municipalities can be found in their relative political insignificance. Despite the disputes I cited earlier, the real institutional base of the nobility in the reformed autocracy lay in the *zemstva*. Still, in the tsarist universe of those years the "needs" of the city placed it in a new and different institutional context, one that we might describe as "Western" in the same sense that the judicial reform of 1865 adopted in legal form the Western principle of judicial independence. In the historical schema adhered to by tsarist officials progress retained a European imprint.

The Western character of the reform is probably the main reason why the principle of estate representation, which led to noble preeminence,

23. V. A. Nardova, "Periodicheskie izdaniia gorodskikh dum v 60-kh godakh XIX v.," *Vospomogatel'nye istoricheskie distsipliny* 6 (1976):226–31.

24. V. A. Nardova, *Gorodskoe samoupravlenie v Rossii v 60-kh–nachale 90-kh godov XIX v.* (Leningrad, 1984), 155.

25. Ibid., 175.

26. Walter Hanchett, "Tsarist Statutory Regulation of Municipal Government in the Nineteenth Century," in *The City in Russian History*, ed. Michael Hamm (Lexington, Ky., 1976), 103; Hanchett provides a detailed discussion of the 1870 municipal statute (98–103).

vanished from the new municipal statute. The model of curial elections by estates that was used in the Petersburg and Moscow dumas disappeared. It was replaced by a tripartite schema that was based on the contributions of tax-paying townspeople, both property owners and those merely assessed commercial fees. Because total contributions, not the number of contributors, determined the membership in the three curia, this mode of representation accorded exceptional electoral influence to the handful of residents in each town whose preponderant share of municipal taxes placed them in the first and second curia.

The model of this reform was the Prussian municipal (and legislative) electoral system, which the Urban Affairs Section studied closely in preparation for the reform. The principle behind this procedure of enfranchisement was the presumed responsibility and competence of the propertied and productive classes, which the Russian reformers identified, using Western precedent, as the prime source of the cities' "best people." Late in 1861 Count Valuev gave his approval to this bourgeois principle. He explained to the state council that "those inhabitants personally concerned with these [public] affairs through ownership of urban real estate, trade [permits], and the fulfillment of various obligations" ought properly to receive the right to vote. He acknowledged inequality in wealth (in the form of real estate or trade) but not inequality of social rank in reconstructing urban public life.[27] Although enthusiasm for reform waned later in the decade and conservative warnings about the danger of introducing pernicious Western institutions dominated the political debate (Valuev himself lost his position of minister of the interior in the process), the principle of municipal enfranchisement by property ownership or trade remained at the heart of the reform project.

The 1870 municipal statute was only one ingredient in the transformation of the Russian city in the late nineteenth century. The economic forces of industrialization and the social pressures exerted by migration and population growth had a more profound impact on the direction and shape of urban life. These trends indirectly influenced municipal activities, reshaping the electoral constituency, bringing tsarist officials into urban affairs in spite of the legal autonomy that ostensibly protected municipal self-government, and forcing civic leaders in migrant cities to undertake an activist agenda even when they had little commitment to reform. Municipalities had begun to address the social and cultural needs of their cities even before

---

27. "Po proektu polozheniia obshchestvennogo upravleniia goroda Moskvy," 22 December 1861, TsGIA, f. 1287, op. 37, d. 2004, 15–16.

the 1870 statute went into effect, and they continued to do so after a new statute, wiping out the broad electorate and ending municipal autonomy, went into effect in 1892. The fixation of historians on Russian institutional history has tended to exaggerate the importance of tsarist policy on public practices and ideological perceptions. In the process it has turned the contemporary images of "liberal" and "conservative" policies and groups into objective criteria by which to interpret changing power relations. Viewed from within the urban context, however, municipal practices played a shadowy but key part in creating a civic constituency that the state was unable to repress.

The meaning of the 1870 municipal statute lies less in its details of electoral procedures, selection of councils and mayors, fiscal sources, and responsibilities for "local needs" than in its implicit creation of a civic public sphere and its recognition of a civil society. Both creations were very severely restricted and rudimentary. The recognition of autonomy in the statute, however, enhanced the importance that civic-minded Russians had already begun to attach to urban affairs. It forced tsarist officials, even when violating the autonomy provision, to acknowledge the new character of power relations within the city. Similarly, the encouragement given to propertied townspeople to participate in public affairs, even though disregarded by most, strengthened the ideal that estate distinctions would be replaced by commonalities of culture, ideology, and action. Legal definitions of electoral rights played only a minor role in the formation of a civic elite, but they created an institutional context in which that elite could find space for action. The city was a rapidly expanding territory that challenged the elite's sense of public service and tempted them to introduce their own methods of "civilizing" the mass of migrants. In this manner the municipal reform slowly gave shape and substance to a civil public sphere in the Russian city.

Municipal Oligarchs and the Civil Public Sphere

After the introduction of the 1870 municipal statute the search for the "best people" and the efforts to get municipalities to confront their own civic needs essentially became affairs of local political elites, local practices, and local programs. In the next decades municipal histories would reveal both the potential for the creation of a civil public sphere and the severe limits that tsarist authoritarianism and public indifference placed on that sphere. Political factions coalesced around personal leaders and divisive issues. Leadership and new policies became the source of bitter conflicts, but they also became the points around which emerged consensus about allies and enemies, political priorities and common practices. Smaller, less economically dynamic towns clung to the old habits of deference to local power cliques, conservative leadership, and little municipal action. Migrant cities, however, were an arena of active municipal politics.

Who should speak for the city and what were municipal priorities? Tsarist officials tended to blame the slow pace of action in the major cities and the inaction of small towns on the urban mob and stingy merchants. Municipal activists employed similar rhetorical epithets to chastise their rivals and to portray themselves as "educated," "enlightened," and "progressive" civic leaders. Increasingly, these activists dominated the politics of the migrant cities. Often their pompous language tended to gloss over the prosaic side of their actions and the small size of their constituency. Before 1892 municipal leaders were subject to informal tsarist reprisals and after that year they were subject to sanctioned controls. In addition, they were hamstrung by limited fiscal resources that were never adequate to deal with the needs of a rapidly growing urban population. In other words, municipal autonomy remained a problematical creation.

As a consequence of both the provisions of the 1870 statute and the social conditions of urban centers, the Russian city could not duplicate the mass politics of the English or German municipalities in that period. The legally enfranchised citizenry included only a fraction of the adult male population. To qualify as a voter a citizen had to have one year of residency and either possess real estate subject to tax assessment, or pay municipal commercial fees. Recent migrants, even if possessing property, were excluded from the franchise, as were the owners of the untaxed hovels in which many poor townspeople lived. All renters, whether rich or poor, professionals, laborers, and anyone else not engaged in some form of commerce were also excluded. These restrictions cut severely into the voting population of the migrant towns, with the highest proportion of the disenfranchised among migrants, renters, and the very poor. In these urban areas probably no more than one-fourth of the adult males enjoyed the right to vote.

Further curtailing voting powers was the division of the electorate into curiae according to their tax payments. The handful of wealthy townspeople who contributed two-thirds of municipal revenues controlled the town duma because they elected two-thirds of the deputies. As wealth flowed into the migrant cities in the 1870s and 1880s, the size of the electorate grew principally because of the expansion of the membership of the lowest, third curia. The first curia, composed of those paying the largest tax burden, scarcely grew at all or stagnated and in some cases even declined (see chapter 2). Nizhny Novgorod, probably typical of the provincial migrant cities, counted a total of approximately sixty voters in its first curia in both 1872 and 1890; its third curia, however, expanded in those two decades by 50 percent (from 2,100 to 3,200).[28] The bulk of the Russian city's enterprising and propertied citizens, gathered from every estate of the realm, were found in the third curia. It was most representative of the male population of the city. As such, the third curia quickly became the epitome of the urban plebe and its members were thought to represent either ignorance or democracy, depending on the social views of municipal activists, intellectuals, and tsarist officials.

The dynamics of municipal elections were more a function of cultural values and social bonds than of legislative statute. The process by which enfranchised townspeople participated in the selection of their best people resembled the workings of a private club for the first two curiae and the confusion of a mass meeting for the third. The Ministry of Internal Affairs kept close watch over elections (of which there were five before a new statute altered procedures). The data, carefully tabulated by statisticians in the Urban Affairs Section, uncovered a high degree of abstention, suggesting pervasive apathy and disinterest, especially in the third curia. Among the "patriarchy" of the first two curiae one-half to one-third of the voters participated; in the third curia the rate of participation fell from about 20 percent in the early 1870s to 5–10 percent in the late 1880s. Only in exceptional cases such as Odessa, where bitter ethnic conflicts were beginning to emerge, did participation reach 30 percent.[29] In terms of voter interest in municipal affairs, the new era very closely resembled the old one.

To the extent one can generalize from limited statistical data the social profiles of the absent voter included both the privileged and the plebe. Our most detailed information comes from a senatorial inspection of the southwestern provinces in 1880, including a number of medium-sized towns as

28. N. N. Baidakov, "Vvedenie Gorodovogo polozheniia 1870 g. v Nizhnem Novgorode i vybory v 1870–90-kh gg." *Uchenye zapiski Gor'kovskogo Gosudarstvennogo Universiteta, seriia gumanitarnykh nauk* 105 (1969):76–77.

29. Figures on elections in the early and the mid 1870s are collected in "Vvedenie Gorodovogo polozheniia v deistvie," TsGIA, f. 1287, op. 37, d. 1290 (1878), 56–63; the last elections (1888–89) were examined in incomplete returns in "Statisticheskie svedeniia ob uchrezhdenii gorodskogo obshchestvennogo upravleniia po piatoi chetyrekhletii," TsGIA, f. 1287, op. 38 (1892), d. 2336, 2337, 2338; extensive data on municipal voter participation are found in Nardova, *Gorodskoe samoupravlenie*, 61–70, tables 1–6.

well as Kiev. In Kiev the greatest proportion of abstention (over 90 percent) was among the nobility-bureaucracy, which constituted nearly one-half of the eligible third-curia voters.[30] Their uninterest carried forward the social disdain they had shown for civic affairs in earlier years. And according to Kiev's mayor their uninterest was reinforced by the chaotic voting procedures of the third curia, which were so "debilitating" they were fit only for "the mass of illiterate [townspeople] and for fraudulent voters."[31] His reference to illiterate masses was based on cultural prejudice, not dispassionate observation. The same senatorial inquiry found that almost all illiterate voters (estimated to represent one-third to one-half of the electorate) never participated in elections.[32] Resembling one another only in the minimal tax payments they made, the missing nobles were probably drawn from the ranks of petty property owners and the illiterate voters from poor artisans and traders. Their absence from municipal voting suggests that the borders to this protocivil society to a great extent excluded those townspeople who were marginal to the urban economy.

The abstention of nobles and illiterates made the political voice of the townspeople of the middle ranks more influential than their place among the enfranchised would indicate. The ministry's voting records and the reports of the senatorial inspection left no doubt that the city voter was most likely to belong to one of the urban estates—merchants in the first two curiae and merchants and petty bourgeois in the third. The motives that drew these voters to municipal elections were discussed in contemptuous and patronizing terms by both provincial governors and municipal activists. The comments of both these groups tell us more about their own lofty self-images than they do about the electorate. Many petty bourgeois voters continued to follow the old municipal tradition of cliques and factions, especially in those towns where the forces of commercial and industrial change were little felt. After reviewing senatorial reports on municipal affairs the Kakhanov commission concluded in 1883 that "a few influential people" could control the "subservient [nesamostoiatel'nye] petty traders." The commission blamed these traders for "the improper conduct of elections, which are often affairs of chance and even corruption."[33]

The Kharkov governor-general gave a contemporary twist to this theme

---

30. "Zapiska Senatora Polovtsova," in *Trudy komissii Kakhanova* (St. Petersburg, 1884), 2:95, table 41; 3:60–61, table 26; 120–21, table 40.
31. Ibid. 2:138–40.
32. Ibid. 3:29, table 12, 33, table 14.
33. M. V. Islavin, *Obzor trudov vysochaishe utverzhdennoi, pod predsedatel'stvom stats-sekretaria Kakhanova, osoboi komissii*, vol. 2, *Gorodskoe i zemskoe upravlenie* (St. Petersburg, 1908), 16.

that was suitable to his provincial capital, where commerce and manufacturing were creating a boom economy. He accused "powerful capitalists" of using the new municipal statute to manipulate "petty homeowners, traders, and shop assistants" by means of "promises, intimidation, vodka, and outright bribes of a very miserly sum."[34] Perhaps he had heard rumors from Kiev about the directors of the Mutual Credit Society, that city's principal home mortgage bank, who reputedly brought pressure on their clients to vote for the directors' political faction.[35] For the Kharkov governor-general, the presence of traders, artisans, and merchants in public life necessarily arose from their personal greed and corruption. By implication they stood for class interests and represented intruders in civic life.

His judgment needs to be set against the evidence that ministry officials collected on voting. This evidence points to another possible reading of urban politics, one that suggests that in the 1870s and 1880s electoral practices incorporated private interests and public needs in a manner that provided, at least in the major cities, a local leadership responsive to both practical issues and social welfare. In other words, an ethos of public service was not incompatible with massive abstentions, the indifference of most petty nobles, and the continued influence of the city's business community among municipal electors. Electoral tabulations, which cited only estate membership in their classification of candidates, reveal a selection of duma deputies that voting based on economic interests would not predict.

Although proportions shifted slightly during these twenty years, estate representation in municipal dumas remained essentially unchanged. The deputies from the upper urban estates—the merchants and honorary citizens (a rank that included both professionals and established entrepreneurs from commerce and manufacturing)—held the majority, and petty bourgeois deputies were but a small minority. Only in small district towns that were little touched by economic and social change was the petty bourgeoisie likely to dominate. In the major provincial and economic centers of the country the urban business elite held up to two-thirds of the seats.[36] There was some justice to the conclusion of one Moscow journal in 1876 that "on the basis of current electoral laws the duma is formed mainly of the

34. TsGIA, f. 1287, op. 37, d. 1296, 18–19.

35. *Kiev v 80-kh godakh: Vospominaniia starozhila* (Kiev, 1910), 70–71.

36. The sources for these figures are the official surveys cited earlier: "Vvedenie Gorodovogo polozheniia v deistvie," TsGIA, f. 1287, op. 37, d. 1290 (1878), 56–63, and "Statisticheskie svedeniia ob uchrezhdenii gorodskogo obshchestvennogo upravleniia po piatoi chetyrekhletii," TsGIA, f. 1287, op. 38 (1892), d. 2336, 2337, 2338; see also, L. F. Pisar'kova, *Moskovskoe gorodskoe obshchestvennoe upravlenie: Avtoreferat* (Moscow, 1980), 11, table 2.

Table 2. The Estate Origins of the Elected Representatives of Each Curia (fifth round of elections, 1890)

	Nobility		Merchant Estate		Petty Bourgeoisie		Total	
	Number	Percentage	Number	Percentage	Number	Percentage	Number	Percentage
First curia deputies	130	10	267	20	31	3	428	33
Second curia deputies	152	12	231	18	52	4	435	34
Third curia deputies	149	12	162	13	107	8	418	33
Total deputies	431	34	660	51	190	15	1,281	100

Source: "Statisticheskie svedeniia ob uchrezhdenii gorodskogo obshchestvennogo upravleniia na 5oe chetyrekhletie," Tsentral'nyi gosudarstvennyi istoricheskii arkhiv, f. 1287, op. 38 (1892), dd. 2336, 2337, 2338.

patriarchs."[37] Nobles and bureaucrats (who were grouped together in ministry statistical tables) occupied an unexpectedly large place in municipal dumas. These two groups accounted for one-third of total duma representation generally, and in some provincial capitals, such as Kiev, they numbered up to one-half of the representatives. Thus, these privileged segments of the urban population had a role in municipal politics that far exceeded their insignificant presence among voters. To this extent, the merchants did not monopolize municipal representation.

The electoral data from throughout the country suggest that, at this modest level of political activism, municipal voters turned to socially as well as economically distinguished townspeople for leadership. By law, each curia had a fixed number of deputies to elect (which depended on the size of the city), but its choices were not restricted to men from the same curia. In other words, the pool of deputies in each town included all eligible voters, whose ambitions, talents, or social ties might earn them a seat in the duma from any curial bloc. Incomplete returns from the 1890 elections, primarily from the provincial centers and larger cities, offer our best insight into these obscure electoral processes. Table 2 provides the estate background of each curia's elected representatives; table 3 indicates the estate

37. Cited in E. A. Pavliuchenko, "Moskovskoe gorodskoe upravlenie v 70–80-kh godakh XIX veka" (Kandidat dissertation, Moscow State University, 1956), 57.

Table 3. The Estate Origins of the Deputies by their Curial Membership (fifth round of elections, 1890)

Members of	Noble deputies		Merchant deputies		Petty Bourgeois deputies		Total deputies	
	Num- ber	Percent- age	Num- ber	Percent- age	Num- ber	Percent- age	Num- ber	Percent- age
First curia	44	3	208	16	13	1	265	21
Second curia	139	11	258	20	39	3	436	34
Third curia	248	19	194	15	138	11	580	45
Total	431	34	660	51	190	15	1281	100

Source: "Statisticheskie svedeniia ob uchrezhdenii gorodskogo obshchestvennogo upravleniia na 5oe chetyrekhletie," Tsentral'nyi gosudarstvennyi istoricheskii arkhiv, f. 1287, op. 38 (1892), dd. 2336, 2337, 2338.

background of the deputies arranged by their curial membership. In these elections about one-fifth of the total number of deputies were from the first curia and nearly half (45 percent) of the deputies were from the third curia. Wealthy town citizens tended to avoid serving as deputies, choosing in their place townsmen who were distinguished either by birth or by public repute but not by their wealth. If in fact a patriarchy of merchants dominated the dumas, they frequently preferred to exercise their influence indirectly through less distinguished deputies.

Although one can only infer political attitudes from these statistics, they suggest that economic interests and social deference were not the only factors at work in choosing a municipal leadership. The post-1870 dumas did not duplicate the narrow merchant representation of the Nicholaevan municipalities. A substantial group of deputies was of noble rank and did not possess great wealth. A "delegation of powers" seems to have occurred from the prosperous commercial and propertied citizens to deputies not noted for their business activities. In Moscow only 7 percent of the first curia representatives were from that body. The education and occupation of the deputy seemed most noteworthy to these electors. The biographical record of the nonmerchant deputies from the upper curiae often included secondary or advanced education and some form of professional work.

The patriarchs of Moscow's first two curiae chose, alongside their merchant-honorary citizen representatives, a sizable number (nearly one-third) from the nobility-bureaucracy. Almost all of these men were by the fiscal measures of municipal ranking from the "plebeian" third curia.[38] By other standards, however, some were quite distinguished. They included people such as V. I. Ger'e, a noble by birth and a professor of history at Moscow University, and the lawyer I. N. Mamontov. Their willingness to participate in municipal politics implies that they were ready to serve for what they understood to be the public interest, not for private profit. To the extent they were typical of groups of deputies in other migrant cities, their presence suggests the existence of a civic elite that was distinguished to some extent by an ethos of public service. Their presence was particularly important for the emergence of a civil public sphere in the city.

Their activity became especially significant because of the low level of participation within the dumas. Duma leadership tended to fall into the hands of small political factions, whose views of municipal needs set the tone for public debate and whose quarrels fixed the public image of municipal politics. Reports from the capitals and the provinces in the years after the reform repeated a common theme of half-empty duma meetings. The senatorial survey of the southern provinces in 1880 concluded that generally only one-half of the deputies participated regularly. As a result, "the same small group of deputies becomes the only activists who take a real part in urban affairs by their participation in the various issues associated with municipal administration."[39] There was no pronounced tendency for one particular group of deputies to abandon their municipal duties; the reports refer indiscriminately to wealthy merchants, poor nobles, and humble petty bourgeois in identifying the missing representatives. Noncommercial groups—nobles, bureaucrats, priests—predominated in the duma of the central Russian city of Tambov, where the 1880 inspection discovered that "meetings of the duma are conducted by a few people, most often by the mayor himself."[40] Despite the broad suffrage of the 1870 reform, municipal power had, as in the early part of the century, fallen into the hands of relatively few townspeople.

Because of their own interest in urban affairs and because of the indolence of most electors the members of this elite tended to become the stalwarts of municipal life over a long period. In the mid 1880s the interior ministry's statisticians found that longevity in office was a characteristic of deputies in all curiae. Not surprisingly, it was most pronounced in the first,

38. Pisar'kova, *Avtoreferat*, 10–11, table 1.
39. "Gorodskoe khoziaistvo Chernygovskoi gubernii," in *Trudy komissii Kakhanova* (St. Petersburg, 1884), 3:247–57, 566–67.
40. "Gorodskoe khoziaistvo Tambovskoi gubernii," in *Trudy komissii Kakhanova* (St. Petersburg, 1884), 6:58.

nearly 60 percent of whose deputies had won reelection in three out of the four elections. In the third duma, one-fourth were in their third or fourth terms.[41] These long-serving deputies were the leaders of municipal affairs and the regular duma participants. Such was the case, for example of Moscow's Professor Ger'e, whose term lasted from 1876 to the turn of the century and who made social welfare his special field of municipal expertise.[42] The fact that he subsequently became active in national politics suggests that in his case, as in many others, the possibility for civic activism had political implications that tsarist reformers did not intend.

Despite voter abstention and deputy indifference, post-1870 municipal dumas were far more active than prereform dumas. With considerable pride—and perhaps exaggeration—government urban affairs statisticians revealed in 1879 that duma meetings were occurring throughout the empire with remarkable frequency. By their count, in the first five years after the introduction of the 1870 statute eighteen thousand meetings had taken place and only 10 percent of these had been canceled for lack of a quorum.[43] The vitality that the statisticians claimed to have uncovered was perhaps a product of the heightened expectations for reform that were already apparent in the 1860s. By this measure of activism municipalities were establishing an institutional framework for the civil public sphere. At the same time, however, the social diversity of the deputies and the pressure of local needs made duma activities a subject of growing controversy. Perceived needs, personal ambitions, and social animosity combined to generate bitter debates that often obscured the real issues.

Municipal politics became an arena of conflict between activists, who sought extensive civic programs, and conservatives, who disapproved of what they thought of as spendthrift policies and instead advocated fiscal frugality. The activists, far more vocal, portrayed these controversies as being driven by the ignorant, selfish members of the urban estates who were blind to the ideals of public welfare, enlightenment, and commitment to public service. Estate stereotypes became a convenient weapon in their hands. The activists, together with the tsarist officials, proclaimed that the merchants and the petty bourgeois had a backward, tribal understanding of the city, that is, a fatalistic view of urban life and a proprietary sense of control of urban society. For example, in the late 1870s the activist mayor

41. G. I. Shreider, *Nashe gorodskoe obshchestvennoe upravlenie* (St. Petersburg, 1902), 18.

42. Pavliuchenko, "Moskovskoe gorodskoe upravlenie," 104.

43. "Vvedenie gorodovogo polozheniia v deistvie," TsGIA, f. 1287, op. 37, d. 1290 (1878), 112–13.

of Tambov explained the ineffectiveness of his municipality by pointing to the deputies he referred to as "half-literate merchants and petty bourgeois."[44] His culturist language permeated the discussions of both urban activists and government officials who were hostile to commercial factions in municipal government. The police chief of the Volga port town of Kuznets, a stalwart tsarist official, explained the inaction of his municipality by referring to its lack of "any cultural aspirations." He noted that this deficiency was the cause of the city's "narrow concern for personal interests" and its unwillingness to do anything that would "disrupt the usual peaceful conditions of life."[45]

The mayor of a south Russian town (who was a university graduate, a gymnasium teacher, and an unsuccessful campaigner for more municipal elementary schools) provided a detailed literary portrait of his ignorant enemies. He regretted the presence in municipal politics of "an unskilled worker whose hovel has neither a brick nor a stone floor" and of "someone who does not even have a simple wax candle or kerosene lamp and gets his light from kindling wood, and even then for economy's sake sits part of the evening in the dark." From such as these, he disparagingly remarked, one could not expect support for improvements in street paving or lighting. He called for the elimination of "illiterates" from municipal affairs. This portrait made his own culturist view of public life quite clear; in fact, all the deputies of his town claimed some level of education.[46] In effect he accorded no public awareness whatsoever to his parsimonious townspeople, whose petty lives and "personal interests" by definition excluded them from his ideal civil society.

The many criticisms of the backwardness of the urban estate deputies tells us a great deal about the educational background, cultural views, and civic ideals of the municipal activists. They adopted a vocabulary that ennobled their aspirations and reforms and demeaned the objectives of their rivals. Their portrayal of urban politics does not, however, constitute a fair characterization of the civic priorities and social outlook of municipal factions. The so-called merchant party, at least in the large towns, usually had a concrete program and was not blind to issues of urban needs. Some factions defended their views by citing traditional practices, others by referring to higher civic goals. The key issues involved the problems of

44. "Gorodskoe khoziaistvo Tambovskoi gubernii," in *Trudy komissii Kakhanova* (St. Petersburg, 1884), 6:69.
    45. TsGIA, f. 1290, op. 5, d. 28, 104.
    46. "Gorodskoe khoziaistvo Chernygovskoi gubernii," in *Trudy komissii Kakhanova* (St. Petersburg, 1884), 3:162.

inadequate resources and, in the migrant towns, burgeoning demands for basic social and public services. All factions addressed these problems to a greater or lesser extent. None had a monopoly on civic action. Each municipal faction claimed in effect to be the voice of the city and sought to occupy the central position in civic affairs.

In the small group of activists "literacy" was both a code word for public service and an indication of a strongly perceived difference between the members of this group and the town public. The isolation of many councils and mayors from their urban constituency was both cultural and political. The figures from the mid 1870s indicate that the estate membership of the mayors and town councillors strongly resembled that of their fellow deputies. In large and small towns alike, merchant councillors were in a majority.[47] There was a substantial difference, however, in the level of education of the councillors. Information is incomplete, but it consistently reveals that the councillors and especially the mayors were men of some advanced educational training. The senatorial investigation of 1880 found that the councillors usually had some secondary education. This tendency was particularly strong in larger towns and cities. The Kiev city council included three merchants with secondary education, an engineer, a professor from the theological academy, and an officer with advanced military training.[48] Mayors also tended to possess an education considerably above that of the average deputy. A mid 1880s survey of thirty-two large towns and cities found that three-fourths of the mayors belonged to the first curia, 60 percent had a secondary or higher education, and over half were employed in some type of state service. By contrast, the same investigation found that only one-third to one-fourth of the deputies had a comparable education.[49] At a time when educated Russians were reordering "society" in their own minds by elevating the "intelligentsia" above estate ranks and honors, the educational level of urban leaders apparently earned them genuine stature and authority in municipal political life.

Whether validated by official degrees or claimed by force of lofty language, educational attainment became a key ingredient in the dynamics of municipal politics. A mayor's language immediately revealed his perception of himself in this ideal world of civic eminence. Tambov's mayor resigned in 1879 after only one year in office because of the "fruitlessness" of his

---

47. "Vedomost' o sostave gorodskikh dum i uprav," TsGIA, f. 1287, op. 37, d. 2190, 147–48.
48. "Zapiska Senatora Polovtsova," in *Trudy komissii Kakhanova* (St. Petersburg, 1884), 2:190.
49. Shreider, *Nashe gorodskoe obshchestvennoe upravlenie*, 19–20.

attempts to implement the reforms he judged to be "excellent and necessary for the good of the city." He blamed the "semiliterate merchant and
petty bourgeois deputies" for the failure of his efforts.[50] When mayors
lacked these ennobling qualities themselves, officials found an easy explanation for municipal inadequacy. The secret yearly reports of provincial
gendarme officials repeatedly referred to an ideal of the "best people" that
incorporated the intellectual qualities associated with education. In the new
industrial region of the western Ukraine the mayors of the mid 1870s were,
in the opinion of one officer, "absolutely unsuitable for their duties because
of their low native intelligence and their lack of any education."[51] At this
level description was equivalent to condemnation. In characterizing the
mayor of the Moscow province town of Kolomna as "an uneducated former
peasant, owner of a local tavern, who takes more care of the tavern's needs
than the town's," the district gendarme officer encapsulated his own social,
cultural, and political agenda for civilizing the city.[52] The similarity of the
language that municipal activists and tsarist officials used when judging
municipal inadequacies suggests that both groups believed that intellectual
(and moral) eminence was essential to the enterprise of making the city a
center of progress.

The implicit assumption that education was the key to virtuous and
progressive municipal leadership was self-serving and misleading, however.
It is not clear, for example, how essential intellectual attainments were to
the politics of the Kiev municipality, whose council's educational distinction
was noted earlier. The city's mayor of the late 1870s and early 1880s,
Gustav Eisman, was professor at St. Vladimir university—and an extremely wealthy man. His power rested on a political "machine" that was
adept at using proxy votes from the clients of a major bank to elect loyal
deputies, many of whom were presumably from among the well-educated
nobles who constituted the majority in the duma.

If we can believe the memoirs of a local journalist, Eisman's faction and
his backers in the Mutual Aid Society included property speculation and
development in their agenda. These policies were as much a potential benefit to noble as to merchant or petty bourgeois property owners. In one
affair the owner of a large commercial and residential building petitioned
the duma to be permitted to construct a church on a nearby town square.

---

50. "Gorodskoe khoziaistvo Tambovskoi gubernii," in *Trudy komissii Kakhanova* (St.
Petersburg, 1884), 6:69.
51. "Politicheskii obzor," Tsentral'nyi gosudarstvennyi arkhiv Okt'iabrskoi revoliutsii
(TsGAOR), f. 102, d. 9, ch. 21 (1887), 45.
52. "Politicheskii obzor," TsGAOR, d. 88, ch. 35, 46; ch. 20, 29.

On investigation, the reporter discovered that the petitioner stood to profit financially as well as spiritually. The presence of a church would end an outdoor market on the square, forcing traders to rent shops in nearby buildings, whose rental value would soar. Our muckraking journalist concluded, in terms that echo other judgments of less prestigious municipalities in those years, that "the majority of deputies . . . exclusively [seek] to obtain personal profit."[53] On a more prosaic level the pervasive practice of setting a low value on town real estate indicated that private interests were at work behind the scenes. This practice reduced taxes and resulted in the loss of municipal revenues. In the late 1880s the Moscow provincial zemstvo conducted its own assessment of urban property; it doubled and tripled the values that had been fixed by the municipalities.[54] This disparity is one crude measure of the inherent contradiction between the objectives of tsarist leaders (and of urban activists), which were to find the best people and to resolve local needs, and the economic and social conditions of the migrant city.

Social and cultural stereotypes reveal a great deal about the perceptions that different groups employed to make sense of the encounter between self-government and the townspeople in the postreform years. However, stereotypes could also obscure the municipal practices that emerged in that period. For example, in early 1892 a newspaper dispatch reported that Kharkov politics was split between the "old" merchant bloc and the "new" *intelligent* faction. However, the journalist only classified the latter's candidate for mayor with the "new" faction because his daughter was married to a pharmacist.[55] Official reports on backward municipalities occasionally revealed other dimensions to public inaction besides ignorance and greed; in particular, they pointed to pervasive impoverishment. A gendarme report on towns in Moscow province complained that the municipalities showed "no effort to improve the well-being of the people" but then noted that they were constrained by "a miserly budget resulting from the poverty of the population."[56] Under these conditions "indifference" to public welfare was less a function of cultural sloth than an effect of hardship; it was a condition that resembled the situation in prereform municipalities. Where new wealth flowed through urban economies, civic leaders, whether shaped in the culturist mold or not, could undertake public works beyond the dreams of those in poor municipalities.

53. *Kiev v 80-kh godakh: Vospominaniia*, 80, 92.
54. TsGIA, f. 1149, op. 11, d. 38 (1892), 296–97.
55. *Moskovskii listok*, 14 April 1892.
56. "Politicheskii obzor," TsGAOR, f. 102, d. 88, ch. 35, 41.

This expanding fiscal base was the singular advantage of the migrant cities. It was the obverse side of the glaring social hardships and constantly growing demands on public services that economic development and the influx of migrants created. Moscow stood out in this respect as the exemplary city. In the years when Nikolai Alekseev was mayor, its politics brought out the new forces in the public life of the city. In his conduct Alekseev combined the traits of his merchant forebears and the qualities of a civic leader (for example, he was educated in a secondary commercial school). To one Muscovite intellectual-activist (and former mayor) Alekseev was a man "born to command and to order."[57] He was both a leader of his business community and a political activist who was elected to the provincial zemstvo and to the Moscow duma, which chose him in 1885 to be city mayor even though he was only thirty-three years old. His ambitious program of public works entailed enormous expense, which led him to launch a program of municipal loans. Part of his duma and the tsarist administration resisted this program. His manner of conducting municipal affairs displeased the tsarist administration because he operated, in the words of one gendarme report, "on too grand a scale and almost without supervision."[58] Until his assassination by a disgruntled municipal employee in 1893, he was a municipal activist whose political ethos bore little resemblance to the stereotypical images of merchants and intellectuals. His example suggests the complexity of the conflicts, political and social, that were contained in the small public sphere of municipal life.

The social rank of municipal voters, deputies, and leaders is of little use in understanding the debates and factional divisions in the body politic of the city. One might expect that the social customs outside the duma would be reflected within its walls, but these customs do not adequately explain municipal politics. When Professor Ger'e pointed to the petty bourgeois deputies' habits of "bowing humbly to 'eminent merchants,'" "preferring silence" in debates, and "voting as their leaders indicated," he was in effect proclaiming his allegiance to the "educated" duma group.[59] The key point is that municipal politics operated in a very small world where debates over local needs confronted the immediate issues of municipal taxes and expenditures. The success or failure of municipalities in resolving these issues is not explainable by praising the self-styled "best people" and singling out the "worst people." One Moscow activist claimed that his city's duma of those years was a remarkable "merging of estates" that was brought about

57. B. N. Chicherin, *Vospominaniia* (Moscow, 1934), 182.
58. "Politicheskii obzor," TsGAOR, f. 102, d. 152, ch. 35 (1893), 12.
59. Cited in Pavliuchenko, "Moskovskoe gorodskoe upravlenie," 104.

by work "in common municipal tasks." Such a phenomenon, he exclaimed, was "previously completely unknown in the social structure of Moscow."[60] In his optimistic reading of municipal politics the mingling of social ranks was the essential condition for the appearance of a sense of collective endeavor and, by extension, the emergence of civic activism in the city. However, his vision of a new public order was as idealized as the one put forth at Moscow's national exposition of 1882.

The new agenda of municipal reform was subject to very divergent definitions. A large number of deputies were reluctant to approve a substantial enlargement of municipal services and, as a consequence, were branded "semiliterates" by their opponents. Their opposition stemmed in part from their own economic insecurity and their resistance to municipal expenditures and in part from their reluctance to define the city in any terms other than minimal services and economic operations. Similarly, the commercial and manufacturing interests of the city tended to view the municipality as a vehicle to bolster their economic and social activities. For these interests, labeled in public debates as "merchants," the public sphere occupied a minor place in urban affairs.

The term "local needs" was understood either as public service to higher causes such as good health, cleanliness, participatory democracy, and learning, or as concern for the immediate needs of traders, manufacturers, or other local interests. This latter, "merchant" program did not call on an ethical commitment to social welfare or to the commonweal; rather, it relied primarily on an awareness among its backers of pressing local problems. The activist approach to municipal politics, by contrast, depended for success on the leading role of a civic elite. In the migrant towns, however, both the merchant and the activist perceptions of public needs led to some degree of political activism. One might refer to these two approaches as "conservative" and "liberal," but these labels suggest differences in political philosophy that were less meaningful in Russian urban affairs than were certain political and social forces.

State officials, on the one hand, and the urban masses, on the other, placed special demands on municipalities. Local factions were deeply divided on the social responsibility that the city had toward the migrant population, but all shared the belief that the city was a place where the laboring population could be disciplined and "civilized." Both state authorities and activists conceived of public service as crucial to the work of

60. V. Golitsyn, "Moskva v semidesiatykh godakh," *Golos minuvshego* (May–December 1919):119–20.

municipal self-rule. However, these two groups were profoundly divided on the latitude to be accorded municipal action.

The "golden words" in the 1870 statute on municipal autonomy pointed to the key area of conflict between activists and the tsarist administration. The principal reason for the disputes lay in the pervasive autocratic habits of domination and supervision. Provincial officials continually claimed in their reports to the capital that urban "improvements" occurred, as the Ekaterinoslav gendarme commander asserted, "only because of the energetic demands of the administrative authorities."[61] All important personnel moves, particularly the election of mayors in major cities, came under close scrutiny from tsarist officials. The new governor of Moscow province, P. P. Durnovo, forced Moscow's mayor out of office in 1873 because the mayor failed to demonstrate proper "respect." Durnovo dismissed the mayor with the scornful comment that he was "still a merchant, even if he has the title of state councillor."[62] The governor denied the municipalities any authentic place in public life, describing the deputies two years later as "a group of people without mutual ties and general interests [who are] morally irresponsible."[63] To officials such as Durnovo, the proper role for municipalities was to be "obligated to carry out unquestioningly all orders" from officials, who would "supervise all their actions."[64]

Had Durnovo's attitude been implemented in the daily conduct of municipal affairs, there would have been no need to reform the 1872 statute to satisfy the reactionary views of Alexander III. The reformist spirit of the 1860s, however, remained to put occasional restraints on administrative intervention. An interior ministry report of the late 1870s regretted that "several governors" had intervened unjustifiably in municipal matters of "public need and benefit to the city" and reiterated the statutory provision that gubernatorial authority did not include "administrative instructions" to municipalities.[65] Although respect for this statute weakened in the 1880s, it still provided the grounds for municipal appeals to the Senate.

More important than official calls to order was the expansion of municipal responsibilities, which came to form a complex web of affairs over which even the most authoritarian governor was incapable of exercising close supervision. Repeated complaints from provincial officials about municipal "inaction," which usually meant the municipalities' failure to im-

61. "Politichestkii obzor," TsGAOR, f. 102, d. 152 (1893), ch. 11, 6.
62. Quoted in Pavliuchenko, "Moskovskoe gorodskoe upravlenie," 119.
63. "Vsepoddanneishii otchet," TsGIA, f. 1284, op. 69, d. 126 (1876), 13.
64. "Vsepoddanneishii otchet," TsGIA, f. 1281, op. 7, d. 82 (1875), 19.
65. "Vvedenie gorodovogo polozheniia v deistvie," TsGIA, f. 1287, op. 37, d. 1290, 86–87.

plement the governors' instructions, reveal the extent to which the governors' powers were limited. We need not accept the governors' accusation, as Richard Robbins appears to do in his excellent history of the "tsar's viceroys," that municipalities were derelict in their concern for "local needs."[66] Perspectives on municipal needs, financial resources, and the ideal city varied greatly. Governors added their powerful voices to the ongoing debates on policy within the municipalities, not necessarily effectively but certainly obtrusively.

The governors succeeded, however, in suppressing overt claims by municipal activists to any higher competence beyond local needs. Only rarely did civic leaders seek publicly to enlarge their sphere of action to national dimensions. In 1870 Moscow's municipal leadership unsuccessfully attempted to lay claim to a voice in the affairs of the nation. A somewhat similar claim came again from Moscow in the early 1880s. The origins of this audacious move lay in the atmosphere of crisis of those years, which was sparked by the terrorist movement. In 1880 Moscow public figures prepared a memorandum that challenged the claim (typical of officials like Durnovo) that "a state as vast as Russia may be run almost exclusively by bureaucrats." Its message was an appeal for "public participation in government" at all levels.[67]

In the uncertain early period of Alexander III's reign, the new Moscow mayor, Boris Chicherin, used his prominent position to restate this claim to some form of popular voice in national affairs. By his own admission this eminent historian and political liberal had been chosen to be mayor by a small clique of duma leaders. Still, speaking to the country's mayors at the time of the tsar's coronation, he presented his views as those of "public self-government." He extolled "public initiative" and proclaimed the readiness of elected officials to aid in the struggle against "internal enemies" when "the state takes note of our collaboration."[68] In the reactionary mood of those years, even these few assertive words provoked the anger of the tsar, who forced Chicherin to resign from his post as mayor.

The affair did not end so simply, however. In its repercussions and consequences it was an exemplar of the conflict between the tsarist administration and urban civic society and of the tensions among the municipal elite. One of Chicherin's supporters, angry at the refusal of the duma to

66. Richard Robbins, *The Tsar's Viceroys: Russian Provincial Governors in the Last Years of the Empire* (Ithaca, N.Y., 1987), 168–71.

67. Cited in P. A. Zaionchkovsky, *The Russian Autocracy in Crisis, 1878–82*, trans. and ed. Gary Hamburg (Gulf Breeze, Fla., 1979), 127–28.

68. Chicherin, *Vospominaniia*, 166, 235–36.

vote a protest motion after the mayor's resignation, blamed the petty bourgeois "black hundreds" (that is, reactionaries) of the third curia for this failure.[69] In his memoirs the ex-mayor himself scornfully explained that "civic courage" in this crisis was unthinkable from "merchants and petty bourgeois, . . . [who were] accustomed for ages to render obeisance to authority [prekloniat'sia pered vlast'iu]."[70] His scorn was self-serving and somewhat misplaced. In fact, the "supine" deputies launched at that time a semipassive protest, similar to the tactic other municipalities adopted when governors refused to approve their choices for mayor. For over a year after Chicherin's resignation the deputies did not elect a new mayor. Finally, they picked Nikolai Alekseev over the governor's protest. In the next municipal elections Chicherin was elected as a deputy.[71] These largely symbolic gestures did not weaken the authoritarian pretensions of tsarist officials, particularly in that era of reaction, but they did often force the administration to compromise. These actions also bolstered an awareness of municipal activism among the urban elite, activism that was created in part by its opposition to tsarist intervention in municipal affairs.

The resistance on the part of municipalities to tsarist meddling is a more concrete explanation for the debate over municipal self-rule than such labels as liberal and conservative. The monarchist and patriotic mayor of Kiev, Eisman, justified municipal insubordination when he attributed conflict to "the governors' fears that they might lose authority in the eyes of the population" and to official "hatred for anything that carries even a shadow of autonomy and independence from the bureaucracy."[72] His emphasis on the issues of tsarist authority and municipal autonomy pointed to the substantial institutional role of municipalities in the new power relations of the reformed autocratic regime. Historians, such as Alfred Rieber, who dismiss the political activities of the Russian merchants, have overlooked this relatively quiet but still rapid emergence of an authentic ethos of civic activism among the urban elite.[73] Without either explicit ideological positions or the power of mass support municipal practices were nonetheless forming a new public sphere in the city.

69. S. A. Muromtsev, "Moskovskaia duma," Vestnik Evropy (February 1885):847.

70. Chicherin, Vospominaniia, 256.

71. Pavliuchenko, "Moskovskoe gorodskoe upravlenie," 144, 149; these semisubterranean municipal conflicts with the administration are described in Nardova, Gorodskoe samoupravlenie, 178–80.

72. "Zapiska Senatora Polovtsova," Trudy komissii Kakhanova, vol. 2, pt. 2, 456.

73. See Alfred Rieber, Merchants and Entrepreneurs in Imperial Russia (Chapel Hill, N.C., 1982), esp. 99–103; Robert Thurston offers a more nuanced interpretation of municipal "liberalism" in the Moscow municipality in the early twentieth century; see his Liberal City, Conservative State, 9.

The authority that gradually accrued to municipal leaders led in the 1880s to tsarist opposition to the very principles of the 1870 statute. The specter of "popular democracy" figured occasionally in the complaints of tsarist officials, but the key issue was the legitimacy of the civil public sphere of the city. In his yearly report of 1887, the governor of Moscow province defined the essence of the problem as follows: the "widening circle of [municipal] activities . . . strengthens the importance of municipal administration and thereby lessens the significance of the [state] administration."[74] In 1885 the tsar had already sealed the fate of the statute when, in a marginal notation on a gubernatorial report, he expressed his "doubts" about the "appropriateness of the [1870] reform based on the principle of self-rule without state supervision [kontrol']."[75] In other words, municipal autonomy had become a defiance of the principles of autocracy.

The revision of the municipal statute dragged on for several years, an affair (as in the 1860s) of less importance to tsarist leaders than the reorganization of the zemstva. Once again the discussion within the central government turned to the problem of identifying the "best people." The interior minister now sought to incorporate in municipal affairs only the "most reliable elements" by excluding from the electorate "petty traders and salesmen, [who are] deprived by their economic position of any independence."[76] The argument echoed the earlier comments of provincial governors; it assumed that well-to-do townsmen, if isolated from the urban "plebes," would form a municipal leadership that would be susceptible to tsarist "supervision." His reasoning was seriously flawed, however, because it completely overlooked the roots of political activism arising from the new conditions within the migrant cities.

As expected, the 1892 reform deleted all references to municipal autonomy. It explicitly authorized tsarist officials to annul any municipal action that they judged to be unacceptable "either for state needs or for the interests of the local population." It also severely cut back the size of the electorate by setting high minimum property valuations (from three hundred rubles in district towns to three thousand in the capitals).[77] By tsarist fiat the municipality, as legally defined, shrank in both power and size. Yet the scope of its responsibilities for local needs remained unchanged.

Although the 1892 reform was reactionary in intent, municipal self-rule

---

74. "Vsepoddenneichii otchet za 1887," TsGIA, f. 1284, op. 223, d. 165 (1888), 17–18.
75. TsGIA, f. 1287, op. 37, d. 2196, 232.
76. Cited in E. N. Kuznetsova, "Kontrreformy 80–90-kh godov XIX veka v Rossii" (Kandidat dissertation, Leningrad State University, 1977), 94–95.
77. The new statute is summarized in Walter Hanchett, "Tsarist Statutory Regulations," in The City in Late Imperial Russia, ed. Michael Hamm (Bloomington, Ind., 1986), 109–12.

was only partially reestablished within its pre-1870 limits. The franchise was restricted to an elite, but the elite was one of wealth, not estate. Municipal autonomy was gone, but civic leaders were still expected to devote their energies to improving public services and addressing social problems. The "widening circle of activities" that had been of such concern to the Moscow governor could not be narrowed because the city was an increasingly important presence in Russian public life. Perhaps more than elsewhere, in the city autocracy and modernity proved irreconcilable forces. Reactionary municipal reform was an anachronism.

Tsarist nostalgia for a golden age of restrictive statutory regulations could not undo the accumulated practices of two decades. The reduction in the size of the electorate cut down the municipal constituency but had little effect on the composition of the town elite. Poor voters had had the chance to participate in elections, but massive voter abstention had effectively reduced the electorate years before the 1892 reform. Although the less well-to-do townspeople could not vote after 1892, they could still be elected to the duma, which was open to any tax-paying municipal resident. As a result, this new *tsenzovoe obshchestvo* ("taxed society," that is, the electorate) bore a remarkable resemblance to the old one in terms of voter participation and elected leadership. Over half of the voters abstained from elections after 1892, and those who voted favored their earlier deputies. When Nizhny Novgorod voters gathered to choose their new municipal leadership, they turned as before to their commercial community; over half of the deputies were members of the local stock exchange or their supporters. Three-fourths of these deputies had previously been elected under the old statute. Presumably, some of them had lost the right to vote under the provisions of the new statute. The small town leadership that had previously dominated municipal life continued to do so. As a local paper remarked, "the spirit of the new duma remains the same as before."[78] Throughout the country the dumas were new in name only; generally, only 10–30 percent of the deputies were new.[79]

In migrant cities the municipal leadership was increasingly composed of entrepreneurial and professional groups even though a handful of activists continued to conduct duma affairs. As before, very wealthy townsmen avoided municipal leadership, leaving civic activism to what by then could properly be called the middle classes. In Moscow throughout the 1890s

78. "O vvedenii gorodovogo polozheniia," TsGIA, f. 1287, op. 38, d. 2636, 20.
79. Shreider, *Nashe gorodskoe obshchestvennoe upravlenie*, 81.

"most [duma] members continued to be those who had earlier belonged to the third curia."[80] The Moscow deputies who were classified as "merchants and honorary citizens," who accounted for fully two-thirds of the total by the late 1890s, included directors in manufacturing enterprises (thirty-two in 1897 compared with only twenty at the end of the 1880s) and many professionals. The old trading merchants occupied a minor place. The label "merchant" duma was becoming as anachronistic as membership in that estate. Secondary or higher education figured in the backgrounds of most deputies—by the end of the decade two-thirds of the deputies had reached this level. As one Soviet historian notes, "the changes in the composition of the duma were based less on the new municipal statute of 1892 than on the economic and political development of the country."[81] These changes, however, did not lead to increased participation in duma affairs. As before, many deputies did not attend regularly. Even in St. Petersburg, only about seventy members (one-half of the total) took an active part in duma meetings. The others, in the opinion of the police prefect, had "an extremely meager interest in public affairs."[82] As a consequence, power and influence gravitated, as under the previous statute, into the hands of a small group of activists.

The changes under way in the migrant cities accentuated the pressures on municipalities to undertake extensive public works. The previous conflicts between those who supported civic improvements and those favoring fiscal prudence seemed to become less pronounced under the new municipal regime. In Kharkov, the elections of 1893 saw the "decisive defeat" of the curiously named "noble party," which was described by a local journalist as "intellectuals united on a program of educational, humanitarian, and progressive aspirations." The victors that year were the members of the merchant party, whom the same journalist characterized as defenders of "frugal administration in the old style, without waste."[83] In the next years, however, the Kharkov municipality undertook a major program of civic improvements, belying the merchant party's reputation for frugality. Local needs demanded increasingly ambitious municipal projects. The activism evident in the civil public sphere of the migrant cities was largely a product of the very social and economic conditions created by rapid urbanization.

80. Pisar'kova, Avtoreferat, 12.
81. Ibid., 14; 12, table 3; 13, table 4.
82. "Otchet za 1900 god," TsGIA, f. 1284, op. 223, d. 332 (1901), 94–95.
83. Bagalei and Miller, Istoriia goroda Khar'kova, 2:307.

Local Needs and
the Sanitized City

The municipalities experienced the migrant city as an ever expanding territory that generated imperative and increasingly complex local needs. The perception of these needs, however, varied greatly from the merchant to the activist factions. The response of the so-called merchant group to the problems associated with migration was to define their city as a workplace whose public areas required municipal investment to facilitate commercial and manufacturing operations. In effect, the merchant party delimited the borders of their city around the places of economic activity. The activists defined their city borders to include all inhabited places that required attention to health, housing, education, and welfare. From both perspectives the lower urban classes needed to acquire orderly habits that were suitable to a civilized, Western-type city. By the end of the century the activist agenda was increasingly the rule among migrant cities.

Among the concerns of the activists public health seems to have been paramount. By identifying and condemning insalubrious urban conditions, medical experts promoted expectations of a healthy, "sanitized" city that was far different from the reality of poor water, filth, and stench. Although many townspeople still referred to "God's will" in order to explain endemic contagious diseases and high mortality, public health officials, state bureaucrats, and an increasingly influential group of civic leaders insisted that major public works projects that focused on preventive measures were absolutely necessary.

The potential improvements to urban life included far more than short-term benefits such as a reduction in mortality rates. The introduction of public health measures removed Russian urban areas from the category of "Asian" city, where epidemics raged uncontrolled, as Koch had reminded the leaders of Hamburg. Public lighting brought the Russian city closer to the "cities of light" of Western Europe. Street paving promised the efficient transportation of goods as well as better health conditions. Municipal public works, in other words, were part of a progressive agenda shaped by Western models of the city. In addition, municipal actions on problems such as clean water, education, and sanitation were the substance and meaning of the "widening circle of activities" that filled the civic public sphere of the city.

The heightened concern for local needs was the product of a new awareness of the public interest, increasing respect for scientific discoveries in areas such as public health, and the threat that mass urbanization posed to public order. In the reform years, visions of urban progress in Russia emerged from this new understanding of environmental, health, and public needs. Tsarist officials were increasingly concerned about conditions in their provincial towns. In 1869 the governor-general of Orenburg province explained that "paved streets, sidewalks, and a water main" had become "real and unavoidable requirements." The recent economic growth and sudden population expansion of the provincial capital had created "needs" that had been "impossible to anticipate several years ago."[84] He omitted any mention of facade planning; rather, he redefined public orderliness [blagoustroistvo] to mean vital urban services. His redefinition greatly enlarged the possible array of municipal activities.

In this perspective Russia's urban centers were even less worthy of comparison with Western cities than in the earlier period of facade planning. By the new standards the civilized city was noteworthy not by its public monuments and ceremonies or neoclassical facades and geometrical street plans but by its infrastructure of services for everyday life—paved streets, lighting, water, etc. Any comparison with Europe on those terms could only be invidious. Even more emphatically than before, contemporary judgments condemned the miserable conditions of Russia's cities in the postreform decades. A municipal agenda for remedial action was imposed by the desire for a better future. Public discussions about the backwardness of Russian cities appeared in municipal and state reports, and by late in the century they even appeared in newspaper accounts of urban life. This new manner of writing about Russian urban history in order to criticize contemporary shortcomings to some extent offered an excuse for the inadequacies of public services. For example, Kharkov's governor-general, lamenting the city's meager accomplishments at the end of the century, admitted that "everything possessed by the cities in the form of basic property . . . was created by the efforts and sacrifice of the last two to three generations."[85] Even so, the contrast between past and present cast a somber light on what municipal activists and observers considered to be Russia's intolerable urban conditions.

These woes became a kind of litany that many observers used in reference to "the provinces," a vast and ill-defined territory beyond the pale of progressive (that is, Western-inspired) municipal self-rule. The provincial gendarme commander of the northern province of Vladimir decried the "terrible desolation" of his provincial capital, where streets were "always

84. "Otchet za 1869 g." TsGIA, f. 1287, op. 37, d. 2139, 299–300.
85. "Otchet Khar'kovskoi gubernii za 1900," TsGIA, f. 1282, op. 3, d. 444, 4.

covered with dirt or deep in mud, depending on the time of the year," a "terrible stench" overwhelmed passersby near any courtyard, and "filth" fouled the city's drinking water. The conditions to which he objected were all very tangible: they could be smelled, seen, touched, and tasted. Yet he claimed to be alone in his distress: "The people treat the needs of the city with indifference."[86]

In his awareness of these problems he was a product of the "perceptual revolution" that the French historian Alain Corbin argues had appeared in early nineteenth-century France. In Corbin's opinion the standards by which one judged the "intolerable" in cities were redefined in those years to incorporate "noxious" smells, which ranged from putrid drains and stagnant water to body odors. These criteria of acceptable and unacceptable odors were part of a process by which the authorities circumscribed those places and people for which remedial action was required. Typically, these areas were inhabited by the poor laboring population. In medical debates over public health, the cause of the spread of contagious disease was thought by one influential school to be "miasma," which was easily recognizable by its foul smell.[87] Corbin's theory of the essential changes in the "social imagination" of odors fits well with the judgments of Russian officials and urban leaders and makes clear one underlying reason for the importance attached in the late century to the issue of local needs in the cities. For example, newsworthy information in the Moscow popular press included the lament of one special correspondent from the central Russian town of Voronezh that in summer "an enormous cloud of white dust hangs constantly over the city." Blown up from the roads, the dust impeded breathing and irritated the eyes.[88] The condition was not new, but the implication that something ought to be done about it was.

The agenda for municipal public services potentially involved all aspects of Russian urban life in those decades. Commerce became an important inducement for paving when goods could not be moved through towns in fall and spring because mud made the streets impassable. Walking through ankle-deep mud in areas where sidewalks could easily be built offended the proprieties of educated townspeople; travel in winter by sleigh or on foot across mounds of unswept snow that resembled small hills was equally offensive. An urban outdoors whose only lighting at night consisted of moonlight, tavern signs, and a few faint kerosene streetlights was a threatening place, especially when crowds of migrants filled the city. Most urgent

86. "Politicheskii obzor," TsGAOR, f. 102, d. 89, ch. 43 (1888), 11.
87. Alain Corbin, *The Foul and the Fragrant* (Cambridge, Mass., 1986), 55–57.
88. *Moskovskii listok*, 17 June 1896.

of all, the dangers of overcrowding and the lack of sanitation stirred concern about health.

It is tempting to attribute the pressures for public services to the members of the new urban middle classes. They were in a good position, both through their reading the urban press and in their daily lives, to become critical of conditions in their cities and to be aware of Western models of progressive urbanism. Their public-spirited leaders had access to civic forums where they could demand that their municipalities create the public services that were imperative for a clean, sanitized city. However, they were not the only townspeople to be aware of and offended by noxious sights and smells and, to judge by their rate of electoral abstention, many of them were indifferent to reform. Although the views of the town poor were missing in such discussions, it is fair to assume that they too had at least some stake in turning urban public space into a useful and healthy place to live and work.

The voices advocating public health reforms spoke for the entire population and did so with the authority of scientific analysis. The public health movement had emerged in Western Europe in the early nineteenth century. It combined new measures by government administrators for the struggle against epidemic diseases, particularly cholera, which first spread across Europe in the 1830s, and medical expertise that could be applied to infectious diseases and to the social conditions that scientists judged were responsible for the spread of these epidemics. The new science of statistics strengthened the claims of these authorities to extensive knowledge of the city. Statisticians applied quantitative measures to compile comprehensive information on urban living conditions (especially in the slums), birth and death rates, and the spread of disease.[89]

By mid century a body of Western literature and an array of policies had come into existence that made public health a new mark of social progress. When examined by educated Russians in the reform years, the writings and official policies in Europe provided models for both analysis and action. In the 1870s Russian medical specialists formed the Society for the Protection of Public Health, and one of its sections specifically focused on urban sanitation. At about the same time Russian medical societies began to appear in provincial cities.[90] Public health officials in the Ministry of In-

89. See, for example, R. A. Lewis, *Edwin Chadwick and the Public Health Movement* (London, 1952); Catherine Kudlick, "Disease, Public Health, and Urban Social Relations: Perceptions of Cholera and the Paris Environment, 1830–1850" (Ph.D. diss., University of California, Berkeley, 1988).

90. E. I. Lotova, *Russkaia intelligentsiia i voprosy obshchestvennoi gigeny* (Moscow, 1962), 11–13.

ternal Affairs were particularly influential because of their work in compiling a comprehensive picture of the most serious threats to public health in Russian cities. Their observations, together with those of municipal health officials, uniformly damned urban health conditions.

Their reports drew a detailed picture of the insalubrious city: polluted lakes and streams were sources of drinking water; winter accumulations of filth rotted in the streets and courtyards each spring; stagnant ponds collected the water from uncleaned streets and unemptied cesspools and gave off an "intolerable stench"; public squares filled with the refuse that accumulated over periods of months; butcher shops and private slaughter houses dumped their garbage into the streets. In 1880 the medical inspector of Voronezh province recorded a conversation with the mayor of a district town, who "naively explained that the cleanliness of his town was maintained by pigs devouring all the piles of filth." The two parties to this conversation were divided by a cultural gulf. The mayor viewed his town as a villagelike place where acts of nature and the "will of God" decided the conditions of life; the inspector expected civic leaders to take action to enforce sanitary standards that would ensure cleanliness and public health. Using some literary license, a tsarist official summed up the case against the municipalities by concluding that "all the cities of the province are drowning in filth."[91] He very likely shared the judgment of Paul Koch (cited in chapter 1) that such befouled places did not belong within the borders of civilized Europe.

That polluted water, unremoved filth, stench, and dirt were related to infectious diseases and high urban mortality rates was an essential truth among public health specialists and their followers. The government assiduously collected death rates and although the statistics were of dubious precision, they nonetheless reveal great divergences in mortality rates between the better maintained central areas of towns and the dirtier—and poorer—outskirts, between the laboring people and the well-to-do, between infants and adults. Gendarme and gubernatorial reports began to assume a connection between the municipal neglect of local needs and disease, citing medical data to back up their demands for action. Where did the source of this appalling backwardness lie? In the mid 1890s St. Petersburg's so-called medical police compiled a comprehensive list of the ills of the capital. The authors started their analysis by discussing the absence of clean water and sewage removal and proceeded to the topics of overcrowded

91. "Gorodskoe khoziaistvo Voronezhskoi gubernii," in *Trudy komissii Kakhanova* (St. Petersburg, 1884), 3:10.

housing and poor food for the "mass of working people," whom they specifically distinguished from the "educated [*intelligentnye*] strata." They concluded that a number of "artificial factors resulting from the necessity for an enormous number of people to gather in a disproportionately small territory distort all the conditions of existence of the individual."[92]

Such descriptions established an agenda for social reform. They raised issues that were debated with particular vehemence in the Society for the Protection of Public Health in the 1880s and 1890s when its members confronted the implications of the "bacteriological revolution." Pointing to the evidence on water-carried germs, some specialists argued for immediate measures to filter drinking water rigorously. The "localist" school argued that public health was attainable only through extensive social welfare. The localist program implicitly pointed to the reform of the tsarist regime itself, which it judged to be ultimately responsible for these ills.[93] On one side of this debate, then, the sanitized city was a sort of metaphor for political revolution.

Within the confines of municipal action, however, the larger implications that these debates over local needs raised never emerged in public view, in part because of tsarist surveillance but, more important, because most civic leaders had a much narrower conception of public needs and responsibilities. To judge by the comments of tsarist officials, many municipalities had no conception of a public sphere of action. The benign neglect espoused by the mayor of the district town in Voronezh province that I cited earlier had its counterpart all across the country. The police chief of Kuznets claimed, probably with considerable inventiveness, that the elders of his minor Volga trading center shared the opinion that "sanitary-hygienic qualities [*svoistva*—i.e., public works] were simply an unnecessary, frivolous distraction that disrupted the normal quiet conditions of life." On a more sober note, he observed that the principal objection to bringing clean water to town by building a water main was that it represented "an unnecessary, unproductive expense."[94] Where the prevalent attitude assumed that a city was a collection of families and private enterprise, this argument carried great weight.

The police chief's observations omitted one vital consideration, namely, the miniscule income of these small municipalities. The pervasive poverty

---

92. I. Eremev, ed., *Gorod Sanktpeterburg s tochki zreniia meditsinskoi politsii* (St. Petersburg, 1897), i, iii.

93. Lotova, *Russkaia intelligentsiia*, 64–66, 76–77; for a general view of the politics of the Russian medical profession at the turn of the century see Nancy Frieden, *Russian Physicians in an Era of Reform and Revolution, 1856–1905* (Princeton, N.J., 1981), esp. chaps. 7–8.

94. TsGIA, f. 1290, op. 5, d. 238, 104.

of the trading and laboring populations was a general condition throughout the country. Saratov's campaign in 1880 against tax dodgers collapsed when it discovered that 90 percent of the miscreants "for the most part proved to be artisans in extreme misery and without work," so needy that the municipality had to arrange charitable contributions.[95] When a relatively prosperous property-owning and business community is absent, one senatorial survey into provincial life concluded, urban centers "do not have, and will not have in the foreseeable future, the possibility to improve their public services."[96] Officials and other critics from the outside tended to discount provincial claims of hardship as self-serving, a point underlined by the Saratov governor when he noted in 1895 that duma deputies "may be accused of stinginess but not wastefulness."[97] Municipal parsimony owed its attractiveness as a policy not only to ignorance, superstition, and sloth but also to the slender margin of livelihood of the large majority of townspeople.

Although forceful and persuasive voices in provincial centers and migrant cities spoke out in favor of municipal activism, they confronted another major obstacle to the realization of extensive public services: the tsarist state placed a considerable financial burden on cities to contribute to state operations. Since Peter the Great's time Russia's vast, underadministered empire had turned local self-government into a device for obligatory assistance in administering, and more often simply financing, state-ordered functions. For major towns and cities the most onerous of these in the mid nineteenth century were the quartering of military garrisons and paying for municipal police. Other responsibilities were gradually added in later years. Part of the tsarist reaction to political terrorism in the late 1870s entailed the expansion of the municipal police forces, the cost of which fell, as in the past, on the municipalities. Kiev's mayor complained to the senatorial investigators that his townspeople believed the new municipal self-government meant more taxes and fewer benefits because the "taxes are increasing not for the welfare of the city but for the payment of those state functions that are obligatory and increasing in scope."[98]

The complaint echoed similar hostile comments of earlier decades, and the evidence suggests that the tsarist regime was making the cities pay heavily. Kiev's cost for the municipal police force doubled in the period

95. *Izvestiia Moskovskoi gorodskoi dumy* 4 (1880):91.
96. "Gorodskoe khoziaistvo Saratovskoi gubernii," in *Trudy komissii Kakhanova* (St. Petersburg, 1884), 4:544.
97. "Otchet Saratovskoi gubernii za 1895," TsGIA, f. 1284, op. 23, d. 28, 18.
98. "Zapiska Senatora Polovtsova," in *Trudy komissii Kakhanova* (St. Petersburg, 1884), vol. 2, pt. 2, 293.

from the mid 1860s to the early 1880s. Moscow's obligatory expenses, which had declined from one-half to one-quarter of the budget between 1860 and 1878 rose again in the following years, with police expenses mounting to 20 percent of its total expenses.[99] Under these circumstances attacks from tsarist administrators on the municipalities' neglect of public services appeared at best hypocritical and at worst a device to shift responsibility onto powerless and impecunious civic leaders.

The principal improvements in municipal finances came about as a result of the economic expansion of certain cities or through the inventiveness of civic leaders. In both cases the locus was the migrant cities. Although the ingenuity of particular leaders was an affair of talent as well as circumstances, increased taxes were the result of urban economic growth. New financial sources included the development, beginning in the 1870s, of revenue-earning municipal enterprises—somewhat on the model of German "municipal socialism" of that period—ranging from slaughterhouses to banks and public transportation. All such enterprises entailed serious financial risks, especially in the depression years of the 1880s. In cities such as Odessa and Moscow they began to return substantial profits by the 1890s. A second innovation was extensive borrowing. Like municipal enterprises, it was largely the prerogative of the provincial capitals and migrant towns, presumably because these cities were both better risks and better governed. By the end of the century the level of municipal debt in those cities averaged 7,000 rubles per capita. In the small towns per capita debt was far lower—2,500 rubles.[100] Municipal borrowing aroused bitter criticism from frugal deputies and townspeople. Moscow's conservative "public opinion," as reported from a tavern gathering in 1892 by one journalist, complained that "future generations will have to answer" for mayor Alekseev's years of heavy borrowing. In an editorial rebuttal the newspaper pointed to Alekseev's program of municipal improvements. "He who hasn't seen the city in fifteen years," the editor boasted, "will not recognize it now."[101]

The editor's civic boosterism suggests that an urban constituency was taking shape behind the activist municipal leadership. By the 1890s many

99. Pavliuchenko, "Moskovskoe gorodskoe uprovlenie," 180.

100. These figures are drawn from the comprehensive statistical survey *Goroda Rossii v 1904 g.* (St. Petersburg, 1907); "small" towns are defined as all those without appreciable population growth, that is, with more than half of its residents locally born.

101. *Moskovskii listok,* 3 May 1892; a very different point of view came from a state duma survey in 1907 that concluded that municipal indebtedness in Russian towns (measured as a proportion of annual revenues) was less than half that of Western European municipalities; see Thurston, *Liberal City, Conservative State,* 47.

municipalities were enjoying a substantial increase in available revenues. Even taking their rapidly expanding population into account, by the end of the century they disposed of twice the per capita income of the small towns.[102] The increase in revenues also outpaced the rise in obligatory expenses, which in Moscow fell to 18 percent of the budget by 1900.[103] However, to say that revenues in these cities were increasing is only to suggest that the needs of the local population could be addressed in part and that the vision of a "civilized" city, whatever this term was understood to mean by competing factions, could be realized in some small measure. Throughout the last decades of the century complaints continued to echo the observation of senators inspecting provincial affairs in 1880, namely, that "all the towns complain of the paucity of their income by comparison with the rapidly growing needs brought out by the spirit of the times."[104] The bitterness of civic debates involved the issue of who was to enjoy the benefits of public services.

By the turn of the century one answer to the question of who would benefit from municipal expenditures was that the urban elite cared for the needs of its own constituency. A map of the location of public services coincided to a remarkable extent with the residential distribution of the well-to-do and entrepreneurial townspeople. A special correspondent for a Moscow paper reported that in the Volga town of Rybinsk the "conveniences from municipal services" were far more accessible to the "owners of brick houses located in the central streets of town . . . than to house-owners whose [wooden] buildings are located on the outskirts." Among these "conveniences" were "more or less acceptable street lighting, relatively decent [paved] streets and sidewalks, [and] more or less vigilant police surveillance." As for the poor inhabitants on the edges of the town, they experienced "impassable mud in the streets and complete darkness after sunset."[105] This physical ordering of the city gave tangible form to central areas, but there was little in the underrepresented (and unrepresented) urban fringes that, by contemporary (ideal) standards, deserved the name of "civilized" urban life.

The reasons for the inequitable distribution of municipal benefits lay in part in the conscious priorities of municipal deputies and councils. But it

102. The source and method of calculation are identical to those used in footnote 100.

103. L. Pisar'kova, "Deiatel'nost' Moskovskoi gorodskoi dumy v oblasti meditsiny, narodnogo obrazovaniia i obshchestvennogo prizreniia posle 1862," *Problemy istorii SSSR* 7 (1978):130.

104. "Gorodskoe khoziaistvo Voronezhskoi gubernii," in *Trudy komissii Kakhanova* (St. Petersburg, 1884), 6:1.

105. *Moskovskii listok,* 20 April 1899.

was also the result of the very dynamism of these migrant cities, which were constantly enlarging their settled areas and pushing their outskirts further and further away. Voices from the town center were heard much more easily than those from the urban fringes (with the exception of the occasional factory owner). For example, Tambov's mayor could count on a sympathetic hearing from his trading constituency when he warned in the late 1870s that the central streets in his "swampy" town were "absolutely impassable in fall and spring." Paving these streets was a business necessity in a city where commerce in agricultural commodities was becoming increasingly important.[106] In 1893 Kharkov's merchant party demonstrated no reluctance to spend municipal funds on a major program of street construction, the paving of all town squares, and lighting as far as the outlying districts.[107] These investments brought tangible benefits to the "solid citizens" and to vital urban economic activities.

Such programs were also visible evidence of substantial civic achievement. Both economic and cultural considerations were probably behind the Ministry of Finance's decision in the mid-1890s to subsidize an extensive program of paving, electric lighting, and electric streetcar construction in central Nizhny Novgorod. The city was on display for the national exposition of 1896 and that urban "hill of light," which so impressed Maxim Gorky, was a part of the ministry's proselytizing effort as well as a convenience for the visitors to the exposition. The town's back streets, however, still belonged to the migrants and the poor and were a territory that, to urban activists, was as much in need of public works as the center.

The less visible services that were needed for public health and sanitation required more sophisticated justifications. Public health publications presented arguments about the connection between infectious diseases and tainted water, filth, and stench; they relied on reason and scientific authority to challenge the received wisdom of traditional practices. In this area in particular activist reformers were critical of their "illiterate" and "half-educated" opponents who were less prepared to accept the major expenses that capital improvements like municipal water mains and sewage systems required.

In Moscow the principal political leader pushing for major investment in water mains was the mayor, Nikolai Alekseev, who held impeccable merchant credentials. He won the fervent backing of the editor of Moscow's first penny press, N. Pastukhov (himself a former tavern keeper), who

106. "Gorodskoe khoziaistvo Tambovskoi gubernii," in *Trudy komissii Kakhanova* (St. Petersburg, 1884), 6:68.
107. Bagalei and Miller, *Istoriia goroda Khar'kova* 2:307–8.

foresaw that a beautiful city would emerge "when the sewer is built . . . and the river water becomes clean." He promised that "instead of the stench from filth Moscow's inhabitants will breathe fresh, clean air, and half the infectious disease will disappear."[108] Such arguments proved sufficiently persuasive to win municipal backing in most migrant cities and provincial capitals by the end of the century. An official medical report of the early 1890s found that sixty cities possessed water mains providing "good water, judging by appearance and taste."[109] In these cities a substantial part of the population enjoyed in their daily lives the benefits of their municipalities' "widening circle of activities."

The mortality records of these cities indicate that the investments in sanitation produced tangible improvements in public health. The reliability of the urban mortality figures is dubious for reasons that involve both population turnover and imperfect data collection, but comparisons of data over time provide a fairly reliable picture of the overall trend. When filtration of public water began in St. Petersburg and Moscow, the death rates in the areas served by the mains suddenly dropped; by contrast, in the newer districts inhabited mainly by the laboring population the rate remained unchanged.[110] Similar changes occurred in other cities that were provided with water mains. The figures for death caused by typhus had declined sharply by the 1890s, and the major urban centers were spared the cholera epidemic early in that decade.

In the outlying, newly settled areas of these cities and in towns lacking these sanitary services epidemics remained a critical problem. Public medical care became more widespread through the construction of municipal hospitals, but it was never adequate to the demand (in either the countryside or the city). Critics of municipal public health measures pointed to the inequalities in mortality figures between the central districts and the city outskirts and to the evidence suggesting that mortality in Russian cities, including Moscow and St. Petersburg, remained higher than in the countryside.[111] The point is not that some cities suddenly became sanitized islands in a sea of infectious diseases. By the end of the century municipal politics in the migrant cities had created a consensus on policies of public

108. *Moskovskii listok*, 3 April 1982.

109. "Otchet Meditsinskogo departamenta za 1892 g.," *Vrach'* 24 (1896):10.

110. *Sanitarnoe sostoianie gorodov Rossiiskoi imperii* (St. Petersburg, 1899), 40–42.

111. The story of St. Petersburg's "deadly districts" is described in James Bater, *St. Petersburg: Industrialization and Change* (London, 1976), 342–52; Moscow's improved conditions are discussed in Thomas McGivney, "The Lower Classes in the City of Moscow, 1870–1905" (Ph.D. diss., New York University, 1978), 185–86. The most searching statistical inquiry into urban and rural mortality rates is S. A. Novosel'skii, *O raslichiiakh v smertnosti gorodskogo i sel'skogo naseleniia Evropeiskoi Rossii* (St. Petersburg, 1911).

health reform; their impact and the visible improvements that these reforms made to the urban environment gave civic leaders tangible evidence
of their own substantial contribution to the construction of a modern city.
The Russian city was also becoming a place of care for the needy. Venerable religious tradition sanctioned private charity. The idea of public
responsibility for alleviating the effects of poverty, however, encountered
open hostility from frugal civic leaders, who argued that such efforts confronted an endless stream of poor migrants. Housing was the most acute
problem in the growing cities: many migrants moved in and out of urban
areas depending on the season and lived on an extremely low income that
provided for only the most miserable housing or, in some cases, no housing
at all. Many municipal leaders, however, approached the housing problem
with the attitude that it was entirely the affair of the workers themselves.
For example, when a government inspector charged the municipality of
Samara with being derelict in caring for the housing needs of its seasonal
dock workers, its mayor, after blaming inadequate revenues and insufficient
help from the district *zemstvo*, added that the stevedors "usually work
loading grain and, receiving a very substantial income, have every possibility to rent lodgings in apartments."[112] His roseate assessment was a
convenient justification for municipal inaction.

The issue of welfare raised questions about the social role of the city that
were as central as the issues posed by public health. Were the conditions of
daily life the affair of individuals only? Should the industrious and enterprising be accorded, and the lazy and incompetent be deprived of, such
items as adequate food and housing on the basis of individual competition?
Were measures to alleviate social inequities a moral imperative for civic
leaders or did public order only require minimal efforts to provide pallia-
tives and then only when hardships threatened social unrest? Such questions were asked in cities throughout the West as well, but the scale of the
problem in Russia was arguably greater than elsewhere. Poverty was acute,
the resources to address the problem very meager, and municipal leaders
and provincial officials were deeply divided on the issues. The various ways
of addressing the problem rested on different assumptions of urban life and,
by extension, of the nascent civil public sphere.

The tsarist administration gave its own authoritative answer to these
questions. It conceived of the problem of urban welfare from the point of
view of public order. In the early 1870s Odessa's police prefect, adopting a
policy typical of other officials, took the problem of unhoused migrants

---

112. "Reviziia komissii Kakhanova," TsGIA, f. 1391, op. 1, d. 23, 4.

very seriously. He ordered the police to open four public shelters to house six hundred people "at the expense of private charity." He justified his arbitrary intervention in municipal affairs by citing the "disease and depravity" allegedly rampant in private flophouses and the ease of "police surveillance" of public shelters.[113] In this disciplinary perspective housing regulation and assistance were inseparable from control of the laboring population. In the mid 1860s the Moscow police chief recommended that the municipality provide lodging for the poor and close slum housing. A municipal commission replied to this advice by asserting that his real intent was to enhance police "vigilance" against "idleness, vagrancy, pauperism, depravity, theft, and other crimes in the city."[114] Tsarist paternalism supported urban public welfare but with a strong element of administrative control. In this respect the municipalities were expected to do part of the work of the police.

Although municipal leaders also viewed the laboring masses from a great distance, they did so from a different perspective than tsarist officials. The concept of civil society is particularly useful in interpreting the welfare policies of Russian municipalities because the presence of a small commercial and manufacturing electorate created a cultural and social barrier between the municipal elite and the urban poor. Arguably, this barrier was even stronger in Russia than in Western countries. Party machines did not mobilize the poor to exchange favors for votes, as in cities in the United States; and no socialist parties could force a social welfare agenda on municipalities, as in German cities. Both Russian municipal statutes of the late nineteenth century identified social welfare as a "facultative" municipal activity and the dumas placed it very low on their agendas. One Russian doctor accused the dumas of failing to "hear the voice of the needy" who were for him a substantial collective presence in the city.[115] The response of dumas to poverty suggests that instead of hearing the "voice" of the masses, they continued in the style of the Samara mayor to view the migrants as laborers who were fit to earn their keep; they relegated the needy poor to charitable institutions. Seen in this light, poverty was essentially a social disorder and a private philanthropic concern. Supporters of public welfare, seeking to win municipal support, at times even presented the problem in terms of "dangerous classes." One appeal for municipal action argued that "hundreds of thousands become corrupted by begging, commit crimes, threaten public safety, and ultimately land in prison and

113. "Vsepoddanneishii otchet," TsGIA, f. 1284, op. 67, d. 165 (1875), 9.
114. Bradley, *Muzhik and Muscovite*, 282.
115. Quoted in Frieden, *Russian Physicians*, 237.

cost several times more than the most expensive cases of relief."[116] The argument was ingenious but could make converts only where poverty assumed mass proportions in the migrant cities.

The appeal for public welfare, whether understood in terms of public order, parsimony, or spiritual duty, brought some action. Moscow's aid, which has been studied by Joseph Bradley, was the most extensive, but it failed to cope with the influx of migrants. In its regulated approach to "misery" it could not make a serious impact on the world of the poor. Characteristically, Khitrovka remained essentially untouched at the end of the century.[117] Short-term crises caused by recession or sudden increases in food prices produced ad hoc measures such as soup kitchens and temporary shelters. In the 1880s and 1890s an increasing number of municipal pawnshops competed successfully with loan sharks by offering inexpensive credit to those with items to pawn.[118] This type of municipal self-help was compatible with the idea of the city as workplace, which was part of the agenda of the merchant parties as well as the economic practices of townspeople. However, the array of policies to cope with widespread urban poverty remained insignificant in comparison with the obvious need.

Under the circumstances it is not surprising that municipal leadership lacked real vision and failed to occupy a major role in the public life of the country. What is impressive is that despite the serious political and administrative obstacles, municipal public life came to occupy a substantial place in the Russian city. Its importance was primarily a result of the activities that grew in response to local needs. The significance attributed to these activities in public debates was grounded partly in an idealized vision of the city as a civilized place and partly in a practical sense of the economic role of the city as a workplace. The factions that coalesced in municipal politics articulated these competing views, neither of which directly challenged autocratic power and neither of which widened civic life beyond the narrow constituency of a municipal elite. Although the accomplishments of the municipalities in the last decades of the nineteenth century fell far short of the goals of the activists, they were nonetheless both substantial and tangible.

Observers tended to describe the urban elite in disparaging terms of

116. E. Maksimov, "Statisticheskie i finansovye voprosy obshchestvennogo prizreniia," *Novoe slovo* (April 1896):8, cited in Adele Lindenmyer, "Why Did They Give? Social Influences on the Motives of Russian Philanthropists" (Paper presented at the AAASS national convention, November 1986), 15.

117. Bradley, *Muzhik and Muscovite*, chaps. 6–7.

118. "Lombardy russkikh gorodov," *Isvestiia Moskovskoi gorodskoi dumy* 10 (October 1891), pt. 4, 1–4.

patriarchy or oligarchy. Still, the actual autonomy of Russian urban civic leadership supports the view that municipal politics in the postreform period supported the emergence of a civic public sphere in the cities of the land. The world of the municipalities was small because it was confined by both tsarist authoritarianism and the social conditions of the very migrant city within which it emerged. Although urban "society" and the "people" shared a common territory that was delimited by city outskirts and the urban environment, the two groups were separate communities divided by social practices and cultural perceptions. Civic life and municipal services appeared unable to bridge this social gulf, which the growth of the migrant cities made increasingly visible.

Figure 1. *The bucolic planned city:* The Town Square of a Russian Provincial City, *approx. 1850. E. Krendovskii. Istoriia russkogo iskusstva, ed. E. Grabar (Moscow, 1964), vol. 8, pt. 2, 238.*

Figure 2. *A mid century Volga river port:* Kostroma, *approx. 1850. Unknown artist. Hoover Institution; Russian Pictorial Collection.*

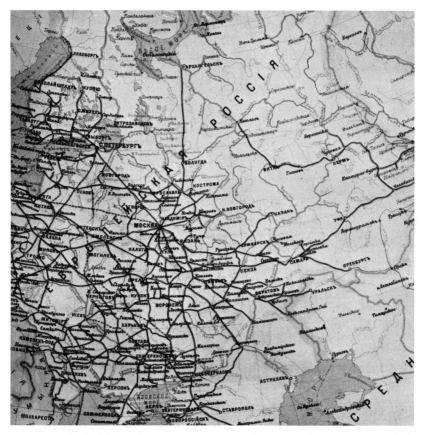

Figure 3. Railroads and Russian cities: "Carte des voies de communications de la Russie." Aperçu statistique des chemins de fer et des voies navigables de la Russie (St. Petersburg, 1900), endpiece.

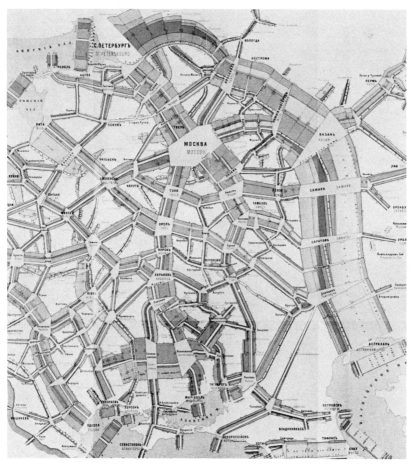

Figure 4.   Schematic flow chart of river and rail shipments of goods, 1897.
"Mouvements des marchandises par chemins de fer et voies navigables de la Russie
d'Europe en connexion avec l'importation et l'exportation par les ports et douanes
frontières d'après les données de 1897." Aperçu statistique des chemin de fer et des
voies navigables de la Russie (St. Petersburg, 1900), endpiece.

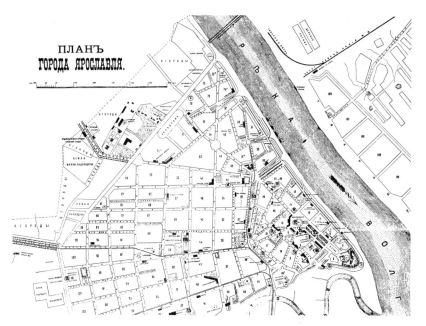

Figure 5.   The imperial planned city: "Modern Plan of Iaroslavl." Iaroslavl' v ego proshlom i nastoiashchem: Istoricheskii ocherk. Putevoditel' *(Iaroslavl, 1913), end-piece.*

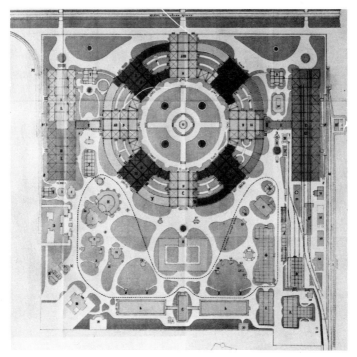

Figure 6.　The fair as planned city: "Plan of All-Russian Industrial-Artistic Exhibition." Ukazatel' vserossiiskoi promyshlenno-khudo-zhestvennoi vystavki 1882 goda v Moskve (Moscow, 1882), following 160.

Figure 7. *The migrant laborer and his sweetheart:* On the Boulevard, *1886–87. V. Makovskii.* Istoriia russkogo iskusstva, *ed. E. Grabar (Moscow, 1964), vol. 9, pt. 1, 345.*

Figure 8. *The lower depths:* The Flophouse, *1889. V. Makovskii.* Istoriia russkogo iskusstva, *ed. E. Grabar (Moscow, 1964), vol. 9. pt. 1, 341.*

Figure 9. The metropolis: Nevskii prospekt, 1887. I. Repin. Istoriia russkogo iskusstva, ed. E. Grabar (Moscow, 1964), vol. 9, pt. 1, 554.

Figure 10. The city of popular entertainment: Mardi Gras Carnival on Admiralty Square in St. Petersburg. 1869. K. Makovskii. Istoriia russkogo iskusstva, ed. E. Grabar (Moscow, 1964), vol. 8, pt. 2, 256.

Figure 11.   Popular images of the city (1): "The Return of the Son, Waiter in the City, to His Peasant Family," 1875. Chapbook illustration. Print Collection, Saltykov-Shchedrin Public Library, Leningrad.

Figure 12. Popular images of the city (2): "Two Migrant Workers in a Tavern," 1878. Chapbook illustration. Print Collection, Saltykov-Shchedrin Public Library, Leningrad.

4

Sobriety, Squalor, and Schooling in the Migrant City

In its ideal form the Russian city of the late nineteenth century was to be both an enlightened and an orderly place. Although facade planning disappeared, the impulse to impose some ideal ordering of public life on the chaotic migrant city did not. Tsarist authorities and many civic leaders possessed a vision of the city as a place that, in one form or another, had to be created—or recreated. They were the heirs of Peter I and Catherine II. The reasons for this common approach to the Russian city are rooted in both Russian authoritarian social practices and culturist views that measured Russian society against Western models. When compared with the West, Russia still seemed to be a borderland and its cities outposts where cultural ideals directly confronted a harsh social reality. The decision of the Ministry of Finance to locate the second national exposition in Nizhny Novgorod in 1896 affirmed the principle that any major Russian city was a place of learning. In this context, enlightenment meant proselytizing for technology, industry, and capitalism in the spirit of Witte's program for national development. It also meant finding a language by which to communicate this message to a diverse and deeply divided population.

The impoverished, poorly educated, and mobile character of most of the urban population challenged the best efforts of those who sought an enlightened city. The problem of cultural change in the city can best be approached in the manner proposed by the sociologist Lyn Lofland. Her conceptual perspective relies heavily on psychology and cultural anthropology. She views the city in modern times as a "problematic world of strangers" in which groups and individuals that are unknown to one another become aware of one another's existence through encounters in public spaces. On the one hand, the responses to this situation involve efforts to create a place for oneself—to "privatize public space." On the other hand, the responses also engage urban dwellers in a process of learning in which they attempt to acquire skills for living among strangers and for placing these strangers in a familiar, knowable order.[1] Lofland devotes little attention to the importance of power in the ways that these "strangers" interact. Logically, one might expect that those who claim authority and are committed to a reordering of the city would use their positions to try to incorporate the strangers into their own ideal city. Her approach suggests that those who study the history of Russian urbanism must pay close attention to the struggles inherent to the transformation of urban culture. Rival agendas for cultural integration competed against each other, and the proponents of each agenda attempted to communicate with and persuade the migrant masses of the rightness of their cause. "Strangeness" was a barrier to the emergence of a new city.

The encounter between elite and popular cultures was strongly influenced by tsarist suspicion of spontaneous cultural activities, a culturist definition of progress among educated Russians, and by the assumption—shared by both the business and laboring population—that the city was essentially a workplace. Perceptions of strangeness varied greatly and the attempts to deal with this condition can be examined from several points of view. One important dimension is gender. Relations between laboring men and women in the migrant cities were deeply marked by the mobility of the population and the numerical insignificance of settled families. A social dimension is readily visible in the multiplication of voluntary associations among educated townspeople, who turned their attention to opening channels of communication and to spreading learning among the uneducated. An economic element is apparent in the support that municipal dumas and merchant societies lent to the creation of schools to raise the educational level of the urban workforce. The political concerns of Russian conservatives emerged in the campaign to organize officially approved public programs of learning and knowledge that were directed at spreading sobriety and piety among the laboring population. Finally, the cultural ramifications of the encounters among strangers brought a fascination with the exotic "squalor" of the slum-dwellers. In popular literature Khitrovka acquired

1. Lyn Lofland, *A World of Strangers: Order and Action in Urban Public Space* (New York, 1973), esp. 15–22.

junglelike qualities and became a sort of "darkest Moscow." The awareness among townspeople that these vast cultural differences existed brought added support for a sustained campaign to spread literacy into those little-known fringes of urban society. The Russian migrant city of the late nineteenth century contained a multitude of competing movements to incorporate the population into an integrated culture. In this chapter I focus on those activities that were directed at the "migrant stranger."

Tavern and Church

The presence of migrants was the dominant social reality of urban Russia. It caused civic leaders and officials to search for the means by which to bring enlightenment and order to their migrant city. Although they often claimed to know the "people," they were aware of a cultural gulf between "society" and the "people" that bred suspicion and made any form of communication a difficult endeavor. The label "migrant" subsumed a variety of social conditions. The occupations of the newcomers varied widely, as did the length of their residence in the city. Although descriptions of housing offer a one-dimensional image of the laboring poor, they provide a general indication of the private places that these strangers occupied in the city. To the extent they can be perceived in contemporary reports, these living conditions help to describe how the world of the migrants was circumscribed with respect to the settled townspeople and how the migrants' efforts to "privatize public space" evolved.

The great disparity between the comfortable housing of the few well-to-do townspeople and the squalid quarters of the poor can be measured using the data gathered in official studies. The distance between the houses in Kiev's center that were classified as "expensive" and the "crowded houses, more like hovels stuck together with mud" (as one medical inspector observed in 1890) on the city's outskirts, where "petty artisans, traders, [and] day laborers" lived, was at once spatial and social.[2] There was no territorial border, however, to separate "decent" from "squalid" rental lodgings; both often existed in the same neighborhood or even next to each other. When in the 1890s the Ministry of Finance introduced a tax on urban renters, it estimated that the floor of the tax on the most "inexpensive" taxable residences excluded three-fourths of all lodgings.[3] This administrative decision gives an indication of the size of the urban poor.

2. "Sanitarnyi nadzor v Kieve v 1890 godu," *Izvestiia Moskovskoi gorodskoi dumy* 12 (December 1891):2.
3. *Gosudarstvennyi kvartirnyi nalog* (St. Petersburg, 1903), 69 n.1, 108.

The structures that the fiscal agents left off the tax roles included the ready-made shacks that one traveler found in Volga port cities that landlords constructed to house laborers in the navigation season. He saw "small lots on the outskirts of town that were so crowded" with these structures that "they represent a serious danger in case of fire."[4] In this domain, as in others, the lives of the poor were beyond the reach of official regulations. Building violations could easily be dismissed with a bribe to the neighborhood police officer, who was the only authority to enforce the municipal statutes. A particularly characteristic form of housing for the poor was the "cot-and-corner" (*koechno-kamorochnaia*) apartment, which was a residence sublet into as many cots and corners as the market and physical space would permit. At the turn of the century a Moscow survey estimated that such lodgings housed nearly 175,000 people (one-sixth of the total population).[5]

In these conditions the borders between public and private space were difficult to discern. The desperate need for cheap housing was the paramount concern. Observers reported that crowding, fetid air, and the stench from courtyard latrines set these areas apart as places of terrible squalor. Gorky's "lower depths," which he used at the end of the nineteenth century to shock his educated audience, were located in a cellar "cot-and-corner" apartment. The term *trushchoba* ("slum") had emerged by the mid nineteenth century to designate the areas where this squalid housing was concentrated—at first the streets around Haymarket Square in St. Petersburg, then also the Khitrovka neighborhood of Moscow. Soon it was used to identify places of visible poverty in any town. The term also conveyed a secondary meaning similar to the usage of the word "slum" in the United States in the late nineteenth century: to middle-class Americans, slums were "strange, novel, large places that people visited as a foreign territory." In America as in Russia, the inhabitants of these places became "slum people."[6] In this manner the language of educated Russians identified a different social world within the migrant cities.

4. E. I. Ragozin, "Puteshestvie po russkim gorodam," *Russkoe obozrenie* 4, no. 7 (July 1891):255–56.
5. *Moskovskie vedomosti*, 14 November 1902; the report was published in *Izvestiia Moskovskoi gorodskoi dumy* 23 (October 1899). This subterranean housing world (I use the term both figuratively and literally because many such apartments were located in cellars) is explored in detail in Joseph Bradley, *Muzhik and Muscovite* (Berkeley, 1985), 211–13.
6. Sam Bass Warner, "Slums and Skyscrapers," in *Cities of the Mind: Images and Themes of the City in the Social Sciences*, ed. Lloyd Rodwin and Robert Hollister (New York, 1984), 187. The Russian term, which originally designated a thicket in a forest, first appeared in literary works in the 1840s and had a pejorative social meaning; at that time it designated the St. Petersburg slums. See *Slovar' sovremennogo russkogo literaturnogo iazyka* (Moscow, 1965), 15:1063.

For the residents of these poor neighborhoods such living conditions were part of a network of relations by which they organized their lives in the city. Where peoples of different languages gathered in the same city, ethnic differences to some extent determined the borders between neighborhoods. In Odessa, for example, the ethnic segregation of Russians and Jews led most Jews to reside in the central areas. Russians congregated in the outlying factory districts.[7] Because residential segregation highlighted the cultural barriers that divided Jews and Gentiles (Russians and Ukrainians), they had the effect of turning certain neighborhoods into targets for mobs when anti-Semitic pogroms erupted.

Residential areas of migrant laborers in Russian cities principally housed working-age men who were living apart from their families. According to Joseph Bradley, in Moscow in the early 1880s between one-half and two-thirds of these men were not living with their families, and we can assume that the same condition existed in the other migrant cities.[8] Urban labor was largely male. In the last decades of the nineteenth century most men no longer moved about as part of a work gang (artel'), but they still frequently changed jobs and residence. They kept the company of fellow migrants both in work and, just as important for their sense of place in the city, in their lives away from work. Thus, places that we might call a "man's world" occupied a visible and important area in the migrant city.

The urban centers where the migrants gathered were "privatized" by their new residents in the sense that Lofland suggests: they sought to find space in the city for their own way of life. In the mid 1890s one young villager, Semen Kanatchikov, entered this world under the protection of his father's village friend, who was a migrant factory worker bringing his own son to Moscow at the same time. In many ways Kanatchikov's story, which he later told in his autobiography, is typical of the migrant laborer. He lived with fifteen other men, who were employed at different trades and worked in different parts of the city; they shared a communal apartment that they collectively rented and for which they hired a cook. He took his meals at the apartment and spent his leisure time in the company of the other migrants who lived there. He ran to fires, read the penny press, joined in collective fistfights, and at payday visited neighboring taverns and brothels.[9] Our

7. Robert Weinberg, "Worker Organizations and Politics in the Revolution of 1905 in Odessa" (Ph.D. diss., University of California, Berkeley, 1985), 84–85.

8. Bradley, *Muzhik and Muscovite*, 217–19.

9. S. I. Kanatchikov, *A Radical Worker in Tsarist Russia*, trans. and ed. Reginald Zelnik (Stanford, 1986), 9–13; see also Bradley, *Muzhik and Muscovite*, 196–211.

meager records suggest that these collective living arrangements, which were termed a residential *artel'*, were common. According to the 1897 census, in the typical migrant city 6 percent of the population lived in "households without family ties," and this figure is probably artificially low.

Artel' residents came and went; new arrivals at times came from the workplace of one of the members or from the neighborhood. At times the village (or regional) connections provided by the members' *zemliachestva* furnished new residents. Experienced migrants assisted the move from the village and initiated the newcomer into the ways of the city. Kanatchikov, presumably like many other new arrivals, soon moved on to separate quarters and found comrades in other places. However, at a key moment of transition in his life the *artel'* had become for him both a refuge and a school in urban living; in personal terms it was as important as his place of work.

The customs and living practices provided by shared housing and comradeship gave migrants, both those employed in factories and those who found work elsewhere, special skills and knowledge that they needed to make some small part of the city their own. The significance that the French writer Michel de Certeau attributes to the everyday practices of residents of modern cities is equally pertinent to the experience of these Russian urban migrants, who were also able to incorporate in the practices of their daily lives "ways of making use of the confining order" in which they found themselves.[10] The large group of married workers in an apartment-commune in St. Petersburg knew that they belonged in the city and their wives and families belonged in the villages. Their life as "temporary bachelors" was forced on them, they explained to a visitor, by their urban transience: "'Today we're here, but God knows where we'll be tomorrow. So that's how we live—each by himself.'"[11] But instead of living in disordered solitude, their way of life gave them a special collective place in the city.

The migrant way of life was in many respects repugnant to both civil society and official Russia. The bonds that united the laborers' society were solidified by rituals in work and leisure; these bonds were cemented by regular and heavy consumption of vodka, by masculinity that was proven in organized fistfights, and by casual sex with prostitutes. Educated Russians and workers who aspired to respectability regarded temperance (or at most moderate drinking) as a mark of cultural development. But in the

10. Michel de Certeau, *The Practices of Everyday Life,* trans. Steven Rendall (Berkeley, 1984), 76.
11. P. Timofeev, *Chem zhivet zavodskii rabochii?* (St. Petersburg, 1906), 13–14.

male brotherhood of laborers, the use of vodka was an essential sign of membership. It celebrated entry into a workplace, it was a reward for a job well done, it commemorated the holidays, and it turned strangers into comrades in the neighborhood tavern. Its use, in the words of one censorious provincial governor, initiated young migrants into the "different style of life of the workers." From his official perspective vodka was the first step toward creating a "riotous" laboring population, which appeared so threatening to public order.[12] If we can believe the tabulations of the municipal statisticians, who were zealous record-keepers of the well-ordered city, in the migrant cities at the turn of the century there were nearly as many taverns per capita as there were churches. Whether it was justified or not, the Russian laborers' reputation of drunkenness made the tavern (*traktir*) a particularly odious symbol of squalor and depravity to educated Russians. As in the West, it was the common target of the temperance movement and respectable workers, both of whom held up high standards of moral behavior by which to reform the laboring population.

The prevalence of casual sex in the laboring community added another dimension to the "strangeness" of their part of the city. In this respect the workers in Russian cities resembled those in Western metropolitan centers earlier in the century. Alain Corbin describes what he calls the "quantitative sexual poverty" that labor migration created in large French cities in that period. In these urban centers the "sexual activity of laborers appeared virtually synonymous with prostitution."[13] The tsarist state, like other European states, attempted to regulate prostitution, which according to its problematic records was the occupation of young, female, peasant migrants who either abandoned or were forced out of domestic service.[14] Officials recognized that "secret prostitution" was probably far more prevalent than the legal form. Women in trades such as seamstress, where unemployment was endemic, often turned to prostitution to escape destitution. The evidence that casual sex was widespread in the city is indicated by the far higher rate of illegitimate birth in migrant cities than in the countryside.[15] The assumption among educated observers that laborers were promiscuous helps explain why medical writings tended to attribute the cause of the syphilis epidemic to this particular segment of the urban population. The

12. "Vsepoddanneishii otchet Ekaterinoslavskoi gubernii za 1898," Tsentral'nyi gosudarstvennyi istoricheskii arkhiv (abbreviated TsGIA), f. 1282, op. 3, d. 3255 (1899), 10.

13. Alain Corbin, *Les filles de noces: misère sexuelle et prostitution au 19e et 20e siècles* (Paris, 1978), 276–77.

14. *Prostitutsiia y Rossiiskoi imperii* (St. Petersburg, 1890), xii–xxxvi.

15. A. G. Vishnevskii, "Rannie etapy," in *Brachnost', rozhdaemost' i smertnost' v Rossii i v SSSR*, ed. A. G. Vishnevskii (Moscow, 1977), 115, table 3.

evidence of male laborers' sexual behavior and the male stereotype to which it gave rise contributed to an image of the migrant city that was very troubling to respectable urban society.

In addition to drunkenness and sex, manliness in the migrant setting found its expression in fighting. Violent behavior among the laboring population assumed a variety of forms, some erupting in deadly earnest but others assuming a spirit of play. As best we can determine, the participants in urban riots were a cross section of the urban laboring population: unskilled laborers and factory workers, shopkeepers and artisans, migrants and townsmen. Similar confusion surrounds the question of who participated in the collective fistfights that were a common affair on the outskirts of major cities and in laboring sections of towns at least until the end of the century. A centuries-old custom, they were banned by the state in the 1832 law code, which stated that "collective fistfights are a harmful pastime and are absolutely forbidden as a violation of public order."[16] Nonetheless, they continued to occur wherever large numbers of male laborers gathered. They pitted neighborhoods against neighborhoods, factories against factories, or workers against peasants. Any holiday was appropriate for this entertainment, although winter Sundays and Christmas and Easter seemed particularly favored moments.

The fights followed a simple, ritualized scenario that new arrivals could easily recognize. Two sides formed "walls" of skirmishing lines to struggle for control of a disputed no-man's-land. The participants relied largely on their fists, although rocks and knives were occasionally used as weapons as well, and fought until one team fled the field. The event usually began with a "young" wall of teenage boys, who were still learning the skills of battle; they were followed by grown men until up to five hundred fighters were present. Enthusiastic onlookers gathered and some placed bets on the outcome. A few well-to-do fight lovers became patrons of champion fighters. The degree of violence occurring in these fights appeared barbaric to both outsiders and those who had passed through this school of manly training before suppressing their fighting skills to adopt respectable behavior. One Moscow businessman later recalled that the fights he participated in as a young man were events where "passions built up [and] men turned into animals; [they] broke each other's ribs, arms, and legs and beat [their opponents'] faces to a bloody pulp."[17] His lurid account probably added

16. V. Lebedev, "K istorii kulachnykh boev na Rusi," *Russkaia starina* 44 (August 1913): 337.
17. I. A. Slonov, *Iz zhizni torgovoi Moskvy* (Moscow, 1914), 23–24.

more gore to the event than was usually the case; the fights were to him a barbaric remnant of old Russia and had no place in a civilized city.

At the end of the century militant workers also sought to distance themselves from these wild customs. In the opinion of one Marxist worker these fights were the result of cultural backwardness, which stemmed from the fact that "the majority of the factory workers were illiterate and lacked intelligent entertainment in their free time."[18] To any Russian for whom culture meant learning and rational discourse, the fights epitomized the uncultured and backward aspects of popular life. A provincial correspondent for a Moscow paper summed up his report on one collective fistfight in his town by damning the activity as a "form of Asian barbarism [tatarshchina] that has lost all sense in our time."[19]

What outsiders judged to be uncivilized had a very different meaning to the laboring population. In the conditions of the migrant city the long history of these battles made them a familiar activity to newcomers and residents alike. In the laboring man's world of the late nineteenth century this ritualized conflict was, like the other forms of social conflict studied by the sociologist Lewis Coser, "a means to 'test' and 'know' the previously unknown . . . stranger, [who] may become familiar through one's struggle with him."[20] Although they were bloody and brutal, the collective fistfights created bonds of comradeship that helped the migrants to form a community to which they could turn in times of need; this community gave the migrants a sense of belonging to a place of their own in the city.[21] Thus, the migrants adapted past practices to the needs of their new lives in the city. In doing so, they created another visible indication of the gulf that divided them from the urban elite.

For this reason, in the last decades of the nineteenth century the Moscow slums of Khitrovka acquired a great power of fascination and revulsion for educated Russians. The concentrated misery, squalor, and—to the outsider—depravity in Khitrovka made it emblematic of the conditions in all migrant cities. Lev Tolstoy's traumatic encounter with the Khitrovka area, which occurred while he helped in the 1882 municipal census, inspired him to meditate in general on human misery, although he placed his meditations in what he called the "different world" he had discovered in Moscow's

18. I. I. Smirnov, "Brianskie zavody v 80–90-kh godakh," *Letopis' revoliutsii* 4 (1923): 88.

19. *Moskovskii listok*, 16 January 1882.

20. Lewis Coser, *The Functions of Social Conflict* (New York, 1956), 122–23.

21. A thoughtful study of this social and cultural world of working men and women is found in Anne Bobroff, "Working Women, Bonding Patterns, and the Politics of Daily Life: Russia at the End of the Old Regime" (Ph.D. diss., University of Michigan, 1982).

slums.[22] The strangeness of Khitrovka's population and its repellent sights, sounds, and smells led writers to use images of exotic and dangerous places to describe their reaction.

In the last decade of the century popular newspapers regularly sent journalists to Khitrovka to write titillating and censorious "eyewitness" accounts. One writer compared it to an "Indian kingdom" in North America's Far West.[23] Exotic comparisons with distant lands, however, were less frequent than those that evoked images of Christian damnation; one popular writer borrowed from Dante in warning his readers that Khitrovka's motto was "All hope abandon, ye who enter here."[24] The journalist Vladimir Giliarovsky, who made something of a profession escorting educated "tourists" into the slums, wrote of the denizens of Khitrovka as if theirs was an anti-society in which the hierarchy, rituals, and honors were a gruesome caricature of respectable society. He portrayed a hierarchy that included lowly beggars and "fences" at the bottom and the lords of the land, that is, the thieves, at the top—all residing in murky taverns or repellent flophouses. Perhaps inspired by thoughts of Hades and the river Styx, he turned Khitrovka's district police sergeant into a sort of border guard who regulated passage between the underworld of the slum and legitimate society beyond.[25] In these popular accounts the masses of migrant workers who gathered at the labor market went unmentioned; they could not satisfy the writers' fascination with depravity and lawlessness. Public interest in Khitrovka was in large measure the result of the implicit challenge that its apparently barbaric ways posed for urban civilization.

The cultural dynamics of Russian urbanism were as contested as the civil public sphere that emerged in the activities of the municipalities. Not one, but several conflicting "common mental pictures" of the city existed among Russian urban dwellers. The "single physical reality" of the urban landscape was interpreted differently by different groups in the population.[26] The public images that civic leaders, intellectuals, and tsarist officials held of urban popular culture made invidious comparisons with an ideal city. For them such comparisons represented a call to action. Tolstoy's encounter with Khitrovka's "different world" is an example of one such moment. Even the penny press, whose commercial needs provided an incentive to take a less activist and more entertaining approach to everyday life in the

22. L. Tolstoi, *What Then Must We Do?* trans. Aylmer Maude (London, 1935), 10.
23. "Khitrovtsy i ee obyvateli," *Russkoe slovo*, 7 May 1897.
24. A. Pazukhin, "Khitrovtsy," *Moskovskii listok*, 18 April 1892.
25. V. Giliarovskii, *Moskva i Moskvichi* (Moscow, 1955), 29–30; these writings date from the 1890s.
26. Kevin Lynch, *The Image of the City* (Cambridge, Mass., 1960), 7.

city, was drawn into these cultural debates, although its moralizing never satisfied disdainful intellectuals or suspicious tsarist officials.

Learning assumed many forms as the urban population adapted to its needs, real or presumed. Townspeople who identified themselves as enlightened relied on formal education and scientific knowledge in organizing cultural activities for the laboring population. It is tempting to adopt their point of view and to assume that their work alone reshaped Russian urban culture. However, I have sought to avoid this assumption. The public images by which urban dwellers gave meaning to their lives were not the sole product of civic activists. Learning emerged from behavior as well as from texts. In other words, the way of life of the laboring population offered an understandable model to the "strangers," who needed to make a place for themselves in the migrant city. Khitrovka, besides being a den of iniquity, was also a place where migrant laborers learned of work opportunities, found the means if necessary to avoid police patrols, and could hope to establish ties with *zemliaki*. Similar places existed in other migrant cities. Their practices were not sure protection from misery in an urban world where finding work remained the essential condition for survival. Still, these practices were far more easily learned by the newcomers to the city that the symbolic language and learning of those who defined enlightenment in literary and artistic terms.

The processes of acculturation operated at times independently and at times in competition with the organized programs of instruction. Some cultural activists promoted what they understood to be Russia's traditional order. Others worked within narrowly defined cultural fields. Still others sought to begin a profound, revolutionary reordering of public life. The migrant cities were the principal arena where these programs could be introduced and tested. In cultural activities the Russian city was the principal symbol of the country's future.

Traditional popular rituals associated with Orthodoxy and the autocracy continued to be observed in the postreform years. It is difficult to judge from contemporary reports whether their message of patriotism and piety retained a strong hold over the urban population. Provincial governors invariably stressed the public enthusiasm that greeted official receptions, the canonization of bishops, and celebrations of tsarist holidays, which they extolled as "triumphal" and "magnificent" spectacles. Nicholas II's coronation in 1896 made the union of the Orthodox church and the tsarist state visible in all cathedral towns, where celebrations were held on the designated day of the Moscow pageantry. The bishop of Saratov described with satisfaction the "triumphant bell ringing" in that city that opened the ceremonies in honor of the tsar's coronation. It was followed by public prayers in the cathedral square, which was "filled by a large crowd of common people, military, and civil servants," and ended with a religious procession. He noted that all schools held their own ceremonies, which were accompanied by "religious and patriotic songs."[27] It would be a mistake to minimize the importance of these popular ceremonies. They had monopolized the public life of Russian cities for generations and continued to figure prominently in urban practices. For example, the movement of pilgrims through religious centers such as Kiev involved hundreds of thousands of people yearly.

Major religious processions (*krestnye khody*) occurred regularly in large and small towns as part of Orthodox activities. A Russian ethnographer concludes that such ceremonies were the principal "forms of public activity available to the common people."[28] Some townspeople had recourse to such traditional religious rituals for protection against diseases. In 1892 a Simbirsk physician sarcastically reported that a "large crowd" participated in a religious procession on a hot summer day to appease "God's wrath," which had been manifested in the cholera epidemic that year. Not unexpectedly, at the end of the ceremony the thirsty participants rushed to drink untreated river and well water. The result, he claimed, was a disastrous rise in the number of cholera cases.[29] His obvious disapproval may well have been shared by other urban dwellers who were more inclined to rely on medical expertise than priestly intercession in their daily lives. But the evidence of anticholera riots that year suggests that medical science could not claim to have numerous converts among laborers in provincial towns.

One indication of the decline in the presence of the state and the church in the Russian migrant city is provided by the architectural reordering of urban space. In Alexander II's reign tsarist authorities abandoned the effort to impose a classical order on streets and buildings of the central city. Parade grounds and administrative buildings remained symbols of autocratic magnificence and power, but after the rapid expansion of the migrant cities they held a diminished place in urban life. As business developed and new residential and manufacturing districts appeared on the city outskirts,

27. "Otchet o sostoianii Saratovskoi eparkhii za 1896," TsGIA, f. 796, op. 442, d. 1639 (1897), 2.

28. L. A. Anokhina and M. N. Shmeleva, *Byt gorodskogo naseleniia srednei polosy RSFSR v proshlom i nastoiashchem* (Moscow, 1977), 259.

29. Cited in Nancy Frieden, "The Russian Cholera Epidemic, 1892–93, and Medical Professionalization," *Journal of Social History* 10 (June 1977):546.

the centers of tsarist and church activities ceased being the focal point of the city.

Contemporary writers and artists are eloquent witnesses to the new architectural identity of the city. For Fedor Dostoevsky the effort to make the city conform to a plan represented a product of alienated intellectuals such as Raskolnikov, the protagonist of *Crime and Punishment*. Living in the Haymarket, Petersburg's worst slum, Raskolnikov dreamed of a "Napoleonic utilitarian plan for rebuilding the city" that would correct the deplorable behavior of the inhabitants.[30] In his journalist's writings of the 1870s the novelist celebrated the "increasingly dynamic life of the city," whose essential qualities were "intensive street movement," crowds, and "an abundance of signs and posters."[31] In words that might be read as the epitaph of the imperially planned city, the poet Vasily Briusov remarked late in the nineteenth century that "because architecture cannot fight life, it must submit to it."[32]

By the close of the century some church leaders were aware that their religious rituals and messages had little influence on the population of the migrant city. Orthodox piety confronted a way of life that was dominated by the workplace and the tavern. Certain Orthodox bishops made this note a prominent feature of their yearly reports to the Holy Synod. The bishop of Ekaterinoslav, one of the industrial centers of the Ukraine, proclaimed in 1902 that "urban civilization" was the enemy. Although he was concerned about those he called "depraved workers," he was particularly outraged at the people who, "calling themselves educated [*intelligentnye*], treat questions of faith and related duties often with complete indifference and treat the priesthood with scorn and even hatred."[33]

Vituperative judgments such as his were a condemnation of the social forces that were remaking the city. The 1890 report of the bishop of Kherson province, whose capital was Odessa, portrayed the Russian city in the lurid colors of Sodom and Gomorrah; it was a place where "church holidays, family life, and work" were all neglected. His philippic identified the cause of the decline of Christian morality and social virtue in the very conditions of life in the migrant city, where the "lower [classes], lacking a permanent place of residence," are drawn to "countless numbers of taverns, restaurants, beer halls, [and] bars, [which were all] open until late at

30. See Adele Lindenmyer, "Raskolnikov's City and the Napoleonic Plan," *Slavic Review* 35 (March 1976):46.

31. E. A. Borisova, *Russkaia arkhitektura vtoroi poloviny XIX veka* (Moscow, 1979), 166.

32. Ibid.

33. "Otchet o sostoianii Ekaterinoslavskoi eparkhii za 1902," TsGIA, f. 796, op. 442, d. 1951, 14.

night."[34] From his spiritual perspective a secular popular culture had become an integral and very undesirable part of the new city. By implication, his message called for new measures of cultural control. Among these measures, schooling occupied first place.

Schooling in the Migrant City

One mark of modernity in the late-nineteenth-century Russian city was literacy, and schooling was the principal tool for its achievement. The assumption that a modern city, in order to function, needed a population that had ready access to print culture was a generally shared culturist attitude among Russian elites.[35] City dwellers occupied a special position in educational affairs because literacy was so closely associated with urban employment and urban cultural activities. In contrast to squalor and drunkenness the urban school represented sobriety and industriousness. In the midst of poverty and insecurity it held out the promise of an improved living and a better social position. In cities that were deeply divided between the Westernized culture of the elites and the folk culture of the migrants, the school appeared to be the means both to open channels of communication between these two cultures and to form a common set of beliefs by which the urban population (or a substantial portion thereof) could find common cause.

Despite fears of the subversive effects of popular schooling, tsarist officials gave strong support to urban elementary and secondary education. Intellectuals volunteered considerable time and effort to spread literacy among the laboring population. The merchant and activist municipal factions, although deeply divided on other issues, united on the urgent need to finance elementary public schooling. This consensus emerged in a Moscow duma motion in 1863. It proclaimed that "there is not a single public need that can compare with the need for public education. Every other need

34. "Otchet o sostoianii Khersonskoi eparkhii za 1890," TsGIA, f. 796, op. 442, d. 1369, 28–29.

35. The meaning I give to Russian culturism closely resembles the definition proposed by Jeffrey Brooks, who emphasizes the importance of "shared literary values" in defining a "cultural identity" among educated Russians. For educated Russians service to the people necessarily meant the diffusion of these values and this identity into whatever social context their work took them; see Brooks, *When Russia Learned to Read: Literacy and Popular Literature, 1861–1917* (Princeton, 1985), 317–18. My focus on urbanism places special stress on the contentious role of culturism when confronted with other modes of cultural representation in the urban community.

can be postponed for a time in view of the unsatisfactory state of municipal revenues, but this need is not deferable."[36]

In a country where elementary schooling had remained a low priority in public affairs until the mid nineteenth century and where the laboring population of the cities was expanding at a rapid rate, the success of the campaign for mass schooling depended on considerable financial and human investments. In the next half-century the results of urban education did not meet the high expectations of educators. However, we ought to measure the success of this endeavor in terms of popular need as well as in terms of culturist hopes. Efforts to expand and improve urban schooling began in the reform years in both the Ministry of Education and the municipalities. Tsarist urban educational policies changed dramatically in the reign of Alexander II. Under the 1785 statute, municipalities had had the right to fund district schools, but a lack of interest in the inflexible and formalistic study program had made these schools solely a state affair. Urban literacy instruction was carried out in the so-called free schools or by tutoring. These informal measures appear to have been relatively effective in spreading learning among the commercial classes, but could not meet the needs of migrant cities in the industrial age.

Two factors altered this situation in the reform years. First, the Ministry of Education prepared a new statute on urban elementary education. Introduced in 1872, it permitted the formation of several types of schools, which were intended, in the words of the minister, to "satisfy the needs of the local urban population." These schools varied widely in academic rigor and in the number of teachers. The range extended from "one-class" schools offering the most basic program of instruction to the advanced (and expensive) "four-class" schools. The choice of program was intentionally flexible to allow municipalities "in the large and rich cities" to form schools with "a greater number of classes and in the poor and small towns fewer classes."[37] In addition, the ministry proposed that the municipalities assume the funding of the state's schools. Curricular decisions remained the prerogative of the ministry but by comparison with the prereform era the municipalities enjoyed far greater flexibility in choosing the type of elementary school that they judged to be appropriate to their community. In effect, the ministry sought to enroll the best people of the cities in support

36. Quoted in Walter Hanchett, "Moscow in the Late Nineteenth Century: A Study in Municipal Self-Government" (Ph.D. diss., University of Chicago, 1964), 430.

37. "Otchet ministerstva narodnogo prosveshcheniia," TsGIA, f. 733, op. 167, d. 62 (1870), 94–96; the discussions leading to the 1872 statute are examined in Allen Sinel, *The Classroom and the Chancellery: State Educational Reform in Russia under Count Dimitry Tolstoi* (Cambridge, Mass., 1973), 215–25.

of its campaign for schooling and expected these people to find the means to pay for that campaign. The ministry also had need of the participation and funds of other groups, both private and public. In addition to the municipalities, the financial patrons of regular schools included merchant societies, factory owners, and individual businessmen. In the 1880s and 1890s the state made a particular effort to develop the parish schools that were run by the Orthodox church. Culturist critics condemned the elementary schooling of the church for its mediocrity, but it did become a real force in the campaign to spread urban learning.[38]

Second, in the 1860s a spontaneous movement for the expansion of formal elementary schools appeared in provincial towns throughout the country. Even before the ministry altered its statute on urban education, municipalities had begun to fund a large number of new elementary schools; most of these schools were the basic one-class variety; their numbers increased at a rate of thirty to forty per year. The readiness to expand urban schooling continued to the end of the century, although the movement slowed appreciably as a result of the 1880s depression. On average fifty to sixty new one-class schools were added each year (see chart 1).[39] Moscow had fifty-five municipal schools by 1882 and Saratov had a total of twenty. The numbers increased in the late 1890s but comprehensive data are not available for the years after 1893. Kharkov's merchant party, elected in 1893, doubled the number of elementary schools. Saratov's duma, which the provincial governor claimed was filled "primarily with trading people," transformed most of its schools into the elaborate four-class variety and enrolled 4,500 pupils. At the end of the decade one local writer affirmed that 90 percent of school-age children were in the town's schools.[40] Once a distant dream, universal schooling became the official goal of Moscow's duma: in 1896 it passed a resolution in support of universal primary education for the city's children.

The impulse behind the drive for urban schooling was both visionary and practical. By the close of the nineteenth century elementary education appeared to be an essential part of reshaping popular urban culture. In the mid 1890s a Moscow school inspector could hope for widespread support for his call for universal literacy. He claimed that popular ignorance was no

38. The only balanced study of the parish school movement is Ben Eklof, *Russian Peasant Schools* (Berkeley, 1986), chap. 6.
39. The trend for other types of elementary schools would probably vary, but the measure provided by the growth of one-class schools represents the most comprehensive common indicator of increased municipal involvement in public schooling.
40. "Nachal'noe narodnoe obrazovanie v Saratove," *Izvestiia Moskovskoi gorodskoi dumy* 21 (1899):52–53.

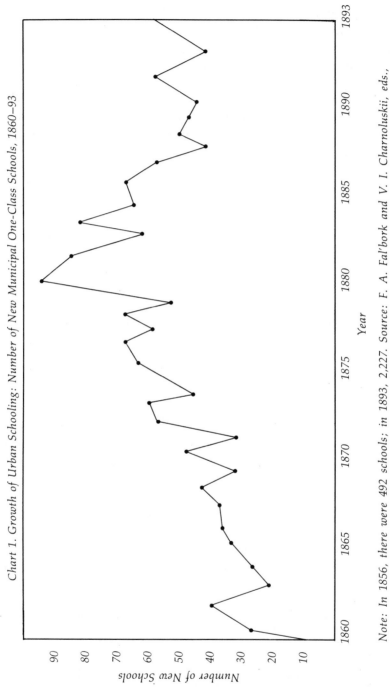

Chart 1. Growth of Urban Schooling: Number of New Municipal One-Class Schools, 1860–93

Note: In 1856, there were 492 schools; in 1893, 2,227. Source: F. A. Fal'bork and V. I. Charnoluskii, eds., Nachal'noe narodnoe obrazovanie v Rossii (St. Petersburg, 1900), l:x, table 1.

longer nourished by "sorcerers, magicians, religious dissenters, [and] wanderers [*stranniki*, that is, religious zealots]" but warned that it had found new sources in "the taverns, the village kulak, the factory, the inn, and other products of contemporary economic relations." The result, he warned, was "degeneration and decay."[41] His apocalyptic version of modernity echoed the uneasiness among elites in the West and in Russia at the consequences of industrialization and urbanization. As much as the Kherson bishop or the visitors to Khitrovka, this Moscow educator was very aware and fearful of the strangeness of the city that was taking shape about him.

Moscow's duma, like those of other migrant cities, heeded this and similar calls (although we need not presume that it accepted the doomsday part of the argument). Smaller towns, however, lacked the resources and the commitment to undertake an educational crusade. In 1890 the Ministry of Education admitted that nearly half of the old district schools (approximately four hundred) had not been taken over by municipalities. It attributed this failure primarily to the "insufficiency of funds" of many t ns.[42] It omitted to mention that the relatively ambitious curriculum of the district schools entailed an expense that the leaders of small towns judged to be an extravagance. The old informal methods, or the simple one-class level of schooling, sufficed for these town elders and presumably for their small electoral constituency.

In the migrant towns, however, economic opportunities provided a powerful incentive for expanded elementary education. There was a strong demand for free public (or parish) schooling. One simple indicator of this demand was the number of unsatisfied school applications in large urban centers. Although the evidence is incomplete, the figures suggest that the interest in elementary schooling was growing rapidly, more so than the financial support that municipalities were willing or able to commit to this activity. In Moscow in 1877 there were six hundred more admission requests than there were openings, and in 1890, despite a sevenfold rise in municipal expenditures on schooling, there were 2,600 excess admission requests. At the end of the 1890s Kharkov's schools, which had doubled

41. Cited in Eklof, *Russian Peasant Schools*, 108; as Robert Nye has pointed out, in the late nineteenth century in Western Europe "degeneration" became a very fashionable code word to decry the conditions of the urban masses; see Robert Nye, *Crime, Madness, and Politics in Modern France: The Medical Concept of National Decline* (Princeton, 1984), esp. 330–32.
42. *Otchet ministerstva narodnogo prosveshcheniia za 1890* (St. Petersburg, 1894), 190–91.

in number since 1893, still had to refuse admission to five hundred children.[43]

The testimony of school directors and instructors, which was collected in a survey by the Petersburg Literacy Committee in 1894–95, reveals the social pressures behind the increase in the number of requests for public schooling. In words that echoed those of many other reports a Moscow priest who directed a large parish school concluded that "the huge demand for the creation of free schools" was caused by the "great size and the poverty of the parish's population."[44] The unstated expectation of the parents who sought to enroll their children was that the basic numeracy and literacy taught by these schools would serve to open access to employment for their offspring. For these parents the city was a place of work, harsh competition for well-paying jobs, and new opportunities for the educated. Second-guild merchants claimed that their "large families and extreme poverty" made financial aid indispensable from their merchant society, to whom they sent many petitions requesting support.[45] Their appeals reveal more about their eagerness for formal learning for their sons than about their standard of living. Their alleged "extreme poverty" bore no resemblance to that of the migrant laborers.

Unsatisfied demands for schooling and appeals for aid are indicators that the settled urban population had new hopes for the future and that these hopes centered on their children's educational preparation for work. Such sentiments probably had more influence on decisions to expand the number of urban schools than the dramatic warnings from the educated elite of the dire effects of ignorance. The combination of popular support and official encouragement brought action from municipal dumas. By the turn of the century several thousand elementary schools (primarily of the one- and two-class variety) with over one-half million pupils existed in urban Russia.[46]

The manner in which learning worked its way from classrooms and instructors into popular culture depended less on curriculum and adminis-

---

43. E. A. Pavliuchenko, "Moskovskoe gorodskoe samoupravlenie v 70–80-kh godakh XIX veka" (Kandidat dissertation, Moscow State University, 1956), 217, 255; *Novoe vremia*, 18 December 1899.

44. "Anketnye svedeniia o nachal'nykh uchilishchakh," TsGIA, f., 91, op. 3 (1894), d. 575, 321.

45. Cited in V. I. Laverychev, *Krupnaia burzhuaziia v poreformennoi Rossii, 1861–1900* (Moscow, 1974), 65.

46. *Nachal'noe narodnoe obrazovanie v Rossii*, ed. F. A. Fal'bork and V. I. Charnoluskii (St. Petersburg, 1900, 1:vii; this four-volume publication summarized the essential quantitative results of the survey (based on over thirty thousand replies) but omitted the perceptive comments of the respondents, which were often included in the completed forms.

trative regulations than on the social dynamics of urban society. Ben Eklof, who has studied Russian peasant schooling, reminds us that the acquisition of literacy and formal schooling are separate phenomena, that the ability to learn is not identical with basic reading, and that parents as well as teachers are influential actors in setting the content and the extent of school learning that is transmitted to the pupils.[47] I take these warnings seriously in examining urban schooling even though there were substantial differences in the social and economic contexts of urban and rural schooling. Our knowledge of the concerns of pupils and parents comes largely from the testimony of teachers and the statistical data that the Ministry of Education collected. The extensive survey of elementary education, which was conducted by mail in 1894 by the Petersburg Literacy Committee, permitted instructors throughout the country to make clear their own ambitious plans as well as the support or opposition they encountered within their communities. These somewhat random clues indicate that at the level of elementary schooling educational authorities and urban parents had substantially different expectations.

Urban schoolteachers were both agents of the tsarist educational system and, to some extent at least, proselytizers in their own right. They created a set of sometimes contradictory objectives for their pupils. Echoes of the values of the Russian intelligentsia sounded in the words of one Moscow school instructor who was an avowed enemy of scholasticism. He defined the goal of teaching, which he presented as the true ambition of his pupils, as "a level of development necessary for an understanding of the surrounding world [priroda] and for a critical [soznatel'nyi] understanding of books."[48] His idealism, which supposed that his pupils would become participants in an interactive cultural environment, bore only a remote resemblance to the prescribed curriculum of these schools. It reflected the view, which was widespread in Russia and the West, that cultural uniformity was desirable. Confronting popular dialects and urban jargon, the teachers hoped, in the words of a Moscow girls' school teacher, to teach uncultured youth not only "to speak and write Russian correctly" but also "to understand literary Russian speech."[49] In this sense elementary schooling and literacy meant basic acculturation into the world of the intellectuals.

At another level the teachers' proselytizing sought a unity based on

47. Eklof, *Russian Peasant Schools*, esp. chap. 1.
48. "Anketnye svedeniia o nachal'nykh uchilishchakh," TsGIA, f. 91, op. 3 (1894), d. 575, 158.
49. Cited in Christine Hinshaw, "The Soul of the School: The Professionalization of Urban Schoolteachers in St. Petersburg and Moscow" (Ph.D. diss., University of California, Berkeley, 1986), 123.

national identity. This political mission, which was also common to public schooling in Western nations, assumed special importance to authorities in the Russian cities because of their fears of social conflict and political subversion. The school curriculum invariably included Orthodox teaching and, usually, elementary Russian history; these were the means to transmit the two official virtues of piety and patriotism. They constituted the essence of learning for the instructor-cleric in a Kiev parish school. He affirmed his commitment to teaching his pupils the "national language" and to conveying to them that "the most holy duty of a well-raised person is faith in God, lofty patriotic sentiment toward the throne and the fatherland, [and] the spirit of love toward one's neighbors and one's family."[50] His language, which sounds stilted and arrogant to our skeptical era, echoed the official nationalism of the tsarist government. Although backed by the power of state and the authority of tradition, it was as remote from the mechanical exercises involved in numeracy and literacy as was the cultural idealism of the Moscow instructor.

Urban social conditions played a decisive role in determining the impact of elementary learning. Schools were part of a community whose members were deeply divided by rank and wealth. Powerful voices among tsarist educators spoke in favor of schooling according to social standing. It was evident in the comments of the director of a Voronezh one-class school, who was convinced that "because almost all the pupils belong to families of artisans and peasants, the students of the school fully satisfy them."[51]

These varied educational objectives provide one indication of the competing cultural agendas for the Russian city. Schooling proposed language skills and basic concepts with which educated Russians (in their capacity as officials, intellectuals, or radicals) could hope to form a common discourse with an urban population whose social conditions and awareness of their own place in society were in rapid flux. At the same time it provided, at a very basic level, practical and vocational skills that offered immediate occupational rewards in economically dynamic urban centers. For many Russian townspeople these two objectives were of unequal importance.

The indirect evidence we possess on popular educational goals suggests that none of these authoritative opinions expressed the dominant attitude of townspeople toward elementary education. When the opportunity arose to place their offspring in more advanced schools, parents seized the chance—very different behavior than most rural families, who appear to

50. "Anketnye svedeniia o nachal'nykh uchilishchakh," TsGIA, f. 91, op. 3 (1894), d. 445, 82.
51. Ibid., d. 321, p. 19.

have been convinced for both cultural and economic reasons that only the most essential learning was desirable.[52] By the 1890s a skeletal framework of a "ladder" of urban education was in place. Indicating the openings for his graduates, a Kiev teacher in a one-class school cited an array of possibilities that included "the two-class school, the artisan school, the medical orderly school, and, for the best students, the *realshule* [technical secondary school]."[53] That these schools represented real opportunities to townspeople is apparent in the enrollment figures. One of the best networks of secondary technical schools were the railroad institutes: over thirty of these institutes were founded in the 1870s and 1880s. The director of the Kiev railroad school, proud of the fact that all his teachers were *gymnazium* graduates, remarked in 1894 that every year his institution of 250 pupils had to turn away from fifty to one-hundred applicants.[54]

These figures, although minute in proportion to the population of youth in a city like Kiev, suggest that families in the migrant cities were aware that education promised economic and social advancement. At some level economic need and social constraints led parents to set a limit to such hopes. A note of fatalism appears in the judgment of a Moscow director, whose pupils' future beyond his school appeared determined by the urban world to which they belonged. "The poor parents," he forecast, "will place their boys in apprenticeship, traders will put their boys in commerce, and the well-off [*sostoiatel'nye*] will put their children in other educational institutions."[55] Prospects for new and better jobs were present in the migrant cities thanks to the multiplication of public services and economic activities. The inspirational motto for this open door to the future was the urban intellectual's exhortation to his son to "study or you won't find decent work" (at least such was the analysis of a rural schoolteacher contrasting rural and urban attitudes toward schooling).[56] Popular literature imitated and shaped reality in this respect. The success of the Russian translation of Smiles's inspirational book, *Self-Help*, is one indication. Another indication is found in the popular novels of the late century, which contained, in Jeffrey Brooks's careful reading, a prominent theme of "education for concrete practical aims."[57]

The hope that successful pupils would find "decent jobs" was under-

52. Eklof, *Russian Peasant Schools*, 440–41.
53. "Anketnye svedeniia o nachal'nykh uchilishchakh," TsGIA, f. 91, op. 3 (1894), d. 445, 15.
54. Ibid., 174–75.
55. Ibid., d. 575, 193.
56. Cited in Eklof, *Russian Peasant Schools*, 253.
57. Brooks, *When Russia Learned to Read*, 282.

mined by social conservatism and cultural prejudice. Anti-Semitism restricted to a handful the number of pupils from the Yiddish elementary schools in the Pale of Settlement who could hope to enter more advanced (Russian) public institutions. Urban schooling was as diverse as the population that was moving into and through the cities and was as much subject to these influences as it was a force in its own right. By the late century the composition of urban elementary schools resembled the social profile of the typical migrant city; among the 8,500 pupils in Moscow's schools in the mid-1880s nearly 40 percent came from the petty bourgeoisie and almost as many came from the peasantry.[58] Both families and teachers set clear limits to the formal learning of children from these groups. One cleric-instructor claimed in the mid 1890s that, because his new parish school experienced an "enormous influx of parents seeking to enroll their children," the "common people" [prostoi narod] were aware of "the necessity of studies."[59] Implicit in his observation was the expectation that education would not alter the lowly social standing of his pupils.

Cultural conservatism and poverty meant that the restrictions on learning for girls were more confining than those for boys. In the mid-1890s Moscow's school population included as many girls as boys, but girls remained tightly bound to the family and there were few occupations for which elementary education could prepare them. An Ekaterinoslav instructor of a one-class girl's school explained that her "poorer" graduates "satisfy themselves with this level of education" but added that those who entered the advanced school in town "take the special sewing section."[60] Employment in positions such as seamstress, governess, or instructor in a girl's school was the best that girls could hope for. The genteel poverty offered by these trades was a more dignified status in the community than that of their families—most schoolgirls were from the petty bourgeoisie— but it represented a paltry reward by comparison to the possibilities increasingly available to boys. Gender was an obstacle to schooling itself; girls continued to assume special family responsibilities. In the opinion of one Moscow teacher, the girls were frequently absent from class because they lacked "warm clothes and [because they had] to replace their mothers in caring for younger brothers and sisters." Another teacher attributed their responsibilities at home to "sick or drunk adult members of the

58. "Vedomost' o nachal'nykh uchilishchakh," *Izvestiia Moskovskoi gorodskoi dumy* 3–4 (1886):154–55.
59. "Anketnye svedeniia o nachal'nykh uchilishchakh," TsGIA, f. 91, op. 3 (1894), d. 575, 211.
60. Ibid., d. 371, 22.

family."[61] Boys were spared this duty because they were not constrained by the family domain.

The indifference on the part of many parents toward "higher culture" set the limits to the boys' contact with formal schooling. Eklof argues that the low percentage of graduates from rural schools was not the result of the need for child labor but because the full program of studies was irrelevant to peasant occupations.[62] Ironically, a similar condition emerged in the cities, albeit in a very different context and to a lesser degree. Although urban schools were able to attract a large and growing proportion of school-age children, at the end of the century they were nonetheless unable to hold more than half of them until graduation. However, the situation appears to have been an improvement over the 1870s. In 1878 a Ministry of Education survey of urban schools found that the schools in the major cities lost three to six times as many pupils as they graduated.[63] The result was that the large majority of pupils, whose ages clustered between eight and eleven, were in the class sections that covered the first two years of study. In that period they acquired what an educator from the southern Russian town of Rostov-on-Don called "the rudiments of reading and writing."[64] Thus, for many Russian townspeople the urban print culture signified little more than the acquisition of basic numeracy and literacy.

Undoubtedly, parents' decisions to limit their children's education involved calculations of relative opportunity costs. In explaining the high dropout rate, educators and pupils often referred to poverty, but this explanation carried with it the parents' perception of their current needs and the future prospects of their offspring, on whom they relied for security in their old age. When asked why they did not complete their schooling, a majority of young Moscow workers polled at the turn of the century referred to a parental decision; at times they explained the decision on the basis of "poverty," but more often they associated it with the parents' will.[65] As in rural areas, formal elementary schooling in the cities did not by itself disrupt family and social patterns of behavior and attitudes. As a consequence, both the critical reading faculties that the Moscow factory

61. Ibid., d. 575, 128, 157.
62. Eklof, *Russian Peasant Schools*, chaps. 11, 12.
63. "Otchet ministerstva narodnogo prosveshcheniia," TsGIA, f. 733, op. 117, d. 68 (1878), 311: the end-of-the-century data come primarily from my reworking of the archival data in the 1894 survey for urban schools in Moscow, Ekaterinoslav, Kiev, and Voronezh provinces.
64. *Izvestiia Moskovskoi gorodskoi dumy* 25 (January 1903):69.
65. Cited in Rashin, *Formirovanie rabochego klassa Rossii* (Moscow, 1958), 592.

instructor sought and the elaborate piety and patriotism that the cleric-teacher preferred had little chance of shaping the malleable minds of their young pupils.

Having acquired the rudiments of reading and writing, town youths had an increasingly diverse and rich print culture available to them. To the extent that publications in the cities were accessible to this minimally educated public—a topic I discuss later—a close tie existed between the learning conveyed by formal schooling and the urban literary culture in the cities. The culturist aspirations of educators worked their influences on youths in school, but an increasingly varied array of readings outside the classroom were also important. When one instructor noted that many of the parents of the pupils in his factory school "subscribe to magazines and newspapers," he unwittingly identified a key explanation for the presence of those pupils in his class.[66] Urban schooling was a part of a larger process of cultural adaptation to the new city. Those families with newspaper and magazine subscriptions had found one means by which to expand their own horizons as well as those of their children. In their own way they had entered the world of print culture; by sending their offspring to the factory school, they were ensuring that their children would be part of that world too.

Those who placed their hopes for the future in an enlightened city promoted cultural activities that made education accessible to adults. The movement for literacy schools, which was directed at the laboring population, was funded and led by volunteers. Like other popular causes in those decades, this movement attracted educated Russians who were aware that their cultural activities were pathetically meager when compared with both the need for action and their own idealistic language. An easy target for cruel satire, their work reveals a great deal about the efforts to reshape urban culture. Volunteer cultural work attracted some of the civic activists, particularly in the field of teaching the skills associated with basic literacy. This area served as a test of the commitment of educated Russians to social progress. In the early 1860s, when municipal support for elementary schooling first appeared, a movement for adult literacy schools also emerged.

This first period of volunteer schooling revealed the traits that would characterize the movement throughout its existence. The campaign was the product of a cultural vision that, in the words of one young idealist, literacy

---

66. "Anketnye svedeniia o nachal'nykh uchilishchakh," TsGIA, f. 91, op. 3 (1894), d. 574, 232.

would let a "beneficial light" shine on the people.[67] Just what this light would reveal depended on the political persuasion of the volunteers. Some were openly hostile to the tsarist regime. In 1862 this hostility led the tsarist government to ban the movement it had authorized just two years previously.

During their brief existence the two hundred literacy schools sustained the hope of their own organizers and teachers that this form of idealism met popular needs and united the urban masses and educated society. One of the women teachers recalled later that volunteer teaching of basic numeracy and literacy constituted "the very first outlet for our aspiration for work, the public good, [and] contacts with the people."[68] Although her vision drew no distinctions between classes of people, literacy schools served the laboring population of the capitals and the provincial centers. They met on workers' one free day of the week and received the title of Sunday schools. For their part, the pupils fixed the goal of this schooling as the acquisition as quickly as possible of the "rudimentary skills" for life in the city. The disparity between the idealism of many teachers and the vocational objectives of the students was enormous.

Despite tsarist fears of political subversion, the authorities were not prepared to ban entirely volunteer efforts to raise urban literacy levels. In 1874 the government reauthorized the literacy schools; its readiness to take this step suggests that the tsarist regime placed a high priority on the diffusion of basic literacy skills among the population. The Ministry of Education reorganized the rules on the organization of the schools to control the suspicious enthusiasm of the volunteer teachers while still tolerating their presence. The hostility of the authorities remained a serious obstacle to volunteer schools; in 1889 Moscow's authoritarian governor-general, for reasons that are not clear, forced the city duma to close nine of the existing fifteen adult schools.[69] Sporadic tsarist repression did not dissuade the volunteers, and in fact it may have encouraged them. Both the government and the volunteers shared a conviction that a literacy movement was a necessary part of the campaign to spread elementary education among the population.

Although tsarist regulations made no distinction between city and coun-

67. TsGIA, f. 1282, op. 1, d. 74 (1862), 191; see also Reginald Zelnik," The Sunday-School Movement in Russia, 1859–62," *Journal of Modern History* 27 (June 1965):151–70.
68. Z. Bazileva, "Arkhiv semei Stasovykh," in *Revoliutsionnaia situatsiia* (Moscow, 1965), 439.
69. L. F. Pisar'kova, "Deiatel'nost' Moskovskoi gorodskoi dumy v oblasti meditsiny, narodnogo obrazovaniia i obshchestvennogo prezreniia posle 1892," *Problemy istorii SSSR* 7 (1978):137.

tryside, the centers of volunteer work were once again the provincial capitals. At times factory owners promoted adult education for their workers, but most often literacy committees took the initiative. The leader (until its forced reorganization in 1895) was the St. Petersburg Literacy Committee. By the end of the century there were almost three hundred schools in seventy-five cities, and total enrollment was estimated to be fifty thousand pupils. St. Petersburg and Moscow were the most active centers of the literacy movement, each with over twenty schools.[70] The literacy campaign, although numerically small in comparison to public schooling, played a significant role in raising urban literacy and in encouraging hopes for an enlightened urban population.

Idealism was once again a powerful motivation for the organizers and teachers. If the attitude of one participant in the Kharkov literacy committee is representative, to become a volunteer was to prove one's rightful place among "the best representatives of the intelligentsia." In his opinion, "Among former and present inhabitants of Kharkov [every name] known for scientific or public activities" was present on the list of members.[71] The Kharkov committee's membership had known both lean and prosperous years. The latter came at the beginning of its existence and at the end of the century, when it counted almost seven hundred members.[72] Its activities, which were typical of the provincial centers, included the founding of both a men's and a women's school. The women's school was specifically intended for girls working in clothing enterprises "because a large portion of the girls of the poor urban population choose the sewing trade."[73] This type of activity was "small deeds" without bureaucratic interference; it was visible evidence that intellectuals and the urban poor could find a common cause.

The lofty ideals of the organizers of the adult literacy schools were far removed from the practical concerns of the pupils. The evidence suggests that most of the adult pupils shared the same single-minded concern for the acquisition of rudimentary skills that the school children in elementary public schools exhibited. The 1894 survey cited earlier contacted some of these schools. The director of one Moscow women's literacy school made the somewhat disabused judgment that "very many [pupils] are satisfied with acquiring the ability to read 'any' little book, to write notes, to cal-

70. L. M. Ivanov, "Ideologicheskoe vozdeistvie," in *Rossiiskii proletariat: Oblik, bor'ba, gegemoniia*, ed. L. Ivanov (Moscow, 1970), 331–32.

71. A. Didrikhson, *Istoricheskii obzor deiatel'nosti Khar'kovskogo obshchestva rasprostraneniia v narode gramotnosti* (Kharkov, 1911), 9.

72. Ibid., 243.

73. Ibid., 59.

culate bills, [and] to do arithmetic; [they] leave school after one or two years." He also noted that his two hundred pupils were largely migrants (three-fourths belonged to the peasant estate), some working in factories, others in workshops, and that they possessed the rudiments of learning before joining his school.[74] For the migrants, schooling was part of an effort to find for themselves as secure a place as possible in their new urban world. The great majority of the pupils in the literacy schools were young; in the mid 1880s only 15 percent were over seventeen years old.[75] The effort to create an integrated urban literate culture reached those whose first priority was to acquire early in life the skills that would be most useful for a successful career in the city.

The encounter with the volunteer teachers left an abiding impression on a few of the pupils. One worker, who recalled that most of his young Petersburg factory friends preferred recreation to learning, recorded his own astonishment that "people of another world [*sreda*]" would "teach for free, that is, solely for the sake of bringing knowledge to the people."[76] In that encounter his search for enlightenment led him into the Marxist revolutionary movement. In the same spirit, another Petersburg worker noted in a school essay that as a result of his education he was able to see "with more open eyes how people of other lands live and work."[77] He expected that this understanding would become a guideline to social and political action. It was a hope that some of their teachers were more than willing to satisfy. These cultural ambitions exceeded by far the goal of most pupils to learn to read "any little book." But both objectives were capable of remaking, in different ways, urban popular culture.

In the last decades of the nineteenth century Russian migrant cities were centers of intensive educational activity. The spread of formal schooling was the most important part of this process. Officials, civic activists, and intellectuals endeavored—albeit with very different goals—to incorporate the largest possible proportion of townspeople into a print culture. The goals of those who organized the campaigns to spread the basic skills of learning are relatively easy to discern. However, it is far more difficult to assess the impact of the acquisition of these new cultural tools on millions of individuals. The subject, one that extends far beyond the scope of this study, is explored very thoughtfully in Eklof's examination of rural school-

---

74. "Anketnye svedeniia o nachal'nykh uchilishchakh," TsGIA, f. 91, op. 3 (1894), d. 575, 2–9.
75. "Vedomost' o nachal'nykh uchilishchakh," *Izvestiia Moskovskoi gorodskoi dumy* 3–4 (1886):158–59.
76. I. V. Babushkin, *Vospominaniia* (Leningrad, 1925), 35–36.
77. Cited in I. A. Shuster, *Peterburgskie rabochie* (Leningrad, 1976), 54–55.

ing. He points out the problematical significance of the simple measure of literacy (that is, the ability to read) in assessing the significance of changes in literacy rates. Nonetheless, literacy figures remain the only quantitative indicators that are capable of summarizing such a massive process.

These indices suggest that by century's end the majority of the urban population had access to some form of print culture. The 1897 census found that 60 percent of the population of migrant cities was literate, a substantial increase from the mid century. Literacy varied enormously among age and social groups. Many adult migrants were illiterate and, especially in the reform years, the intensive migration from the countryside to the cities had undoubtedly slowed the increase in literacy levels. There is good reason to believe, however, that by the close of the nineteenth century rural families understood that basic literacy and numeracy were a valuable skill for urban migration, and many found schooling for their offspring.[78] To judge by the conscription reports and by the factory records of young workers (most of whom were migrants), by the 1890s literacy had spread among almost all young men in the cities.[79] The migrant cities in these crude terms were becoming places where the printed word could reach most of the adult population.

Whether or not this access to the world of print culture entailed a fundamental change in beliefs and learning skills is a question that cannot be answered with certainty. The evidence is scanty and contradictory. Urban daily life offered both practical and leisure-time inducements for the urban population to use the rudimentary skills that they acquired in elementary education. Scholars have subsequently confirmed what firsthand experience revealed, namely, that "achievement in handling the tools of reading and writing is one of the most important axes of social differentiation in modern societies."[80] The retention of literacy and numeracy was a perennial problem among the rural population, but it does not seem to have been an issue among the urban population. The return to the village of the successful urban migrant was potentially an ample reward for literacy. In the city, proof that literacy and numeracy were rewarded in both work and leisure was everywhere available. In this sense cultural modernity was present among the urban population.

Tsarist officials, religious leaders, and educators were deeply divided on

78. Eklof, *Russian Peasant Schools*, 268.

79. "Gramotnost' i stepen' obrazovaniia prizyvnykh," *Sbornik statei po voprosam otno-siashchimsia k zhizni russkikh gorodov* 11 (1901):258–61; S. V. Bernstein-Kogan, *Chislen-nost', sostav i polozhenie Peterburgskikh rabochikh* (St. Petersburg, 1910), 66.

80. Jack Goody, "The Consequences of Literacy," in *Literacy in Traditional Societies*, ed. Jack Goody (Cambridge, Mass., 1968), 58.

the question of the moral efficacy of schooling and literacy. No educated Russian aware of the migrant strangers in their city would mourn the decline of superstition as a result of education (if indeed such were the case), but what was its effect on religious faith? Formal learning had its own practical rewards, but could it counteract the forces of the tavern and the brothel to instill the desirable personal traits of sobriety and industriousness? The debates about learning and popular culture in the cities touched on issues of personal conduct, labor relations, and public morality. Although some cultural leaders found hope in the spread of schools and popular reading materials, others sounded a somber note. They worried that "decay and decadence" would overwhelm their crusade for enlightenment.

More sanguine observers, however, stressed the spiritual benefits of learning. The bishop of Saratov seemed to have constructed his own ideal "city on a hill" when in 1896 he contrasted the "simple, childlike faith" of the "rural, illiterate population" and the heightened "level of religious knowledge" of the Bible, the liturgy, and church ritual that he attributed to the "literate [urban] population."[81] In personal accounts of the impact of schooling on urban youth, some instructors echoed this optimistic view. According to the cleric-instructor in one southern town, the parents of pupils in the parish school were "very pleased that their children can read and sing at church services, and [they] require them to read at home."[82] Thus, learning and urban religious practice were compatible. One instructor of a factory school in a provincial town in Moscow province noted in the 1894 survey that schooling appeared to him to "diminish drunkenness" and to augment his students' interest in "reading more books on religious subjects."[83]

Whatever the veracity of such judgments, they reflected a deeply embedded assumption about print culture. Like the radical intellectual who brought socialist doctrine to pupils in a literacy school or the factory manager who was convinced that literacy, sobriety, and industriousness formed a single personality type, no one spoke out against education; all assumed that the processes of learning were part of the transformation of urban culture as a whole. They were as preoccupied with the moral impact of education as they were concerned about the strange, threatening world

81. "Otchet o sostoianii Saratovskoi eparkhii za 1896," TsGIA, f. 796, op. 442, d. 1636, 20.
82. "Anketnye svedeniia o nachal'nykh uchilishchakh," TsGIA, f. 91, op. 3 (1894), d. 448, 3–4.
83. Ibid., d. 574, 227–28.

of ignorance and decadence in slums such as Khitrovka. Despite evidence that the cultural values and social relations among the urban population could not be controlled, other movements in addition to the campaign for schooling attempted to guide cultural change in the Russian migrant cities.

Sobriety, Learning, and the Penny Press

Although the warnings that a cultural crisis existed in the Russian city of the late nineteenth century were exaggerated, they reflected a widespread consensus that action was necessary. The agreement among cultural activists on the desirability to expand efforts to promote schooling and literacy was in large part produced by these fears. Laments about drunkenness, ignorance, and immorality fit well with contemporary stereotypes of both the "barbarism" of a backward land and the decadence produced by industrialization. The tavern, whose presumed life summed up the nature of the crisis, was the enemy of those who defended godliness, enlightenment, and industriousness. The nascent penny press also appeared to be a nefarious influence on popular culture. Many educated Russians thought that its sensationalist accounts of local events and its emphasis on the "human interest" aspects of urban life were crass commercialism that pandered to base popular tastes. Because of these apprehensions an officially sponsored movement to use the tools of print culture to promote sobriety, moral behavior, and industriousness received strong support in provincial cities. These culturist activities found an audience among the urban population and all to some extent helped to reshape urban culture.

In the last half of the nineteenth century the commercial press became an active cultural force in its own right in the cities. As in Western cities earlier in the century these publications included a national and a penny, or "boulevard," press. Both were commercial operations. The national press, however, set ambitious cultural objectives: it offered an encapsulated version of a "newsworthy" world that extended far beyond the mundane events and ordinary practices of the migrant city. Appealing to a relatively well-to-do public, the commercial success of the national press was assured if it attracted a substantial number of subscriptions, for its sales price was relatively high. The so-called penny press thrived on the commercial formula of low prices, mass sales, and advertising. As a result, it drew its inspiration from and depended for survival on a large urban reading public.[84]

Both the national and the penny presses were cultural innovations whose essential conditions for survival appeared only in the reform years. In the last half of the nineteenth century, urban education and effective literacy were sufficiently widespread in towns throughout European Russia to create a large market for publications. Public interest in social and political events in Russia was stimulated by the reforms themselves. The government was aware of the need for public and unofficial daily publications, which were conceivable only if they enjoyed relatively few administrative restraints. For all its defects the new censorship statute of 1865 permitted the daily press to become a public forum. Although it set strict limits on the types of events that could be reported, it did not repress the rapid flow of information. It did this in a spirit of what contemporaries called "openness" (*glasnost'*). Newspapers could request the right to publish without "preliminary censorship," but remained subject to various penalties (the most potent of which was a temporary ban on public sales) if censors judged articles to be unacceptable. At about the same time the spread of the railway network opened up a larger market: the speed of distribution was crucial to make daily news salable. In effect readership followed the rail lines beyond the city of publication. Finally, the openness instituted by the tsarist reforms made abundant information on public happenings accessible to journalists. The national press created its own blend of news for its propertied, respectable public. The penny press found greater rewards in unusual daily events such as crimes, fires, and collective fistfights. Scorned by the elite, these stories were the kind of titillating and sensational news that attracted a mass audience.

The migrant cities were both the market for the boulevard and national papers and the source of much of the information out of which the editors created their daily text. In their social diversity, economic dynamism, and multitude of personal stories of work, success, and social ambition, the migrant cities became a sort of theater of everyday drama that was often unfamiliar and unsettling, but potentially enthralling for a public that was curious to learn more about the world by means of these immediate daily events. The ways that newspaper stories satisfied their readers is a problem to which historians of urbanization have no definitive answers. Gunther Barth, studying "city people" in the United States in the nineteenth cen-

---

84. The distinction between the national and the penny presses is discussed in detail in Louise McReynolds, "News and Society: *Russkoe slovo* and the Development of a Mass-Circulation Press in Late Imperial Russia" (Ph.D. diss., University of Chicago, 1984), chap. 1.

tury, argues that the market for newspapers was created by "the longing of urban masses for identity." This psychological theory rests on the dubious assumption that the city destroyed both personal and collective identities. The "need for information about a bewildering place" that he finds among U.S. readers can be more readily explained by the cultural unfamiliarity of the peoples and the places that the migrants encountered in the city. In Russia, as in the United States, the movement of migrants into the cities was largely a collective endeavor that involved the assistance of family, fellow villagers, and countrymen. The migrants were nonetheless strangers in the sense that beyond the few known locations of neighborhood, taverns, and workplace they confronted unknown places and people in the city. Similarly, established townspeople observed the rapid growth and transformation of their cities, which offered them a strange spectacle of vast human proportions. In this sense, one might agree with Barth that "modern city life" was potentially "the greatest news story of the nineteenth century."[85]

Finding the subjects and style of these stories was the work of the pioneering editors of the new national and penny presses. The national press took shape in papers such as *Novoe vremia* (New Times) and *Birzhevye vedomosti* (Stock Gazette). These papers found a large circulation by appealing to educated readers and to members of the business community in St. Petersburg, where both were published, and beyond. Besides an emphasis on business news, *Birzhevye vedomosti* also included extensive coverage of European events and even occasional articles titled "What they are thinking and doing in the provinces." Its contents fitted the interests of its national audience so well that by the end of the century its circulation reached 100,000, the first Russian paper to do so.

The national press became a key ingredient in setting the tone of public opinion (*obshcestvennost'*). All positioned themselves on a political spectrum from conservative to liberal. In this respect their cultural voices helped to create, in Habermas's terms, a literary public sphere in the same decades that the municipalities and other official and informal institutions were contributing to the rise of a civic public sphere.[86]

The national newspapers were also commercial enterprises whose contents and readers were found largely in the merchant city. Their editors sought to sell a cultural product by appealing to the tastes and interests of the propertied and educated public. Thus, some of the stories were cultural

---

85. Gunther Barth, *City People: The Rise of Modern City Culture in Nineteenth-Century America* (New York, 1980), 59.

86. Jürgen Habermas, *L'espace public*, trans. Marc de Launay (Paris, 1978), 189–93.

creations that involved an "imaginary city" in which the readers believed themselves to be at home. This skill in making the city a known place appears clearly in another genre of popular writing that emerged in those decades, namely, the city guides.

The authors of city guides were in their own way engaged in creating an imaginary city. In their case the city was a place of known, tangible locations with which the readers easily identified. They were responding to the practical needs of a reading public that lived in and traveled to the major Russian cities. Implicit in their collection of factual information was a model of the city with concrete spatial and temporal dimensions.[87] Their books provided "mental maps" for readers with the reading skills demanded by such guides, the money to purchase such relatively inexpensive items, and the powers of imagination to locate the city in space and time. The guides were specifically intended to turn the city into a recognizable location for its residents and, particularly, for outsiders. With a guide in hand, its owner would cease to feel like a stranger in the city.

When the guides began to appear in substantial numbers in the 1860s and 1870s, their content and style were calculated to appeal to a public in need of knowledge. Baedeker's series of guides, which had originated earlier in the century, provided the model. The Russian authors repeatedly stressed the importance of the reader in choosing relevant material. As one guide to Moscow stressed, the reader's verdict "will determine the future of the series." Claiming to contain "all necessary information for travelers," this guide contained the "indispensable addresses" to public agencies and services, the "notable sites" where the city's glorious history could be seen, and a special chapter on the marvelous future that the technical and manufacturing exposition, which was being held at the time of publication, promised.[88] The guides became available for an increasing number of provincial cities later in the century. They gave a cultural and "businesslike" description of urban space. They told dramatic historical stories, assigning to cities their own significant role in the national epic. For example, an Odessa guide stressed its rise from a "half-savage Tatar village" to "progressive" city in less than a century.[89] Travel across the territory that separated these Westernized centers presented a real challenge. A guide to the Volga basin warned its readers that "the development of civilization" in

87. My interpretation of these city guides is inspired by Iurii Lotman, "K probleme prostranstvennoi semiotiki," in *Semiotika prostranstva i prostranstvo semiotiki*, ed. I. Lotman, *Trudy po znakomym sistemam*, no. 19 (Tartu, 1986), 1–16.
88. V. Dolgorukii and V. Anofriev, *Putevoditel' po Moskve i ee okrestnostiam* (Moscow, 1872), vi.
89. *Putevoditel' po Odesse* (Odessa, 1867), 5.

this area, although unlike "southern Africa," had not brought conditions up to the level of Western Europe or the United States.[90] Although somewhat redefined by Russia's entry into the age of steamboats and railroads, the province remained an exotic, backward territory within which the cities were islands of refuge and comfort.

The practical knowledge necessary to survive and prosper in the merchant city assumed an increasingly important place in the guides. By the end of the century the literary-historical themes had dwindled in importance. The city's role in history mattered less to the readers of those years than its sites of administrative and business affairs. The editor of a new guide to Odessa set a businesslike tone to his work by informing his readers that "following the rule that time is money, I tried to avoid wordiness." His book was intended to be a handbook to daily affairs, for its contents were "prepared on the basis of everyday experience" and provided "a rapid familiarization with the city."[91] It omitted any mention of historical events or monuments, for Odessa's time had become businessman's time. For his public, real and imagined, the city's present and future mattered more than its past, and its official and workday practices were more important than the hallowed symbols of cultural glory.

Unlike the earlier fairs, the 1896 national exposition in Nizhny Novgorod was the subject of several guides. They incorporated everything needed for the traveler, including railroad timetables and glowing accounts of the exhibition park, the buildings, and the exhibits. These publications were as important as the reports of journalists in creating an aura of reality around an event that sought to bring the future to the present by constructing an artificial Volga city of technology and industry. Although the guides were perhaps illusory in their depictions, their language of productivity and technology represented only an extreme version of a theme that was of growing importance in other urban guides of the time. For the reading public of these guides the Russian city as workplace assumed the shape and color of industrial modernity.

The intended audience for these guides, like that of the national press, belonged to the Westernized cities of business and public affairs. It was quite different from the presumed readers of the penny press. The images of the city created on the pages of the guides or in the daily articles of the elite newspapers explicitly or implicitly honored the ideals of civilization and enlightenment. In spirit and content they maintained ethical standards

90. Ia. Kuchin, *Putevoditel' po Volge* (Saratov, 1865), 1.
91. *Odessa v karmane na 1896* (Odessa, 1896), 1.

of patriotism and propriety. Their writing belonged to the cultural domain of literary Russia; it was satisfying to those educated Russians with a culturist agenda for the new city.

The penny press belonged to a different cultural world. The distinction that Jeffrey Brooks draws between "edifying or instructive publications" and "popular commercial literature" can be applied to the journalistic genres of the national and the penny presses.[92] For boulevard newspapers as for popular fiction, salability largely determined both form and content. Certain writers moved back and forth between the penny press and popular literature because they shared with editors an overriding concern to exploit the topics and themes that would capture a mass reading audience. The boulevard newspapers created a panoramic picture of urban daily life that bears more than a passing resemblance to the issues that emerged in the debates of the municipal dumas. At times their writers and editors addressed civic affairs, speaking in the name of the city and its people. However, publishers put sales before sermonizing. The penny press combined commerce and knowledge in a way that was often judged as scandalous by tsarist officials and urban reformers alike.

Like similar papers in Western cities, the Russian boulevard press represented a new and problematic cultural venture. Their editors abandoned the familiar world of the intellectual and business communities. By seeking to appeal to the popular urban reader, they were forced to invent on the pages of their papers a way of representing the Russian city for which there was no precedent. As in the West, the popular newspaper had to "create itself" before "creating its public."[93] Educated observers saw the triumph of vulgarity over culture in the unintellectual character of these newspapers. When the first one appeared in St. Petersburg in the 1860s, a critic considered it to be an outright rejection of the culturist "heavy journals" that set the tone of intellectual debate in those years. Employing the formulaic social distinctions of urban activists, he explained that "obviously" the literary language and complex subjects of the heavy journals were beyond the grasp of "petty bourgeois, artisans, and the poorest townspeople, who, if they read anything, buy cheap newspapers."[94]

For its commercial survival the penny press had to discover and appeal to the tastes and interests of a large public. Many of its readers probably possessed a level of education not much above the rudimentary knowledge

92. Brooks, *When Russia Learned to Read,* 296–97.
93. Olga Hughes, *News and the Human Interest Story* (New York, 1940), 7.
94. *Knizhnyi vestnik* 13 (1865):254; cited in "Russkaia gazeta vtoroi poloviny XIX veka," by B. Esin (Doctoral dissertation, Moscow State University, 1973), 1:296.

of reading and writing that urban youth sought in primary schools. Social context defined the content and style of the penny press. In the years when a culturist movement was organizing public readings on suitably respectable subjects for a population that the Minister of Education referred to as the "worker estate and the lower levels of society," the penny press was attempting to sell a very different form of print culture to that same public.

In doing so it incorporated into its selection of newsworthy information many scenes from daily life and presented its articles in popular, idiomatic speech. Sometimes, these human interest stories became the centerpiece of the daily news, continuing a practice that editors of culturist publications had already baptized as the *fel'eton*. Following the model of the French *feuilleton*, this rubric appeared in the national press in the form of literary criticism or witty stories. In the 1870s Dostoevsky published his *Diary of a Writer* in a *fel'eton* format.[95] It reemerged in the penny press in a somewhat new form to designate human interest stories (and occasionally serialized popular fiction) that was written in a "folksy" manner. It avoided the appearance of serious news, using titles such as *Mezhdu prochim* (Among Other Things) or *Tsentki* (Little Incidents) and signed with absurd pseudonyms such as "Not I" (the modest writer's ready reply to the query of who had written such trash). The authors adopted an unassuming, "natural" pose; they selected very ordinary but lively topics that were drawn from everyday life and they wrote their stories in an unliterary style. Their articles bore no resemblance to serious literature. Maxim Gorky, who began his writing career in his mid-twenties as a *fel'etonist* for a provincial paper, soon had moral qualms about this manner of pandering to popular tastes. He later accused such writers of "encumbering the memory of people with the trash of photographic images of their lives."[96] Yet it was just this type of entertaining account of daily life that could assure the commercial success of a boulevard newspaper.

Human interest stories were literary creations that made use of a strong dose of imagination and that suspended standards of accuracy to give dramatic significance to their subjects. The formula that produced these stories proved to be very effective, and by the 1890s the fame and commercial success of Russian popular newspapers depended partly on the skill of their *fel'etonisty*. The authors of the *fel'eton* were sufficiently influential to shape, as well as to reflect, the views of the mass reading public. In the

95. Dostoevsky's feuilleton writings are examined from a literary point of view in Gary Saul Morson, *The Boundaries of Genre: Dostoevsky's "Diary of a Writer" and the Tradition of Literary Utopia* (Austin, Tex., 1981), esp. 14–17.

96. Maksim Gorkii, "Chitatel'," *Sobranie sochinenii* (Moscow, 1949), 2:202.

opinion of one American sociologist, similar writers in the American penny press were able to lead their readers "through the human interest in a personal story toward an acquaintanceship with a simplified and trivialized but wider world."[97] In late-century Russia, that wider world was primarily the readers' own city, which was presented to them in a dramatic, imaginative but identifiable form.

The recourse of the penny press to items that respectable society judged to be scandalous made it especially objectionable to critics. By comparison with later boulevard papers, the news that appeared in the first penny press publication. *Peterburgskii listok* (founded in 1865), was deferential to authority and sober in tone. However, the efforts of its editor to include incidents from the city's daily life, its crimes, and the abusive treatment of its less fortunate population earned the paper the reputation for yellow journalism. The editor was frequently brought to court by readers who accused him of defamation. Most serious of all, the Petersburg Censorship Committee subjected his paper to constant harrassment, periodically banning street sales (once for five years). The committee's hostility seemed to be based as much on its fear of the reading masses as on the paper's content. One censor condemned the editor because he allegedly sought "above all to pander to the crude tastes" of the "Petersburg demimonde [*polusvet*]." In the category of "demimonde" the censor included "artisans, tradesmen, and various types of petty individuals [*melkie liudi*]" who lacked a "well-developed revulsion against crime."[98] Those who shared the censor's conservative outlook preferred to keep the urban scandals hidden from view. But the penny press needed to keep the city's lower depths on the pages of their papers in order to attract readers.

Despite tsarist censorship, the Petersburg paper proved by the late 1870s that the steady production of popular and scandalous news was a formula for commercial success. Its reading public learned on its pages of both a known and an unknown city. The stories that the paper told relied to a certain extent on popular stereotypes: the drunker trader, the helpless wife, the dangerous tramp, and the greedy Jew. But the paper also told of the new railroads, of curious Western customs, and of a cleaner, healthier city that would be constructed in the future. Its urban drama was both an oft-told tale and an account of the new city.

In the 1880s boulevard newspapers sprang up in other cities, first in Moscow and then in the provinces. The fame—and notoriety—of *Mos-*

97. Hughes, *News*, 277.
98. "Zhurnal zasedaniia soveta Glavnogo upravleniia po delam pechati," 6 January 1872, TsGIA, f. 776, op. 2, d. 10, 586.

kovskii listok surpassed other similar papers from the time of its founding in 1881 until the last years of the century. Like its Petersburg cousin, it drew its material from the city and the surrounding region, with occasional notes "from the provinces." The politics and diplomacy of European affairs occupied a very small place on its pages, and the affairs of the tsarist state appeared only to the extent that political exigency required. As Jeffrey Brooks emphasizes, the credit for its effectiveness as "the first model of the Moscow street press" belonged to its colorful, self-made editor, N. A. Pastukhov.[99] Although its articles exploited and dramatized events in the daily lives of Muscovites, its popularity among that public assured its commercial success. By transforming the sensational and ephemeral events of the city into a sort of daily street theater, Pastukhov and his writers turned the paper into the popular voice of the migrant city.

Within the limits set by tsarist censorship *Moskovskii listok* portrayed a city that was divided into, on the one hand, a familiar, and often humorous, cast of characters that consisted largely of propertied, settled Muscovites and, on the other, a violent, sometimes tragic, and sometimes threatening world of the other Moscow of migrants. Its police chronicle offered an ongoing tale of theft, murder, and mayhem from Moscow's taverns and slums. Pastukhov himself entered the ranks of the *fel'etonisty* when he decided in 1882 to write a serialized bandit story that was drawn from the life of a local worker turned robber. The events contained in the police record, which were uncovered by a young journalist cum research assistant, Vladimir Giliarovsky, bore only a remote resemblance to the fictionalized epic that the author recounted at great length. The tale, *Razboinik Churkin* (The Bandit Churkin), which was presented in serialized form, gave a brutal yet sympathetic portrait of the hero. Ultimately, the authorities—identified in various accounts as Moscow's governor-general, the censor, or the conservative editor M. N. Katkov—put pressure on the editor-author to bring his hero and tale to a speedy end.[100]

At times the newspaper's tone veered from the comic and adventure-some to the tragic. In May 1882, when a major fire destroyed worker barracks in the nearby textile town of Orekhovo-Zuevo, Pastukhov sent Giliarovsky to write a first-hand account of what the paper would call the "terrible spectacle" and to report the casualties ("at least" fifteen dead and thirty injured). The town's factory owners complained to the authorities that the report provoked the anger of the workers against their bosses. The

99. Brooks, *When Russia Learned to Read*, 119–23.
100. Ibid., 123–25.

specter of urban riots brought the wrath of Moscow's governor-general, Dolgorukii, down on Pastukhov. Summoning the editor to his office, Dolgorukii threatened (or so Giliarovsky later claimed) to have the reporter arrested and exiled. Only Pastukhov's cleverness in hiding his source allegedly spared his young reporter.[101] Tales of fires, banditry, and everyday trivia made *Moskovskii listok* a commercial success and its editor a millionaire. Urban culture proved to be a very salable commodity.

Despite the risks of censorship and the scorn of many educated Russians, provincial editors sought to imitate the penny press of the capitals. They could not rival the excitement and color of the metropolitan papers, but they made a place for themselves by mixing genres and content. At times they adopted the serious approach of the national press, but invariably they also incorporated the popular feature of the *fel'eton* stories. By the end of the century three hundred daily newspapers existed in European Russia, a relatively small number by comparison with Western lands but a remarkable increase for a country that had only twelve dailies just forty years before.[102] Their growth provides one indication of the emergence of a mass print culture in Russia.

The editors of the penny press kept clearly in mind the types of readers for whom their papers were destined. In this sense, the reading public was a figment of their imagination, which employed an array of social stereotypes to describe that public. We should be very careful before we accept uncritically their observations in characterizing the actual newspaper readers. For example, Pastukhov is reported to have rejected a manuscript for *Moskovskii listok* because he found it unsuitable for his paper's supposed reading public of "janitors and shopkeepers." In effect, Pastukhov was inventing an imaginary reader whose essential qualities were rudimentary literacy and unsophisticated cultural tastes.[103] He had no interest in defining precisely the real social identity of his customers. However, he was vitally concerned with defining that public's taste in news. Like other editors of the penny press, he understood that the financial survival of his paper depended on attracting as wide a general public as possible. For two decades Pastukhov was remarkably successful at finding a mass audience.

---

101. Written under the pseudonym *Svoi chelovek* (My own man), the account appeared in the paper on 4 June 1882; in his memoirs Giliarovskii wrote somewhat romanticized accounts of his various adventures with Pastukhov and in "Moi skitaniia" included his own version of the events surrounding the story of the fire; see V. A. Giliarovskii, *Izbrannoe* (Moscow, 1958), 1:231–32.

102. Publication figures are found in Daniel Balmuth, *Censorship in Russia, 1865–1901* (Washington, D.C., 1969), 113–14.

103. Cited in Brooks, *When Russia Learned to Read*, 128.

His paper held pride of place in popular taverns, and his tale of the bandit Churkin was read aloud in factory barracks and the housing communes of laborers.

These editors were aware that the subject of urban squalor was very popular with their public; readers were both repelled by and attracted to the city's lower depths. In 1892 Pastukhov sent one of his star reporters to write about Khitrovka's denizens. Subsequently, provincial papers sought *fel'etonisty* with similar talents. Gorky developed the theme of squalor while working as a cub reporter for a Samara paper in the mid 1890s. In Rostov-on-Don a young vagabond-journalist named A. Svirskii made a national reputation with tales written for a local paper on what he would later call his urban "slum world."[104] The public that read such articles believed itself to be above the slum dwellers of these squalid places.

Journalistic portraits of the city could arouse a powerful response from the readers, but not the sort that would gratify the culturist elite of urban Russia. Although scorned by intellectuals as a "petty urban intelligentsia [*obyvatel'skaia intelligentsiia*]," readers of the boulevard papers were as capable as more sophisticated townspeople of conjuring up an imaginary city whose actors played out a social drama in which justice and injustice each found their emblems. One such example is the memoirs of the worker-militant, Petr Moiseenko, who in the mid 1880s used Pastukhov's "Bandit Churkin" to raise the social consciousness of textile workers in the provincial factory town of Orekovo-Zuevo. He sensed the resonance that this tale of robbery and murder by a worker turned bandit enjoyed among working-class readers and listeners. He overestimated, however, his ability to define the ideological lesson of the tale for his audience. After listening to the tale his audience concluded that because the factory owners "plundered us," the workers ought "to plunder" them.[105] In this reading Churkin became a mixture of Robin Hood and Stenka Razin.

Thus, the authorities were not far wrong in their fears that the sensationalism of the penny press could unwittingly—or intentionally—feed an undercurrent of urban violence. These papers created simplified portraits of social types that included anti-Semitic stereotypes as well as comical figures of merchants. The simplistic official view made scant distinction between information and incitement to action. A police report on Pastukhov's paper

---

104. A. Pazukhin, "Khitrovtsy," *Moskovskii listok*, 18 April 1892; A. Svirskii, *Mir trushchobnyi* (Rostov, 1898). Svirskii's writings are discussed in Joan Neuberger, "Crime and Culture: Hooliganism in St. Petersburg, 1900–1914" (Ph.D. diss., Stanford University, 1985), 118–40.

105. P. Moiseenko, *Vospominaniia starogo revoliutsionera* (Moscow, 1966), 70.

warned that its articles "with information about all kinds of criminal and bloody events in Moscow, the provinces, and other parts of the empire" might spread unrest. The report concluded that these "scandalous elements of the paper undoubtedly have a harmful effect" on "petty traders and the lower levels of society."[106] That the penny press was in close touch with the lower levels of society was a common assumption of censorship and police reports. This thought worried and offended authorities. Because they were a potential menace, the urban masses became the target for a culturist campaign whose goals were orderliness and enlightenment.

When the project first appeared, it bore the marks of an effort to mobilize public support behind an essentially conservative tsarist policy to discipline the lower social orders in the city. In 1872 at the initiative of the St. Petersburg police prefect, the tsar authorized the formation of a commission for public readings. The measure originated in official concern about worker unrest in St. Petersburg. The capital's swelling labor population and sporadic factory disorders were visible signs that the capital had ceased to be only the center of power and a showcase of imperial grandeur. In a spirit reminiscent of the founders of the Salvation Army (which had been founded in London in the previous decade) the city prefect, General A. A. Trepov, advocated public readings of suitably uplifting literature as a means to promote "the struggle against drunkenness, the elimination of coarse manners, and the improvement of the moral and intellectual level of the people."[107]

In his paternalistic manner Trepov attempted to promote culture through the diffusion of officially approved inspirational and entertaining learning. It was never clear how public readings might incite sobriety. The establishment of public readings was an admission that the church lacked the moral authority to combat the tavern and other destructive cultural forces. The boulevard press was proving that print culture was a potent means to reach the masses, and some authorities believed that its scandalous contents called for some official rejoinder. The readings were intended to be attractive educational public gatherings that would win converts to respectability. The organizers of the readings sought to introduce some of the dramatic features that had long been a part of the popular carnival (*gulian'e*). Centuries old, the carnival was evolving in the nineteenth cen-

---

106. "Politicheskii obzor Moskovskoi gubernii," Tsentral'nyi gosudarstvennyi arkhiv Okt'iabrskoi revoliutsii (abbreviated TsGAOR), f. 203, d. 59, ch. 45 (1883), 9.

107. *Ocherk deiatel'nosti postoiannoi komissii narodnykh chtenii, 1872–1892* (St. Petersburg, 1897), 3, cited in L. Ivanov, "Ideologicheskoe vozdeistvie," 323; this essay contains a detailed study of the history of public readings.

tury through the addition of new attractions, such as the "Petrushka" puppet theater and simple vaudeville shows on patriotic themes.[108] Tsarist authorities closely supervised the public readings. When they began, they included "magic lantern" illustrations to enliven the stories, which were often on historical and patriotic subjects. In this manner, they bore some resemblance to the content of the carnivals. At the same time, however, the readings also sought a tone of moral righteousness and seriousness that was similar in tone to the national theater.

By choice and necessity the audience consisted of townspeople. Setting the guidelines for the choice of readings, the Minister of Education D. M. Tolstoi explained that they should be "adapted to the needs and level of understanding of the people of the worker estate [sic] and, in general, [to that] of the lower levels of society."[109] The number of authorized readings slowly increased until by the late 1880s some three hundred booklets had been approved by the three central public reading commissions. The printings totaled approximately three million copies. Mainly "religious and informational," the subjects ranged from the discussion of natural phenomena such as thunder to a biography of Peter the Great and an inquiry into the role of women in Christianity.[110] A mixture of old piety, modern nationalism, and rationalist science, the readings tried to embody a form of schooling that would be useful for literates and illiterates alike. The readers of such works spoke from a sort of secular pulpit, attempting to inspire their audience with the virtues of morality and sober living.

That public readings were a means to a much larger end became apparent in the next decades. By the 1890s Trepov's call for a struggle against drunkenness had entered the list of officially supported good causes. So important was this goal that in 1890 the government approved a program for the partial prohibition of alcohol consumption through the opening of state liquor stores and the closing of taverns that sold hard liquor. The campaign, which gradually went into effect over the next decade, was largely the work of the Ministry of Finance. Its responsibilities included the creation of provincial "guardianships of popular sobriety," which were intended to offer cultured alternatives to the tavern. Among these activities were the opening of tearooms (chainiki) whose strongest beverage was kvass, the sponsorship of decorous carnivals, and, in the spirit of Trepov's stress on

---

108. The evolution of the carnivals is the subject of A. F. Nekrylova, *Russkie narodnye gorodskie prazdniki, uveseleniia i zrelishcha: Konets XVIII–nachala XX veka* (Leningrad, 1984).

109. "Otchet ministerstva narodnogo prosveshcheniia za 1872," TsGIA, f. 733, op. 117, d. 62, 135–36.

110. Brooks, *When Russia Learned to Read*, 312–13.

officially sponsored learning, the dissemination of enlightenment through the establishment of reading rooms and the holding of public readings.

The reasons for the prominence of sobriety as a goal are not clear. Nothing in the records suggests that demon liquor had suddenly become a devastating plague. Perhaps an important issue was reducing worker drunkenness on the job in a period of rapid economic expansion. In its immediate political context the crusade against liquor fit well with tsarist efforts to shore up the institutional and ideological foundations of conservatism, giving it (consciously or unconsciously) an up-to-date, "modern" character in keeping with contemporary cultural ideals of industriousness and decorum. Just how popular this crusade was is not clear from the records. With state funding and official patronage a network of "hundreds" of committees (if official claims are to be believed) spread throughout urban Russia.[111] Its members came not only from official and church circles but also from business and intellectual groups. In some cases the local organization grew to an impressive size. The Kazan committee had over 2,500 members by the turn of the century; it had opened a tearoom, a public shelter, and a clinic for alcoholics; and it had also organized a reading room and public readings.[112]

Even if much of the success of the temperance movement was the result of official sponsorship, the vision of a sober, patriotic, industrious, and knowledgeable population attracted many educated Russians. Fears of squalor, ignorance, and decadence aroused widespread concern, especially in urban areas. Drunkenness was only the most visible social evil that was presumed to arise in these conditions of social and cultural backwardness. The program of the temperance movement was formulated in a manner that addressed this larger problem. It struck a responsive chord among the members of the urban elite, who were preoccupied with an ethical campaign in defense of culture in the city.

State patronage remained a factor in public readings and related cultural endeavors, but it became relatively insignificant when voluntary groups became active. Although the choice of nonofficial initiatives was limited by tsarist regulations, in the last decades of the century many such associations emerged in provincial towns. Largely the work of the urban middle classes, their activities ranged from charitable work and artistic endeavors to consumer cooperatives and mutual aid.[113] The character of these organizations

---

111. *Izvestiia Moskovskoi gorodskoi dumy* 24 (May 1902):113.
112. "Statisticheskie svedeniia po gorodam Kazanskoi gubernii," TsGIA, f. 1290, op. 5 (1904), d. 190, 8.
113. The question of the importance of these associations in Russian history is addressed

varied enormously. On the one hand, they included groups close in spirit and organization to official Russia, such as the temperance guardianships and the parish brotherhoods. The tsarist government authorized the formation of the brotherhoods in the 1870s and by the end of the century they numbered over one hundred.[114] They were often sponsored by bishops and numbered among their members both monastic and secular clergy. However, secular volunteers constituted the majority of the membership. These people were prepared to participate in charitable activities as well as public readings and the camaign against drunkenness. A few, such as Yaroslavl's Brotherhood of Saint Dmitrii, included several hundred members. Its membership rolls revealed that most volunteers belonged to the petty bourgeois and peasant estates, a fact that suggests that the brotherhood was a fairly representative cross-section of the population of the town.[115]

On the other hand, many of the voluntary associations had no direct ties at all with official Russia. The literacy committees represented one of the most influential movements not so much for their size as for their social prominence and their ability to make visible their activities in their communities. They took a particular interest in finding buildings to house the growing array of urban literary and cultural undertakings. These centers were called "people's clubs" (*narodnye doma*) but the leading role played there by culturist activists turned them into urban temples of enlightenment. Creating such centers did not come easily in some cases. At the end of the century Kharkov's committee still lacked a people's club even though they already existed in cities such as Odessa and Tambov. Its chairman prodded his members by conjuring up a vision of Kharkov as a new city. "Is it possible," he asked, "that Kharkov, the center of enlightenment, trade, and industry in southern Russia, is not capable of erecting a building for a people's club?"[116] In his circle of cultural activists, a center of urban culture had as much importance in the life of the city as the presence of a university or the railroad.

The significance of voluntary work was far greater than these small deeds would suggest. Through their activities the voluntary associations contributed to the public life of their towns and, indirectly, to the urban civil public sphere. Some of the activists, together with certain officials, were conscious of the potential anti-tsarist implications of the associations'

---

in Joseph Bradley, "Voluntary Associations" (paper presented at the conference on Russian *Obshchestvennost'*, Purdue University, September 1987).

114. A. A. Papkov, *Tserkovnye bratstva: Kratkii statisticheskii ocherk* (St. Petersburg, 1893), 11.

115. *Otchet Bratstva Sviatitel'ia Dmitriia za 1888* (Yaroslavl, 1889).

116. Cited in Didrikhson, *Istoricheskii obzor*, 215.

work. The political connection appeared in what might seem very unusual places, such as Saratov's Society of Lovers of the Fine Arts, which became active in the 1880s. The provincial gendarme officer left a detailed if tendentious description of the society: Its official purpose was to enlarge the community of "the lovers of fine arts" by promoting musical performances, literary readings, and plays that were performed by local talent. Its modest but exalted culturist agenda attracted idealists who were spiritual kin to Chekhov's three sisters. It also provided temporary refuge for radicals such as the populist Mark Natanson, who joined after his return from Siberian exile. The gendarme officer took a very suspicious view of the entire society. He warned his superiors of the possibility that political subversives would exploit their membership in the group in order to "enlarge at will the circle of their acquaintances and entice new people into their movement."[117] Natanson may well have shared the officer's expectation. In this respect, police officials had grounds for concern. The voluntary associations were becoming so prevalent that in their daily affairs they were beyond the control of the authorities.

These cultural activities tell us more about visionary hopes for the city than they reveal about the transformation of urban popular culture. No matter how impressive (and inflated) their statistical claims to success, the public readings were largely an exercise in preaching to the converted. In the mid 1890s the Moscow reading commission claimed that it organized 1,600 readings yearly for approximately three hundred thousand people but noted that at first its public thought the gatherings were "new entertainment where for two or three kopeks they could see a magic lantern show."[118] Moscow was one of the three centers for the writing and distribution of approved materials for public readings. The provinces were less rich in volunteers and financial backing to conduct these public activities. Saratov's readings, which began in 1877, depended on school teachers and the local church brotherhood. They offered a mixture of spiritual tales and "useful knowledge of a secular character."[119] In Saratov the public readings created more intellectual dissonance than clarity.

In the last years of the century the public readings were a regular feature of life in all provincial centers. Their success in those years, however, was in good part the result of the funds that came from the Ministry of Finance

117. "Politicheskii obzor Saratovskoi gubernii," TsGAOR, f. 102, d. 152 (1887), ch. 35, 4.

118. "Deiatel'nost' Komissii po ustroistvu v Moskve publichnykh narodnykh chteniia," *Sbornik statei po voprosam otnosiashchimsia k zhizni russkikh gorodov* 4 (1896):104.

119. "Svedeniia po Saratovskoi gubernii," TsGAOR, f. 102, d. 67 (1881), 1–2.

through the temperance societies; their audiences were relatively small. Although the campaign sought to reach the laboring population, there is little evidence that either the readings or the other culturist offerings in the cities proved attractive to them. Perhaps in cities such as St. Petersburg a portion of the skilled, urbanized workers were drawn to these alternative leisure activities, but in newer industrial centers in areas such as south Russia, police reports in the mid 1880s noted the "absence of the common and working classes of the population" from the audience.[120] An organizer of the Kharkov literacy committee's readings observed that attendance at the gatherings was "not large" but consisted of "a permanent contingent of listeners who did not miss a single reading."[121] With such a faithful audience frequent readings appeared to reach an impressive number of townspeople. But the frontier between the respectable townsfolk and the "uncultured" laboring population was not bridged when the readings reached the same townspeople time after time.

The popular resistance to state restrictions on the use of vodka was symptomatic of the problems that activists faced when they tried to influence the lives of the urban masses. Although a greater number of places of relaxation may have attracted some laborers away from taverns, greater choice did not necessarily lead to the reduced consumption of vodka. One skeptical traveler through the provinces concluded that frequenting a tearoom might "more often than not" save "the worker several kopeks on tea and snacks [and] give him the chance to drink an extra glass of vodka."[122] Closing taverns hindered the customary social drinking of the former patrons, but in the opinion of St. Petersburg's police prefect it merely moved the drunks into the streets. He found no evidence in the capital that the temperance movement had had any significant effect on drunkenness. He did, however, note a rise in serious wounds to the palms of drinkers' right hands, which was caused when their vigorous efforts to pop corks out of bottles broke the bottle instead.[123] The "men's world" of migrants and laborers did not abandon its customs in the face of idealistic crusades.

The array of educational and preventive measures, however, helped to establish a model of urban "respectability" that stressed sobriety, learning, and industriousness. The distinction was similar to that which in England made clear the difference between the urbanized worker and the "rough"

120. "Politicheskii obzor," TsGAOR, f. 102, d. 59, ch. 27 (1885), 11–12.
121. Cited in Didrikhson, Istoricheskii obzor, 204.
122. A. P. Subbotin, Volga i Volgari: Putevye ocherki, 15.
123. "Otchet za 1902," TsGIA, f. 1282, op. 3 (1902), d. 545, 105.

laborer.[124] It was, however, only one among many paths to urban acculturation. A model of "petty bourgeois urbanity" [*meshchanskaia svetlost'*]
also existed. It promised that fine clothing, dancing, and drinking would
turn the young migrant into a real city dweller. In a very different spirit,
militant workers drew a clear distinction between unpoliticized "gray"
fellow workers and "conscious" comrades like themselves. They envisioned
a sort of ideal type of proletarian that conveyed what Reginald Zelnik has
called "a universalistic though, paradoxically, class-based vision of the
future."[125] The migrant city was a world of both learning and work. The
voices of those who promoted one form or another of enlightenment—
some buttressed by claims to tradition, others by appeals to utopia—had
only limited success among an audience that was either indifferent to or
suspicious of their message.

By the end of the century learning and schooling had altered both the
practices and the culture of the migrant city. The opportunities for economic advancement and social respectability had spread, and the ideals of
sobriety and industriousness were a meaningful alternative to the man's
world of the migrant laborers. Both tsarist officials and urban activists used
a measure of progress that placed special emphasis on orderliness and enlightenment, but their understanding of these goals differed greatly. For
each of these groups the world of the migrant represented a challenging and
threatening presence that they were scarcely able to touch. The state remained a force for authoritarian control and repression. Its temperance and
reading campaigns represented a timid but idealistic attempt to encourage
and inspire cultural bonds among the population. Civic activists shared the
tsarist officials' fears of the lower orders but were deeply committed to
voluntary campaigns to create cultural bonds in urban society. The success
of the penny press was not reassuring to those who judged that scandal,
crime, and sensationalism were marks of decadence. An underlying current
of violence, which was sensed by authorities and intellectuals alike, remained a deeply troubling reality. Like Khitrovka, the inner life of the
migrant city remained a mysterious place to those who hoped to guide its
future course.

124. Brian Harrison, "Pubs," in *The Victorian City*, ed. H. J. Dyos and Michael Wolff
(London, 1973), 1:181.
125. Reginald Zelnik, "Passivity and Protest," *Journal of Social History* 15 (Summer
1982):504.

5

Policing the Riotous City

The growth of the cities and the advent of new economic and social practices fundamentally altered the understanding of what public order was at the same time that these developments were undermining the foundations on which that order had rested. The "public orderliness" (*blagoustroistvo*) of the city, which had been embodied in prereform city plans, architectural monuments, and municipal regulations assumed the primacy of the state in civilizing the Russian city. Until the 1860s the tsarist regime judged that the repression of urban disorders was a secondary affair, both because the official policy toward urban crime was ill-defined and because the countryside, not the towns, was thought to be the locus of social unrest. The official vocabulary implicitly associated uprisings and disorders with peasant revolts. Until the 1870s the reports of provincial gendarme officers virtually ignored urban conditions and subsumed the urban working population under the category of the peasantry. Until the reform years Russian cities continued to function as outposts of tsarist rule, housing provincial and district administrators and providing quarters for military forces.

Migration, economic growth, and political rebelliousness altered the tsarist view of public orderliness in the cities from the domain of culture to the domain of power. These processes led to both greater state regulation of the urban population and the redefinition of the concept of order by those in positions of authority. In part the story is a familiar one that includes the rise of collective violence in the cities, particularly in the form of riots and pogroms. It also touches on the radical movement's urban activities, which included organizational and propaganda work among the laboring population. With the example of the 1848 revolutions still fresh in their minds tsarist officials came to view public order in their cities in a new context. They began to focus attention on the threat that the urban masses posed for collective action that would be capable of overthrowing the state itself.

The expectations about the role of the police—and of the proper domain of "policing"—altered among both educated townspeople and tsarist authorities. Although the authorities continued to consider the urban police to be a regulatory body, they assigned it increasing responsibilities to repress collective violence in the cities. At a time when the state was calling for increased popular initiative in local municipal and educational affairs, tsarist officials were becoming increasingly involved in the problems of urban public order: property rights and employers' responsibility toward their workers; the protection of individual life; and relations between police and townspeople. The state retained sole authority to define and enforce urban public order, but its powers were limited. The Russian migrant city was a place of struggle between the laboring population and the state long before the outbreak of the twentieth-century revolutions.

Cities and the Policed
Society in the Reform Years

Policing the city became a tsarist priority even before municipal reform was placed on the political agenda. Thirty years after London obtained its own urban police force, the Russian Ministry of Internal Affairs decided to give the major cities of the country a special agency for the enforcement of public order. The example of urban disorders and the police reforms of Western Europe may have played some part in the origins of this reform, but the ineffectiveness of the old police system was also an important factor. The concept of specialization was already apparent in the decision in the mid 1850s to abolish the last remnant of communal self-policing: municipalities were freed of the responsibility for assigning townspeople to be night watchmen. The old system was unfit to cope with the tasks that were created by economic growth and migration. Reports from provincial towns, collected in preparation for the municipal reform, added their own lists of grievances to those of the central authorities. The members of Rostov-on-Don's commission placed first on their list the police's failure to meet "the needs of the urban population."[1] Town leaders and tsarist officials shared a common concern for reform even though the two sides had different interests and objectives.

The police reform of the early 1860s bore the statist imprint of the central bureaucracy. The new urban police remained under the control of the Ministry of Internal Affairs. Their jurisdiction was only extended to the major cities of European Russia, including the capitals, the provincial centers, and the cities under special police prefects (such as Odessa).[2] Towns that lacked an administrative character, even though they might be expanding at a rapid rate, remained in the ranks of district (*uezd*) towns or settlements. In those places the police were still few in number and were responsible, as in the past, for a vast rural area as well as the urban areas. In the cities that the new police staffed, however, their presence became a tangible factor in the daily lives of the townspeople.

The reforms entailed an expansion in the number of police and an increase in their salaries; both actions were paid for by the municipalities. Even so, the police forces remained relatively underpaid and understaffed in view of the multitude of tasks they performed. Although the state set an ideal ratio of police to population as one in five hundred, the actual ratio often fell to below one in seven hundred. This shortage meant that there were few police posts on the city outskirts, where the concentration of laboring migrants was highest.[3] In the first years after the police reform the state brought staffing levels up to or above the ideal size, even though in doing so it provoked municipal leaders to make loud outcries against the additional expense. Kharkov, with a population in the 1860s of over fifty thousand, increased the size of its police force from fifty to over two hundred; Moscow's force grew to over one thousand. Because of municipal tax constraints and bureaucratic routine the number of police expanded very slowly. Occasionally, however, when urban disorders occurred, this slow growth was punctuated by sudden spurts in staffing and equipping the urban police. Official criticism of the inadequacies of the police usually neglected to mention the increasingly complex demands that were being placed on this force. Once in a while, however, it hinted at the pressures

1. "Po predstavleniiu gubernskim nachal'stve," Tsentral'nyi gosudarstvennyi istoricheskii arkhiv (abbreviated TsGIA), f. 1287, op. 37 (1834–62), d. 2152, 212.

2. E. Anuchin, *Istoricheskii obzor razvitiia administrativno-politseiskikh uchrezhdenii v Rossii* (St. Petersburgh, 1872), 224–37; see also "Obzor deiatel'nosti i reorganizatsii uchrezhdenii politsii ispolnitel'noi s 1862 po 1880 g.," Tsentral'nyi gosudarstvennyi arkhiv Okt'iabrskoi revoliutsii (abbreviated TsGAOR), f. 109, op. 3, d. 866, 16–17.

3. Neil Weissman, "Regular Police in Tsarist Russia, 1900–14," *Russian Review* 44 (January 1985):48–49.

that urbanization was creating. For example, in the late 1860s Saratov's provincial governor complained that the province's urban police forces were "inadequate and insufficient in relation to the number of inhabitants and to the local conditions."[4]

In addition to the increasing responsibilities that resulted from urbanization, the police faced a much deeper problem: underfunding seriously weakened the quality of their personnel. In the past, because of the poor pay, retired soldiers were the primary pool for recruitment by the state police. These recruits were survivors of twenty-five years of military service; their exposure to the draconian regime of military command and their habit of obedience constituted their only training to be lowly agents of the tsarist state. Despite the new political climate and the police reform in the 1860s, the police forces seem to have improved very little according to the reports of provincial administrators and gendarme officers. Although few complaints were made about the full officers (nadzirateli), whose pay rose to 600 rubles a year, the same was not true of their subordinates. The lower ranks constituted the bulk of the urban police—300 in a regular force of 350 in Saratov at the end of the century—and their yearly pay rarely exceeded 150 rubles.

Official reports often contained critical observations of the poor quality and high rate of turnover of the regular policemen in both large and small towns. Conditions in the turbulent port city of Tsaritsyn were extreme but they were still indicative of the staffing problems in other migrant centers. In this city in 1887 resignations occurred at the rate of almost one per day; as a result, three hundred new policemen had to be appointed that year to maintain a force of just sixty.[5] Summer was apparently a time of great turnover because in all towns in which agricultural commodities were traded actively the demand for seasonal labor in good years sent wages soaring far above those of the police. The police prefect of Odessa noted that his police abandoned their work regularly every shipping season because "they do not value their . . . very difficult, inconvenient, demanding service" and instead preferred dock work, where they earned wages three times higher.[6] Retired soldiers remained the main source of recruits, and even they considered police work as a temporary post until better employment became available. At the very end of the nineteenth century St. Petersburg's police prefect praised the pool of recruits from the army, whom he judged to be "impressive, disciplined, and literate." He com-

4. "Otchet o sostoianii," TsGIA, f. 1281, op. 7, d. 82 (1869), 17.
5. "Otchet o sostoianii," TsGIA, f. 1284, op. 223, d. 168 (1888), 19.
6. "Otchet o sostoianii," TsGIA, f. 1284, op. 69, d. 341 (1878), 19.

plained, however, that they remained only briefly because such men "are needed everywhere" and easily find "more rewarding positions."[7] Although the police were essential agents of state power, police personnel proved to be as much a product of the migrant city as were the laborers.

Despite the obvious weaknesses and shortcomings of the urban police forces, in theory they had a key role to play in the state's new policy of maintaining public order in the cities. Nicholas I's Corps of Internal Guards disappeared in the reform years, and its duties were assigned to the police, who were backed by the regular army garrisons stationed in each military district.[8] The army forces remained substantial. As it had in Nicholas I's time, St. Petersburg gave the appearance of a garrison city, with a total military force of eighty thousand. In the 1870s Kharkov, a provincial and industrial center that was also a headquarters for a military region, had a garrison of three thousand troops.[9] This relatively modest level was the norm in the provinces to the end of the century. The rules that authorized civilian authorities—urban police officials or governors—to use army units were set in the late 1870s. The conditions under which provincial officials could call on the military included the prevention or repression of popular disorders and the maintenance of order at public assemblies. Troops were the ultimate recourse for the authorities when urban unrest overwhelmed the police forces.

The presence of military garrisons was far less tangible to townspeople than were their daily encounters with the police. Implicitly, the tsarist regime had come to accept the desirability of a "policed society," that is, the delegation of authority to a special agency that was empowered to exercise direct coercive powers over the population in the course of its work in maintaining order.[10] The police now had to deal with aspects of public conduct that they had previously disregarded (the collective fistfights for example). The potential for the police to abuse their powers was great. The possibility of an increase in confrontations with crowds was also great if the new police activities were judged by urban dwellers to be either unjustified or illegitimate. The organization of the urban police force and the enlargement of its responsibilities involved the police much more closely than in the past in the affairs of the population but did not ensure an improvement

7. "Otchet o sostoianii," TsGIA, f. 1282, op. 3, d. 545 (1901), 99.

8. John Keep, *Soldiers of the Tsar: Army and Society in Russia, 1462–1874* (Oxford, 1985), 313–14.

9. D. Bagalei and D. Miller, *Istoriia goroda Khar'kova za 250 let ego sushchestvovaniia* (Kharkov, 1912), 2:177.

10. Allan Silver, "The Demand for Order in Civil Society," in *The Police*, ed. D. Bordua (New York, 1967), 7–8.

in the enforcement of the laws or greater popular respect for the police. One might agree with a historian's observation that by the turn of the century the city police had become "the most important link tying the citizens to the government."[11] That link was not, however, a guarantee of public orderliness.

In the process of redefining public order the police assumed important new criminal tasks in addition to the old duties of enforcing the municipal and tsarist regulations. In the 1870s special investigative branches took charge of crimes against persons and property.[12] The importance of criminal work was particularly great in the turbulent migrant cities, but these new responsibilities were not accompanied by a reduction of administrative duties. On the contrary, at the end of the century the Ministry of Internal Affairs reiterated its commitment to use the regular police "to care for the universal welfare of the people [and] the peace, quiet, and good order of the whole empire."[13] This policy was not only anachronistic but also far beyond the capacity of the urban police. The municipal statutes requiring police action added a further load to the state's administrative edicts until the police could not possibly deal with all the regulations. For example, in 1880 the Kiev police were responsible for a total of forty-six thousand official orders.[14] The results, if the report of the mayor of the town of Chernigov is representative, offered little satisfaction to townspeople. He noted sarcastically that his citizens expected to find police "on a few of the populous streets and in public meetings" but they were were "absolutely not accustomed to think of the police as an institution that was established mainly to serve their interests." As for the inhabitants on the outskirts of town, he was certain that they "literally never see the police in their areas."[15]

Under these circumstances law enforcement remained fitful and capricious, ideal conditions by which to sustain the public's perception—which was often enough accurate—that the police were inefficient and arbitrary. Frequently, law enforcement practices assumed the customary form of protection for those with the means to pay. In the 1880s the Odessa police prefect complained that the owners of bars and taverns regularly violated

11. T. Hasegawa, "The Formation of the Militia in the February Revolution," *Slavic Review* 32 (June 1973):303.

12. See Robert Abbott, "Crime, Police, and Society in St. Petersburg, 1866–1878," *Historian* 40 (November 1977):80–82.

13. Cited in Robert Thurston, *Liberal City, Conservative State* (New York, 1987), 86.

14. "Otchet po Kievskoi gubernii," in *Trudy komissii Kakhanova* (St. Petersburg, 1884), 2:3.

15. "Zapiska Senatora Polovtsova," in *Trudy komissii Kakhanova* (St. Petersburg, 1884), 3:552.

official regulations by "corrupting the low-ranking police," whose "salaries are inadequate for the satisfaction of basic needs," which leads them "to succumb easily to temptations and financial gifts."[16] These practices turned law enforcement into favoritism. As a consequence, civic leaders in the municipalities were generally skeptical regarding tsarist promises of a policed society in their communities. The Chernigov mayor spoke for his respectable citizenry when he concluded in 1880 that "it is the general conviction of the masses that the police serve government officials and institutions, not the city and its inhabitants."[17] This opinion was shared by the senatorial inspector of southeastern Russia. He acknowledged that the police were zealous in enforcing regulations for "the external cleanliness of the central parts of the city, [and] filling out forms for official registers." In his judgment their failure was evident in that fact that they provided "no real police surveillance of the population."[18]

He raised the key issue of which people belonged in the migrant city and which groups posed a threat either to public order or to other townspeople. The question focused on the "lower orders," particularly on the presence of the transients and beggars, who defied official regulations and the expectations of the respectable citizens. The specter of dangerous classes in Russia often appeared in the guise of vagrants. By the 1860s their increasing numbers in the central city confronted townspeople with the sight of abject poverty. Charity was a public virtue, but the migrant city increased the scale of demands and placed the problem of social inequality in an economic context in which townspeople thought that labor was a better solution. Although vagrancy remained an offense that was punishable by forced return to place of origin, the regulations proved more and more difficult to enforce. In the 1860s Moscow's police chief confronted major problems of "crime, pauperism, vagrancy, and idleness." He had to admit that "the level of vagrancy and idleness . . . grows and grows and those expelled from Moscow reappear within a few months"—some returning ten times or more.[19]

In the following decades the police sporadically enforced these regulations. Toward the end of the century they began sending vagrants to new workhouses that had been created as part of the welfare program of the

16. "Otchet o sostoianii," TsGIA, f. 1284, op. 223, d. 113 (1883), 14.
17. "Zapiska Senatora Polovtsova," in *Trudy komissii Kakhanova* (St. Petersburg, 1884), 3:552.
18. "Otchet po Kievskoi gubernii," in *Trudy komissii Kakhanova* (St. Petersburg, 1884), 2:3.
19. "Doklad ob ustroistve," *Doklady Moskovskoi gorodskoi upravy* (Moscow, 1866), 2–3, cited in Joseph Bradley, *Muzhik and Muscovite* (Berkeley, 1985), 271–72.

municipalities. Still, the censorious voices continued to complain of police inaction. In the 1880s one reporter, speaking for respectable society, lamented what he called the invasion of Moscow by vagrants who crowded the city boulevards. In his opinion the problem existed solely because the police were "paying no attention to beggars."[20] To such townspeople, the police were at fault for not ridding their cities of this disreputable crowd. Other educated Russians, however, defended what one critic who studied the beggars of Moscow referred to as the "street proletariat" that suffered from "inescapable need."[21] In other words, both sides blamed the police.

The authorities did not draw a clear distinction between vagrants and migrants lacking proper papers. New arrivals in the city had to register and, beginning at the end of the 1870s, obtain residence permits (*vid na zhitel'-stvo*). Under the vagrancy laws, if their papers were not in order, migrants who found employment could still be convicted and sent back to their villages. They might, however, be given temporary papers by the justice of the peace (the case in St. Petersburg, as discussed in chapter 2) until they were properly registered. One indication of the degree of surveillance of migrants is found in the statistics on convictions for passport violation in St. Petersburg: in every year in the 1870s the number of convictions totaled between six and nine thousand.[22] These figures do not make clear how stringently the regulations were being applied, but they do prove that the police were sporadically enforcing the law.

In the cities in the Pale of Settlement the presence of a large numbers of Jews added a strong tone of anti-Semitism to the treatment of migrants. In 1880 Kiev's mayor made the police his scapegoat when he complained that his city was "overflowing with people lacking the right to live here," but "the police know nothing of their existence."[23] Unofficially, some policemen were very knowledgeable, turning their authority into a source of considerable profit according to a Kiev journalist of the 1880s. He claimed that they traded bribes from Jews for new residence permits and even proposed that the legally settled first-guild Jewish merchants "hire" a variety of "salespeople" and "servants" in exchange for a substantial payment.[24] Throughout the country the regulations governing the pres-

20. *Moskovskii listok*, 3 February 1882.
21. "K voprosu o nishchenstve," *Sbornik statei po voprosam otnosiashchimsia k zhizni russkikh gorodov* 3 (1896):87; Moscow's problem of vagrancy is discussed in Bradley, *Muzhik and Muscovite*, 250–57.
22. Abbott, "Crime, Police, and Society," 74, table 1.
23. "Otchet po Kievskoi gubernii," in *Trudy komissii Kakhanova* (St. Petersburg, 1884), 2:353.
24. *Kiev v 80-kh godakh: Vospominaniia starozhila* (Kiev, 1910), 29.

ence of migrants in the city were irregularly and often abusively enforced and created great opportunities for bribery.

Not surprisingly, observers concluded that the real income of police officials was far greater than their lowly wages. One provincial gendarme officer estimated that Rostov police clerks "lived on their [illegal] income from passport registration, earning 30 rubles a month." More significant than the alleged amount of illicit income (the accuracy of which is seriously open to question) is the fact that the officer did not judge the situation out of the ordinary; within his circle of tsarist officials, police bribery was accepted as a fact of life.[25]

Opinions varied regarding the treatment that the police meted out to the town population. Tsarist officials and municipal leaders believed that the police operations in urban areas were ineffective and inadequate. The head of the gendarmes judged that the district police lacked "even the possibility to organize any police surveillance at all of localities with heavily populated manufacturing centers." As a consequence, the police became "passive spectators of the criminal acts that are committed there and are accused of inactivity." Perhaps their most grievous shortcoming in his eyes was that their actions "undermine the people's trust in them."[26] Laws were enforced selectively and in some places not at all. This condition was as true for the migrant city as it was for the factory settlement. In its own way Moscow's Khitrovka area was a sanctuary from the law. The gendarme chief was arguing, in bureaucratic terms, for a policed society that would bring order and discipline to those urban areas where industrialization and migration were undermining state authority.

Police attitudes toward authority and society also helped to determine their role in the city. The ethos of autocracy reached to the level of the precinct. In the 1880s one policeman gave a lesson in public order to a rebellious young worker in Kazan. Maxim Gorky vividly recalled the words of a Kazan police sergeant, who described in his own popular imagery his understanding of the power and authority with which he believed himself endowed. He thought himself a part of an "invisible thread like a spider's web" extending from the emperor through his ministers and governors "and down the ranks to me and even the soldier in the ranks. Everything is bound together by this thread. In this invisible strength the kingdom of the tsar is held together for all time." Recalling these words many years later, Gorky concluded that the policeman's explanation made "the ma-

25. "Politicheskii obzor," TsGAOR, f. 102, d. 88, ch. 4 (1884), 24.
26. "Mnenie Shefa Zhandarma," TsGIA, f. 1149, op. 8, d. 96 (1874), 167–68.

chine of the state and its processes" clearer than did all the pronouncements of his teachers.[27]

To the extent that Gorky's policeman was typical, the police supplemented expediency and profiteering with a sense of legitimacy when they confronted decisions regarding possible illegal activities. The police judged criminality according to customary practices as well as personal convenience and administrative statute. For example, although collective fistfights had long been forbidden, the police turned a blind eye to them and to the personal injuries they caused. This custom carried into the migrant cities, although civic spirit and the culturist ideals of civilization set new borders there to the free fight zones. The police did not allow popular mayhem to occur in the central city, where respectable society gathered. In 1882 when some artisans and laborers organized a fight in the middle of Moscow during the Easter holidays the police immediately intervened to stop the battle and arrest the culprits. One of the participants recalled later that "the police showed such zeal only because the setting was the city center; on the outskirts such fights occurred without interference."[28] The fistfights were newsworthy events in the popular press, which reported only the most spectacular battles. The survival of the collective fistfights into the twentieth century suggests that police had chosen to draw sociogeographical borders to separate the laboring-class districts from the "bourgeois" parts of the city. On the outskirts of towns personal injury and even death created no official difficulties. Fight patrons bribed the police to ensure that casualities were listed as "sudden street death."[29] In the domain of the laboring population the police of their own choosing let custom override tsarist statute.

The police were very active, however, in the area of passport regulations and registration. Frequent arrests represented a form of sporadic harassment of migrants. Ostensibly, enforcement was directed at the migrants lacking proper documents. However, corrupt police turned the regulations into a means of extracting bribes. The extent of police powers over the migrants was apparent in the exploits in the mid 1880s of the district police officer in the southern mining town of Iuzovka. The regional gendarme officer, a hostile source but apparently well informed, claimed that an enterprising policeman in this settlement regularly threatened even legally

---

27. M. Gorkii, *Detstvo. V liudiakh. Moi universitety* (Moscow, 1948), 484–85.

28. E. I. Nemchinov, "Vospominaniia starogo rabochego," in *Na zare rabochego dvizheniia v Moskve* (Moscow, 1933), 158.

29. D. A. Pokrovskii, "Kulachnye boi," *Ushedshaia Moskva*, ed. N. Anushkin (Moscow, 1964), 158.

registered migrants with forced return to their villages unless they paid the appropriate bribe. After several years in his post he allegedly boasted that he could retire, "having put aside 20,000 rubles."[30] Such brutal treatment was less likely to occur in urban areas with a regular city police force, but even there the poorer outlying neighborhoods were kept under much harsher police surveillance than the central districts.

In their daily operations the police often appeared to be the enemy of the laboring population. The way the police treated the lower classes in St. Petersburg at the end of the nineteenth century was close to the norm in other cities. One worker recalled that the precinct police "treated any poorly dressed person crudely [grubo]." He listed abuses that ranged from simple insults to the beating of prisoners.[31] In retaliation for real or rumored abuses workers, individually or in mobs, occasionally attacked the police near factories or in the streets. The potential for serious confrontations grew as the migrant cities expanded and the police increased their controls of the population. For example, the arrest in 1872 in Kharkov of two workers sparked two days of mob action in which crowds looted and destroyed two police stations.[32] Mob violence revealed most forcefully the undercurrent of hatred toward the police among laborers. A decade later the gendarme officer in the southern factory town of Lugansk described random violence against police there, which he claimed was the work of "wandering groups of young workers who walk the streets always armed with revolvers and [who] fire at [police] patrols."[33] As among the peasantry, the hostility of the urban lower classes extended to other figures of authority, but it focused with particular intensity on the police because they were the visible agents of the tsarist regime. Semen Kanatchikov, a young metalworker in the 1890s, recalled that Petersburg workers disliked "factory management, police, and priests" with equal intensity but added that they considered beating or even killing a policeman to be a "victory."[34]

The violence directed at the police was a product of the migrants' precarious place in the city and of the centuries-old popular hostility toward authority, not from incipient revolutionary consciousness. Kanatchikov noted that his Petersburg workers would tolerate no criticism of the tsar or

30. "Politicheskii obzor," TsGAOR, f. 102, d. 9, ch. 21 (1887), 58–59.
31. A. S. Shapalov, V bor'be za sotsializm: Vospominaniia starogo Bol'shevika (Moscow, 1934), 46.
32. Bagalei and Miller, Istoriia goroda Khar'kova 2:472–73.
33. "Politicheskii obzor," TsGAOR, f. 102, d. 9 (1887), ch. 21, 43.
34. S. I. Kanatchikov, A Radical Worker in Tsarist Russia, trans. and ed. Reginald Zelnik (Stanford, 1986), 153.

God, legitimizing their verbal and physical abuse of officials by quoting the proverb: "Break the cup but don't touch the samovar."[35]

The result of such conflicts was endemic unrest resembling latent civil war. Kanatchikov's description of his "gray," that is, politically apathetic, comrades makes clear that even though workers retained a residual veneration for God and the tsar, they turned the police into a proximate enemy. According to one student who became a factory worker at the end of the century, arbitrary police treatment of the laboring population perpetuated the conviction among workers that "laws do not exist."[36] As Neil Weissman suggests, confrontations between urban mobs and the police remained a constant threat as long as the policing of the city remained in popular perception as well as in reality the imposition of "the personal power of a capricious state police force upon the largely autonomous operation of traditional social groups."[37] Under the impact of print culture and the migrant experience, traditional behavior was giving way to a new awareness of personal dignity and social justice. Because of this trend conflicts between the police and the laboring classes became more dangerous than before.

Urban unrest and riots in the 1870s gave a clear warning that the police were inadequate to the task of maintaining public order. These riots indicated the new directions that urban violence was to take in the coming decades. The outbreak of labor conflict, beginning with the Petersburg strikes of 1870, undermined what Reginald Zelnik describes as "the old official optimism about Russia's immunity from the labor question."[38] Labor unrest had ample precedent in Western countries in the midst of industrialization, and tsarist officials recognized that the factory disturbances in their own cities were similar.

No modern Western European parallels existed, however, for the violence that was directed against the Jewish populations in Russian towns and cities. Anti-Semitism had a long history in Eastern Europe. The events of the 1870s revealed that Russia's migrant towns had become the locus of anti-Jewish violence. The origins of these events defy simple explanations. Political, social, and ethnic enmity pitted laboring people against officials, workers against traders, employers against laborers, and Christians against Jews. The major anti-Jewish riots were concentrated in the cities of the

35. Ibid.
36. P. Smidovich, *Rabochie massy v 90-kh godakh* (Moscow, 1930), 13; these memoirs were written in 1901.
37. Weissman, "Regular Police," 66.
38. Reginald Zelnik, *Labor and Society in Tsarist Russia* (Stanford, 1971), 331.

Pale, but disorders erupted in later years wherever Jewish migrants appeared. Cultural and ethnic stereotypes triggered an outburst of hatred against these outsiders, who were often accused of exploiting the laboring population. The Jews of Russia's cities were often scapegoats for the tensions of the larger world of police, employers, and traders.

Social tensions were apparent in the major rioting against Jews that erupted in Odessa at Eastertime 1871. By this time the city had become a booming port and commercial center that mixed Jewish and Gentile migrants, wealthy traders and poor laborers. The origins of the rioting and the pattern of violence were so similar to subsequent anti-Jewish riots that they stand as the archetype of the pogrom. Popular religious enthusiasm, at its peak in the Easter season, turned to anti-Semitic hatred when, according to police reports, rumors circulated Jews were undertaking "some sort of torturing and mutilation of Russians." The rumors set off disturbances directed against Jews and Jewish property that quickly became a massive urban riot that lasted three days. The mob appeared to be recruited at large from the poor laboring population of the city. The rioters looted and destroyed hundreds of stores, taverns, and houses and overwhelmed the police, over one hundred of whom were injured. Belatedly (and setting a precedent for later official actions) the authorities called out troops and Cossacks to suppress the rioters.[39] There is no evidence of official complicity in the pogrom, but the police forces were neither eager nor sufficiently prepared to put down the rioting.

The authorities had their own peculiar anti-Semitic explanations for the violence. Their suspicion of merchants and traders in general gave a simplistic social veneer to their stereotype of the Yiddish-speaking population. In a report written shortly after the pogrom the governor-general of southeast Russia blamed the "special status and privileges" of Odessa's Jews for the violence, an argument that conveniently ignored the poverty of most of the Jewish inhabitants of that city.[40] The renewal of anti-Semitic rioting at the end of the decade in the southern cities of Kiev, Nezhin, and Elizavetgrad was accompanied by complaints from authorities that "the Jews have grabbed all the trade." These riots mingled old and new elements of ethnic hostility. The role of rumor and the easy credence that many Russians gave to supposed Jewish ritual practices against Christians suggest how important cultural stereotypes and abiding prejudice were in fomenting the actions of the anti-Semitic rioters.

39. "Otchet o sostoianii," TsGIA, f. 1284, op. 67, d. 180 (1872), 7–9.
40. Hans Rogger, *Jewish Policies and Right-Wing Politics in Imperial Russia* (Berkeley, 1986), 128.

By the late 1870s these events and reports on the shortcomings of the existing urban police forces obliged the central government to review its policies for public order in the cities. Authoritarianism remained the guiding principle for new measures to instill orderliness into the urban population. The discussions that preceded the reforms as well as the reforms themselves reveal that the tsarist authorities took the problem of urban violence very seriously. The special state conference that recommended new legislation stressed the difficulties that the police confronted in "quickly and energetically putting down street disorders and, especially in the capitals, preventing [the formation of] or dispersing hostile crowds," which often "get the upper hand."[41] This report repeated the conclusions of the many previous official discussions of the inefficiency of the urban police. The search for more repressive powers represented an old formula in dealing with an urban population that at times took on the terrible features of a riotous mob.

To deal with urban unrest, in 1878 the government created a new cavalry force of two thousand men that was to be stationed in the major provincial capitals of European Russia. In effect, this decision revived Nicholas's Internal Guards Corps, but now in police uniforms. A few years later similar cavalry units were assigned to factory settlements. In 1878 the government also increased the number of regular police and equipped them with improved firearms.[42] At the same time, it extended its controls over the migrant population by imposing the requirement of residence permits (*vid na zhitel'stvo*) on urban dwellers. These permits had to be obtained from police officials. The trend toward new central controls continued in the panic that followed Alexander II's assassination in 1881. The regulations permitting the declaration of "intensified security" or "emergency security" brought urban public agencies as well as individuals under close police and administrative surveillance. These regulations were extended to the cities of St. Petersburg, Moscow, Kiev, and Odessa, their respective surrounding areas, and several other important urban centers.[43] The emergency measures were directed at the terrorist movement but their exceptional powers supplemented the other repressive measures that were intended to maintain public order. For state officials, submission to authority and popular tranquility defined the essential nature of urban public order-

---

41. "Zhurnal Osobogo soveschaniia," TsGAOR, f. 109, op. 163, d. 502, 1:252.
42. I. V. Orzhekhovskii, "Vnutrenniaia politika rossiiskogo samoderzhaviia v 1866–1878 gg" (Doctoral dissertation, Leningrad State University, 1974), 72–73.
43. P. A. Zaionchkovsky, *The Russian Autocracy in Crisis, 1878–82*, trans. and ed. Gary Hamburg (Gulf Breeze, Fla., 1979), 256–59.

liness. By this measure state policies in the next two decades proved a failure. They were incapable of preventing social conflict from erupting into riots or of persuading the public that the state exercised effective control over the urban population. Violence seemed to be intrinsic to the Russian city.

Riotous Cities

Urban disorders had profound political and social implications for tsarist Russia. Many historians focus on the political dimensions of this unrest from the perspective of the revolutionary events of the early twentieth century. The social character of the disorders, however, points to issues that are central to the nature of Russian urbanism. The key problem for con-temporaries was to diagnose the origins of the disorders. In the urban setting collective violence was a threat to all who had visions of progress, no matter what their political persuasion. Both educated Russians and revo-lutionary activists regarded rioting in the same way that they viewed fist-fights, namely, as manifestations of a backward society. Like the French intellectual Gustave Le Bon, "by summoning up the nightmare of the crowd, [educated Russians could] reaffirm their own superiority and explain their impotence."[44] They were deeply aware of the threat that urban dis-orders posed to their hopes of progress and their vision of a civilized city.

As in the 1870s, anti-Semitism remained the most potent force behind urban violence in the last two decades of the century. The level of hostility toward Jews appeared to grow as the century waned. The assassination of Alexander II in March 1881 triggered a wave of rioting. One study of the spread of violence concludes that it was "essentially an urban phenome-non," the work of workers and migrants. "As a rule the pogroms moved from large towns and townlets to nearby villages, and along railroad lines, major highways and rivers to towns and villages further away."[45] That summer the Saratov governor was deluged with telegrams from the capital urging special measures to keep the city calm. He kept part of his troops quartered in their city barracks even though he was concerned not to arouse "potential rumors among the local population by taking unusual and ex-ceptional measures of a preventive nature."[46] Soldiers were his last line of

44. Susanna Barrows, *Distorting Mirrors: Visions of the Crowd in Late Nineteenth-Century France* (New Haven, 1981), 192.

45. I. Michael Aronson, "Geographical and Socioeconomic Factors in the 1881 Anti-Jewish Pogroms in Russia," *Russian Review* 39 (January 1980):26.

46. "Politicheskii obzor Saratovskoi gubernii," TsGAOR, f. 102, d. 67 (1881), 8–9.

defense, and the population of Saratov itself represented in his eyes the principal source of rioting, which the slightest rumor could ignite. To such officials, the disorders presented dramatic confirmation of their fears that the police were unable to control the urban population.

As a rule, the reports that came from the provincial governors and gendarme officers in the following years had ready explanations for such violence. I have been cautious about relying on official judgments, however, because the authorities made use of their own social stereotypes when they diagnosed what they viewed as a collective pathology. They did have access to information on social conditions in the provincial cities and the district towns. Despite their own anti-Semitic prejudices, their authority was seriously weakened whenever riots occurred. Thus in explaining the disorders in their reports to the tsar, they had to attempt to give a comprehensive, dispassionate picture of events. If studied critically, their accounts provide clues to the character and origins of the violence.

The authorities never precisely identified the rioters. They tended to refer to an anti-Semitic laboring population that was thought to be liable at any time to mobilize for a pogrom. They tended to blame migrants, laborers, the unemployed, and poor townspeople in general. The migrants attracted the greatest attention perhaps because many lived in evident misery and tended to congregate in particular areas of the city. In 1883 the presence in Ekaterinoslav of fifteen hundred construction workers building the railroad bridge across the Dnepr river prompted the governor to conclude that this city confronted "a very dangerous situation for public order and peace." He considered the workers to be rootless migrants "from various parts of Russia." All were "inclined to violence and disorder." As evidence, he pointed to the anti-Jewish riots of that September, which had been started by rumors that Jews had ritually murdered a young Christian girl. A mob of over six hundred, fortified with vodka seized from a tavern, attacked Jews and burned and looted property until the governor called out troops and Cossacks. The mob action left "several victims" and extensive damage to property.[47] From his perspective the very growth of the cities was the key to the outbreak of riots because it brought together crowds of laborers prone to violence and ready to form a mob when unpredictable rumors spread through taverns and workplaces. Official reports also noted that rioters usually looted stores, hinting that they were undertaking a crude sort of social retribution against traders and shopkeepers.

47. "Politicheskii obzor Saratovskoi gubernii," TsGAOR, f. 102, d. 185, ch. 11 (1883), 1–2, 20–21.

The authorities emphasized that the crowds emerged from a laboring population beyond the borders of educated, respectable urban society. At the end of the century the governor of Saratov province drew the attention of St. Petersburg to Tsaritsyn, whose summer river traffic attracted tens of thousands of "migrant laborers [who were] generally undisciplined and . . . extremely inclined to drunkenness and disorder." In his opinion a mere rumor about the "evil deeds" of Jews would immediately launch them on a riot.[48] The fact that there were very few Jews in the Volga ports was an irrelevant consideration to the laborers. Jews were scapegoats no matter how few in number. The danger of a pogrom was great when unemployment spread hardship among the population. To the Rostov-on-Don gendarme officer the source of the disorders in his city during the early 1880s was the "mass of unemployed local and migrant workers wandering about the streets and filling the taverns." In his opinion they were responsible for attacks on both Jews and the police "in a sort of common occurrence."[49] His account is noteworthy because he located this "mass" of unemployed workers in public places—streets and taverns—where they could form a crowd at any time. It is also revealing because the victims of mob action were police as well as Jews. The rioters were acting out a communal drama of ethnic hatred (Christians versus Jews), but they were also attacking the urban police, symbols of tsarist power.

Although officials often referred to the riotous public as strangers and outsiders, this explanation was facile. The association of uprootedness and disorder, like the implicit identification of the migrant with peasant, neatly fits the stereotype of the "dark people" of the villages. Observers, however, recognized the presence of townsmen among the rioters. In 1884 Maxim Gorky made this discovery when he watched the inhabitants of his hometown of Nizhny Novgorod participate in a pogrom. To him it seemed as if social identity lost all meaning when people became like animals whose uproar "merged into one heinous and gloating sound."[50] Using less color and making a greater effort to fix the circumstances when the rioting might occur, a gendarme officer of the southern factory town of Bakhmut pinpointed the holiday gatherings of the men of the town. It seemed to him that "efforts to arouse the population against the Jews always occur during the holidays when the petty bourgeois, having become drunk, gathered at

48. "Otchet Saratovskogo gubernatora za 1897," TsGIA, f. 1282, op. 3 (1898), d. 300, 21–22.

49. "Politicheskii obzor za 1884," TsGAOR, f. 102, d. 59 (1885), ch. 27, 20; and d. 89 (1888), ch. 12, 7–8.

50. This short sketch, published at the time of the Kishinev pogrom of 1903, is translated in Filia Holtzman, *The Young Maxim Gorky, 1868–1902* (New York, 1968), 69–72.

the stream for fistfights."[51] Vodka and holiday leisure were the setting for the organized mayhem of the fistfights. With the addition of anti-Semitic rumors the gatherings became the crucible for pogroms.

In the volatile atmosphere of ethnic and social antagonism, leadership was a scarcely visible but still essential factor in the origins of the riots. A sort of language of rioting was well known to the lower-class population as a whole. But the riot itself required voices to transform the anger triggered by the rumors into action and to select the targets of the mob. Rioters too needed leaders, as the governor of Nizhny Novgorod was convinced. In 1886 he punished the presumed riot leaders even before they could act, assuming that when his power was made manifest it would dissuade violence. He claimed to have learned by his mistakes in failing to act decisively in the 1884 riot (witnessed by Gorky). Two years later, he reacted immediately when the police informed him of new rumors of a pogrom. He had the ringleaders, whom the police identified, ruthlessly and illegally flogged. Claiming to have blocked the riot and receiving the tsar's approval, he had no reason to doubt the efficacy of repression.[52]

When and how these lurid rumors appeared were questions no one could answer. They seemed to emerge as naturally from the cultural nexus of Christian popular mythology and the communal antagonism of Russians and Ukrainians toward Jews as did the rumors of land distribution that moved periodically through the countryside and ignited peasant disorders. These rumors found their audience among a poor population that lived in miserable, unstable social conditions, but social hardship could not explain what made the messages so credible that now and then they crystallized into mob action.

Prejudice was not the monopoly of the illiterate, and the elements of the print culture of the cities could become a new source of anti-Semitic rumor. The penny press appealed directly to a mass readership and its audience extended into the laboring population. "Creating a public" with an anti-Semitic coloring sold some newspapers and satisfied the prejudice of some journalists and editors. The Odessa police prefect warned that local papers that printed "sensationalist [and] often false information" could "arouse the population against the Jews" and provoke "major street disorders of crowds moving against the property and person of the Jews."[53] The possibility of press-inspired rumors added a new and disturbing element to the official view of collective violence; it suggested that the "riotous classes" of

51. "Politicheskii obzor," TsGAOR, f. 102, d. 9 (1887), ch. 21, 42.
52. Richard Robbins, *The Tsar's Viceroys* (Ithaca, N.Y., 1987), 212.
53. "Otchet o sostoianii," TsGIA, f. 1284, op. 223, d. 29 (1896), 4–5.

the cities consisted of more than just the ignorant, backward, rootless, and impoverished. Newspaper articles with their own claims to anti-Semitic "truth" multiplied the potential for pogroms and made the problem of policing the city even more complex.

In the drama of the pogrom the visage of the enemy strangers included traders and bosses, Jews and police, and even medical personnel. In times of epidemics this last group assumed the appearance of the police. The onslaught of cholera created the atmosphere for rioting, even at the end of the century when physicians could claim the authority of science. The authorities dealt with epidemics as "social diseases." The resulting measures of isolation and quarantine provoked an outburst of hostility among laborers in some towns that was comparable only to the pogroms—and produced a similar amount of bloodshed. In the cholera epidemic of the summer of 1892 a mob in Astrakhan destroyed the cholera hospital, crying "this is where they bury the living" before being dispersed when Cossacks and police opened fire.[54] Seeking an explanation for the rioting that same year in the Volga town of Khvalynsk, the gendarme officer looked beyond "absurd rumors" and the "panicky fear" of the mob to underlying social conflicts in the town. In the previous years he claimed that the mayor had antagonized poor townspeople by raising rents on city land that they had farmed and that at the same time he and his supporters had enriched themselves at the town's expense. When the riot was over, he (and the district doctor) had lost their lives to the mob. Cholera panic had turned into a type of mob justice.[55] What at first sight had been blind rage on closer view assumed the dimensions of a social crime in which the victims were the representatives of a repressive authority and economic exploitation.

This mixture of wild destruction and social retribution also appeared in rioting in factory settlements. In 1892 in the Ukrainian mining center of Iuzovka the fears aroused by the isolation of cholera victims sparked widespread violence that took on the proportions of a revolt. The mob, which was called into being by the factory whistle, was estimated in the official report to number fifteen thousand. Before troops moved in the rioters had destroyed, by official count, one hundred eighty stores, twelve taverns, seven houses, and the Jewish synagogue. For all its irrationality and wild force the police did not believe that the disorder was an isolated, inexplicable incident. The victims all had a place in a diabolically twisted but still

---

54. *Moskovskii listok*, 30 June 1892.
55. "Politicheskii obzor," TsGAOR, f. 102, d. 152, ch. 55 (1893), 1–2.

coherent cosmology of persecution that identified an array of enemies from doctors and foremen to traders and Jews. The official report noted that "disorders at Iuzovka settlement are repeated every year to a greater or lesser extent." It attributed the origins of the violence to "the exploitation in the broad sense of the word of workers by all mine owners without exception and by the Jewish traders and innkeepers."[56] At this level of collective violence there was little distinction between cholera riots, pogroms, and labor protests. The report bears the mark of Russian officialdom, which was prone to blame capitalists and Jews when popular unrest broke out. Still, its glib reasoning points to popular attitudes, which turned riots into acts of social vengeance.

Police reports from the 1880s and 1890s suggest that disorders were increasing in scope and number. The question of the nature and incidence of urban collective violence is itself open to controversy both because of the absence of comprehensive, reliable data and because of the ideological assumptions that contemporaries and, subsequently, historians made about worker behavior. Officials tended to report events of importance but to omit those "disorders that were repeated every year." They associated disruptive behavior with the unsettled existence of the urban poor. For example, at the end of the century the Vladimir governor concluded that the unemployed and the migrants were "the two most dangerous elements of the population."[57] The historical logic of the argument rested on the prescriptive judgment that social position determined the proclivity toward orderly or disorderly behavior.

Given a dialectical twist, a similar logic informed the opinions of the Marxist radicals. For them it was conceptually impossible to imagine that workers' riots were the affair of an industrial proletariat. A pamphlet issued in the mid 1890s by the Moscow Workers' Union admitted that "the period of 'riots' has still not ended" but reassured its readers that "the time has come in our country when strikes are emerging on a level with [naravne] 'riots.'"[58] This argument was self-serving because their theory of the rise of the working class required that mob action dwindle as strikes increased. Soviet historians repeat this assertion, and Western studies of the Russian

56. "Politicheskii obzor Ekaterinoslavskoi gubernii," TsGAOR, f. 102, d. 152, ch. 11 (1893), 11–12; see also Rabochee dvizhenie v Rossii v XIX veke (Moscow, 1961) vol. 3, pt. 2, 207–13. This massive riot is the subject of a special study by Theodore Friedgut, "Labor Violence and Regime Brutality in Tsarist Russia," Slavic Review 46 (Summer 1987): 245–65.

57. "Otchet," TsGIA, f. 1263, op. 3, d. 5387 (1899), 790.

58. "Stachki i ikh znachenie dlia rabochikh," Rabochee dvizhenie, vol. 4, pt. 1, 78–79; the unease experienced by the authors in referring to collective violence is revealed in their use of quotes to bracket the term bunt (best translated in this context as "riot," although it can also refer to "rebellion").

laboring population have tended to ignore the issue by focusing instead on the organized working-class movement and strike action.[59]

The spread of collective violence in Russian cities is understandable without recourse to deterministic social theories. The models of the worker of the future, which were created by officials and radicals, embodied their idealized views of social progress in a new city. Tsarist authorities searched for the qualities of sobriety, industriousness, and submissiveness; the radicals substituted class consciousness for submissiveness. Both confronted evidence that appeared to contradict their social program, and both explained the contradiction by constructing an "anticity" of uprooted migrants and *Lumpenproletariat*. It was not difficult to find supporting evidence, but certain events suggested that the actual practices of the laboring population of the cities did not follow either model. My view of the urban migrant community suggests that the violence found among the lower classes represented an adaptation of well-established customary behavior. The language and practices of protest indicate that the migrants brought a mode of violent behavior and an adversarial conception of society into the city. They identified new enemies and adopted new forms of action. Many workers, both among migrants and settled townspeople, rejected this mode of behavior, some to seek private rewards, others to take up the cause of social and political justice. Both were found principally among the educated and the relatively skilled laborers. Within the laboring population violence was a distinct and potent manifestation of social and cultural hostility that appeared to increase as the migrant cities expanded.

Increasingly, official reports and observers' accounts tended to focus on collective actions, rioting as well as strikes, that erupted in and around factories. The distinction between an anti-Semitic pogrom and an anticapitalist riot was often blurred. The prominence of factory disorders seems to have resulted in part from the ease with which officials could identify and respond to this type of unrest (as opposed to urban mobs) and in part from the zeal of labor militants in recording their experiences. However, context is also important because the factories frequently had a large labor force and were potentially the locus for massive disorders.

Southern Russia represented the area of greatest factory unrest. In the

---

59. For example, Robert Johnson, *Peasant and Proletarian* (New Brunswick, N.J., 1979), whose table on labor unrest in Moscow province (126, table 7.1) provides one indication of the relative weights of "strikes" and "disturbances." His source is the Soviet documentary collection *Rabochee dvizhenie*, which may in a variety of ways understate worker collective violence (see Daniel Brower, "Labor Violence in Russia," *Slavic Review* 41 [September 1982]: 418–19, 450–51).

south living conditions around the factories were particularly harsh, and the concentration of migrants was higher there than in other urban settlements. The 1892 cholera riots at Iuzovka were one example of this unrest; so, too, were the disorders in Ekaterinoslav later in the decade. In 1898 rioting workers at the new Briansk metallurgical factory so frightened the provincial governor that he proclaimed the violence to be "the wild consequences of the awakened mob on the march." The rioting at Ekaterinoslav began when a plant guard killed a worker in a dispute over pilfering. An estimated two thousand rioters quickly gathered and burned factory buildings. Then, "in a nearby village, in one hour [they] destroyed twenty-four houses of people who had no ties to either the factory or the workers."[60] On close examination, one finds in this riot the same nexus of ethnic hatred, economic hostility, and blind rage as in Iuzovka. The burning and looting included the stores, homes, and synagogue of the nearby Jewish community, whose livelihood came largely through trade with the workers. Eyewitness accounts suggest that the rioters were largely young workers; older workers, who were usually skilled, either stayed away or fought the rioters to protect their workplaces.[61] The workers' community was not a unified group in such protests. Like the pogroms, worker protests expressed the complex, contradictory characteristics of a particular culture of violence and social antagonism as well as the grievances arising from working and living conditions. The worker riots were a product of both the factory and the migrant city.

Contemporary reports stressed that urbanized factory settlements and the industrial outskirts of towns were the major centers for unrest. Industrialization was a key ingredient in creating conditions for the disorders, but urbanization was also essential. Worker disturbances in rural manufacturing centers—the "settlements" of several thousand people and their factories—were far less frequent and massive than in the major industrial communities—for example, Iuzovka in the south and Orekhovo-Zuevo in the north, each of which was a large town by the 1890s—and around urban centers such as Ekaterinoslav or even Moscow. As the cities expanded and manufacturing centers multiplied, incidents of urban unrest and strikes also multiplied. A count of the use between the 1870s and 1890s of troops to repress civil disorders (including both strikes and riots) found a notable increase in military intervention, an indication that the specter of the ri-

60. "Otchet o sostoianii," TsGIA, f. 1282, op. 3, d. 3255 (1899), 10–11.

61. Charters Wynn, "Donbass Labor Unrest: General Strikes and Pogroms in the 1905 Revolution" (paper presented at the Conference of the American Association for the Advancement of Slavic Studies, 1984), 5–9.

otous city had concrete meaning to the authorities.[62] My own incomplete study, which is based on a sampling of the available archival reports, indicates that in the 1880s and 1890s riots among the laboring population waxed and waned in phase with other protest actions. They were particularly frequent in the period 1887–88 and again in 1896–98. Riots were the most dramatic indication of the potential for disorder in the migrant cities. A careful examination of the origins and dynamics of these riots reveals the extent to which disorders had undermined public order in urban areas.

The origins of the disturbances were closely linked to employer-worker relations, the network of trade around the factories, and the actions of police forces. A poorly developed commercial network, particularly in the new urban centers of the south, placed workers at the mercy of the small traders. The workers' low pay—and customary drunken celebrations on paydays—led many to fall deeply in debt to the traders or to the managers of the company stores, which were more often found in the northern factory settlements. An investigation into the origins of the 1892 Iuzovka riot indicated that owners and traders collaborated to collect the workers' debts directly from the enterprise. As a result, the report noted that "most workers (many without passports) never receive their full wages, just a page of accounts, including purchase of goods (for example, tea and sugar) at very high prices."[63] Stores offered a visible—and vulnerable—target for the workers' anger and frustrations, particularly if the traders were Jewish. The laboring population placed shopowners as much as employers in the category of enemy outsiders. Their attitude toward trading and traders rested on assumptions of a sort of "moral economy" in which high prices were the sign of the enemy.

The contrast between worker and boss did not appear as readily as that between worker and trader. The typical small enterprise in the city was a very different workplace compared with the large factory. In many respects manufacturing plants, large and small, reproduced within their walls the conditions of economic dependence and paternalism that the laborers experienced in their relations with the tsarist authorities. Wages were fixed according to the rule "as much as the master wishes." The economic power of the boss was reinforced by the frequently arbitrary fines deducted from workers' pay, the beatings at the hands of foremen or owners, the arrests that occurred at the whim of the owner, whose word was sufficient for the local police, and the sexual abuse of women workers. In these conditions the

---

62. William Fuller, *Civil-Military Conflict in Imperial Russia, 1881–1914* (Princeton, 1985), 89–90.

63. "Politicheskii obzor," TsGAOR, f. 102, d. 152 (1893), ch. 11, 11–12.

potential for sudden outbursts of violence was great. Still, scattered reports suggest that patriarchal authority was a substantial barrier to resistance. Although the "exploitation of workers by manufacturers is very great," noted a gendarme officer from a northern industrial region, the workers would "easily support any kind of oppression from small manufacturers" if they had risen from the laboring class. In these circumstances the domination of the owner rested on the workers' conviction that "'He is one of us.'"[64] Patriarchal authority in the factory manifested itself at its crudest in the physical beating of workers; yet one metalworker, writing in 1906, recalled that in the early years workers "respected a well-paying foreman even if he used his fists."[65] His authority and power to control the work force resembled that of the authoritarian provincial official.

Where enterprises were large and factory relations more impersonal, this social connection was broken. The style of command, however, was not substantially different. In the mid 1890s one Moscow factory inspector drew up a list of abuses that he judged to be "common occurrences in our factory life." These included "crude, demeaning insults by foremen and even owners . . . who use their fists on workers of all ages and both sexes, [and] the rape of young and married women . . . and the dismissal of those women who do not submit." Despite laws against these "abusive powers [samoupravstvo]," the inspector concluded that factory authorities persevered "without fear of legal action."[66] Gendarme authorities, revealing their nostalgia for a vanishing past, lamented the inability of foremen and owners, especially in the foreign-owned enterprises with Westerners in charge, to establish the same moral authority over workers as that enjoyed by the Russian owners of smaller manufacturing establishments. In the late 1880s, when disorders were increasing in number and violence, the gendarme commander of Vladimir province regretted "the inability of the factory administration to communicate with the workers and to guide them."[67] His complaint rested on the assumption that factory owners could exercise disciplinary power in the same manner that noble landlords dominated peasant villagers.

The weakness and lack of authority of the urban police were particularly apparent. In the capitals the very size of the forces of order, which included

64. "Politicheskii obzor Dmitrovskogo uezda," TsGAOR, f. 102, d. 88, ch. 35 (1885), 53.

65. P. Timofeev, Chem zhivet zavodskii rabochii? (St. Petersburg, 1906), 97–98.

66. Cited in V. F. Kut'ev, "Dokumental'nye materialy Moskovskikh gosudarstvennykh arkhivov po istorii rabochego klassa goroda Moskvy v 90-kh gody XIX veka" (Kandidat dissertation, Moscow State University, 1955), 117–18.

67. N. I. Voronov, Zapiski o sobytiiakh Vladimirskoi gubernii (Vladimir, 1907), 25. Voronov served in the province gendarmerie between 1886 and 1900.

large garrison forces and Cossacks as well as regular police, was a major deterrent to public disturbances. Even in the capitals, however, the police exercised little influence among the workers in the daily course of events. Their power protected the owners, and their activities were limited to enforcing certain laws and requiring conformity with the administrative regulations concerning passports. As the Moscow gendarme commander remarked in the late 1880s, "the local police cannot stop workers when disorders are beginning [because] the workers do not trust the police, considering them—and not without reason—to be in the pay of the factory owners and therefore always on the side of the owners."[68] By implication, the officer claimed that enlightened officials like himself could act in the role of both mediator and repressive agent in the disorders. Many workers accepted this claim to special authority.

The socialist militants who sought to organize a working-class movement dismissed both rioting and worker reliance on the tsarist authorities as backward and misguided. In its pamphlet of 1896 on "Strikes and Their Meaning for Workers" the Moscow Workers' Union emphasized that the riots were senseless. In its opinion these disorders revealed that the workers "poorly [understood] the causes of their worsening condition; they blame the heartless owner or foreman for their bitter fate or think that their troubles are caused by machinery." The workers "poured out their pent-up rage on innocent machinery and smashed factory buildings to get even with the owner."[69] Worker activists and socialist militants both did their utmost to build a disciplined working-class movement by promoting strike action. They sought to organize and lead orderly work stoppages, training the workers in the fundamentals of class solidarity and protest action. Sometimes their message found a receptive audience. During the 1896–97 textile strikes in St. Petersburg one militant overheard by a police spy explained to a workers' gathering "how to behave in the forthcoming strike: the *intelligent* recommended that the workers shun rowdiness [*skandal*], breakage of machinery and windows, and so on."[70] The message, however, was only effective on certain occasions and for reasons that suggest that the Moscow Marxists were giving a tendentious explanation of the role that riots played.

Laborers sometimes turned violent protest into a ritualized appeal for official intervention. Behind their animosity toward the factory management and the police rioters hid an unexpressed expectation that the tsarist

---

68. "Iz politicheskogo obzora za 1888," *Rabochee dvizhenie*, vol. 3, pt. 1, 649–50.
69. "Stachki i ikh znachenie dlia rabochikh," *Rabochee dvizhenie*, vol. 4, pt. 1, 75–76.
70. *Rabochee dvizhenie*, vol. 4, pt. 1, 583.

authorities would right the wrongs. The hidden meaning of riots was apparent to the few militants present in factory settlements when strikes and rioting erupted. The socialist activists used a language of class struggle, but the workers understood it in their own way. Ivan Babushkin was agitating among the metallurgical workers in Ekaterinoslav shortly before the 1898 disorders at the Briansk factory. He noted later in his memoirs that the pamphlets he distributed made clear the "undesirability of riots," which "bring the workers nothing but harm." But the reaction of the workers was in "absolute contradiction" to this message; they concluded: "They're ordering us to organize a riot." He concluded that "the old traditions of struggle were so strong that the workers could not imagine the possibility of a strike without beating up a foreman or destroying the [factory] offices. . . . Talk of former riots always led to the urge to organize a 'good riot.'"[71] Babushkin found the answer to his contradiction in the traditions of the past, implicitly reassuring himself that strikes belonged in the future.

Ten years earlier Petr Moiseenko had discovered a more complex set of attitudes when he was organizing workers in 1884 at the Morozov textile factory in the settlement of Orekhovo-Zuevo. He attempted to stimulate discussion of class conflict in his audience by reading them the new novel *The Bandit Churkin*, which as mentioned earlier aroused images of plunder for the workers and led them to thoughts of rioting. One worker remarked that "the Morozov factory has a spell protecting it from riots. Morozov is a sorcerer; otherwise there would have been a riot long ago." Another announced that "we've got to have a riot; without that nothing will happen."[72] Perhaps their reference to the "diabolical" boss was a figure of speech. Still, it brought a mythological sense of good and evil to matters of economic injustice and power, a sense not unlike the workers' attitude toward the Jews. If fear of sorcery had previously protected Morozov, it ceased to do so a few months after this incident. In 1885 a strike broke out in the factory, and within two days it turned into a riot. Tsarist authorities estimated the total damage at over three hundred thousand rubles. They also proclaimed that the workers' complaints of unjust treatment were correct and demanded rectification from the owners. Abusive fines by the owner were canceled and a foreman to whom the workers objected was dismissed.[73] The violence resembled that at other factories. Workers without visible leadership responded to a provocative incident by a rampage of violence in which the targets included not only surrounding buildings and

71. I. V. Babushkin, *Vospominaniia* (Leningrad, 1925), 86.
72. P. Moiseenko, *Vospominaniia starogo revoliutsionera* (Moscow, 1966), 70.
73. Voronov, *Zapiski*, 7; *Rabochee dvizhenie*, vol. 3, pt. 1, 25–26.

at times factory personnel and traders but also the very buildings and machines where they worked. What possible purpose could this violence have? Moiseenko pointed to one answer: the fear of retribution from the authorities, who were viewed at times in folk terms as "sorcerers," was broken by the violence itself.

The impulses behind such a workers' riot resembled those that propelled the mobs that cried, "They're burying the living," to burn the cholera infirmary or that incited pogroms in which the rioters proclaimed, "They killed a Christian child." In these cases crowds responded to a mythic world of mysterious and evil forces with violence and bloodshed, defying these powers and destroying their physical manifestations. In the villages sorcery might be conjured away by the community or families; in the urban areas the actions of mobs was a substitute act of conjuring. The results in the two locales were very different, because far more quickly than in the countryside urban crowd action turned into a riotous confrontation with the forces of order.

The targets of the violence were chosen from the visible adversaries of the laboring population in the migrant towns and settlements. Signs of rational calculation in the rioting appeared alongside the mythic elements. The destruction of factory records wiped out the administrative-police documents of the migrant workers. The burning and looting of stores revealed the anger of poor laborers at the practices of traders. The attacks on town leaders, doctors, foremen, and factory police released the hostility of the laboring population toward arbitrary and oppressive authority. We need not employ the discredited term "crowd psychology" to find in the actions of these urban mobs a form of violent social protest that laid bare the gulf of incomprehension and distrust that separated them from "society." This cultural chasm had long set the context for popular protest; it took on a new form in the cities and evolved into a more dangerous assault on the tsarist order as the century came to a close. The complaints of tsarist officials that both police and factory personnel lacked authority over the workers suggest that the institutional relations of power, embedded in culture as much as in the instruments of repression, were shifting in those decades. Despite increased police and garrison forces and new, augmented administrative powers, the laboring population of the migrant towns lived beyond the control of the state. Labor violence, like strikes, had a history of its own.

The riots followed a recognizable logical progression from their outbreak to their repression by the authorities. The records are most explicit for the 1890s and tell primarily of conflicts in textile factories, which were concentrated in northern Russia and staffed by workers who frequently moved from one factory to another. The evidence is of limited significance, and we can only presume to extend the interpretation by analogy to the larger world of urban factory life. Often the conflict between workers and management began with public protest over harsh work conditions such as long hours, night work, unjustified and exaggerated fines, and abusive treatment of workers. Such was the case at the Khludov textile plant in Egorovsk. Twice in 1893 it was the center of rioting. The story itself is well known. What is important here are the clues it provides to the attitudes of workers toward the authorities. The immediate targets of the workers were the plant managers and the stores in the vicinity of the factory. Both times troops repressed the riots. After the first outbreak of violence the provincial governor personally intervened to demand that the factory owners rectify the worst abuses. The reluctance of the owners to respond was the crucial factor in the outbreak of the second riot several months later.[74] Both times retribution and social antagonism played a part in the selection of targets. As important to the logic of the worker action, however, was the fact that the workers launched the second riot after official action to redress their grievances had failed.

Worker expectations of intervention by tsarist officials appeared in many other riots during the 1890s. Perhaps workers turned with similar intentions to violent protest and strikes. In the typical scenario a small conflict, usually coming after an accumulation of grievances, provoked a work stoppage in some part of a factory. In the hours that followed a crowd would gather, unorganized but with individuals formulating complaints and even negotiating with factory authorities. After the negotiations failed workers would begin the attack on the factory. Frequently, the rioters obtained vodka by threatening tavern owners or by looting. Drunkenness became the catalyst that turned the group of protesters into a violent crowd, welding the individuals togehter into a mob of terrifying force against which the police were powerless. So common was the connection between drunkenness and rioting that workers and radicals who sought to control a work stoppage invariably tried to close all taverns in the vicinity of the factories immediately following the outbreak of a strike. The destructive phase usually dissipated within a day, and the riot often had run its course before Cossack or army units arrived.

Repression, however, was not the end of the drama. Soldiers often beat protesters and arrested the presumed ringleaders. As a rule, a government investigation also occurred. In it government authorities—factory inspec-

74. *Rabochee dvizhenie*, vol. 3, pt. 2, 310–16.

tors, gendarme officers, and even the provincial vice governor or governor—requested the satisfaction of some of the workers' demands. At this point they became, to use Richard Robbins's term for describing the governor at the Egorevsk riot, "mediators in the dispute."[75] This two-pronged policy of repression and appeasement had been in existence ever since the government first confronted large-scale worker protest in the 1860s.[76] One provincial gendarme commander of the 1890s recalled, somewhat complacently, his method of pacifying rioters. "Most important," he noted, "everything depended on concessions and agreement from the factory owners, who rarely refused to cooperate; without their cooperation we could do nothing."[77] The way in which he conceived of his role reveals a deeply rooted official paternalism. By pursuing this policy of concessions the tsarist authorities became, despite their repressive measures, party to the riotous protest.

The evidence suggests that the workers themselves were aware of a kind of official complicity. To the extent that they expected that their rioting would lead to an official investigation of their grievances, they were using violence as a form of communication. Although in a very chaotic manner, their actions were a sort of ritual whose meaning was clear to both them and the authorities.[78] Such a message was conveyed to the Bakhmut district gendarme officer by the miners near Iuzovka who had rioted in May 1887. They complained of inhuman working conditions and exploitation by mine owners and traders. In the words of the officer, "Not knowing where to turn for help and protection, the workers decided to protest together, not separately . . . ; they presume that they will be punished for the disorders but at the very least others will understand their situation and improve it, even if just a little."[79] If, as is likely, the source of the officer's information was the testimony of the worker delegates, they were implicitly calling on him for help.

The attitudes revealed in his account of the encounter were deeply embedded in customary relations between tsarist officials and their subjects. The workers had good reason to claim powerlessness and to admit guilt, thereby appealing implicitly to official clemency. Their attitude bears some resemblance to that of the peasants, whom Daniel Field has called "rebels in the name of the tsar." To revolt and then to appear as the tsar's repentant

75. Robbins, The Tsar's Viceroys, 209.
76. Zelnik, Labor and Society in Tsarist Russia, 164–68, 367.
77. Voronov, Zapiski, 22.
78. See Natalie Davis's work on sixteenth-century religious riots, "The Rite of Violence," in her Society and Culture in Early Modern France (Stanford, 1975), 152–87.
79. Rabochee dvizhenie, vol. 3, pt. 1, 503.

subjects was a protest technique that the peasantry had learned earlier.[80] For his part the officer assumed the flattering role of judge and mediator; he could appease the people while chastising the ruthless capitalists. In those years anticapitalism and anti-Semitism were prominent themes in many of the reports from gendarme officers, who took a populistlike stance in condemning the new industrial and commercial interests.[81] The paternalism of the two-pronged policy linked workers and the state's emissaries: repentance after the fact sanctioned the workers' collective protest; the repression of the disorder entailed state intervention in defense of the workers. In this mutual dependence violent protest was the one sure signal for action.

Early in 1887 miners in an industrial settlement in Ekaterinoslav province, deprived of their wages for several months, had openly threatened to riot to obtain assistance. "A day was even set for the violence [*razgrom*]," reported the gendarme provincial commander, "if the authorities did not help them in their 'rightful cause'." Help came quickly from "on high." It brought the miners their pay by means that were, if not quite legal, at least expeditious.[82] The fact that the miners were migrants helps explain their capacity to organize their protest so effectively; like urban migrants, their action was shaped and their expectations set by the power they could exert in a new social setting in which crowd action had a dramatic impact and where the authorities could be expected to step in immediately. The rioting workers of the 1880s and 1890s wanted not only retribution or vengeance but sometimes also state intervention and the rectification of injustice. Therefore, the authorities had some reason to reassure themselves that, as one report on an 1887 textile factory riot remarked, the disorders had "no antigovernment aims."[83]

Collective actions by workers were shaped partly by economic conditions and partly by the cultural symbols by which the laboring population gave meaning to their new lives. The destruction of property and even the very factory installations where the rioters worked suggested the blind fury and irrational nature of the mob. In the first period of Western European industrialization earlier in the century, the destruction of machinery had a different meaning. Even the Luddites in England had specific goals in mind:

80. Daniel Field, *Rebels in the Name of the Tsar* (New York, 1976).

81. The most forceful of these attacks is found in the report of a Moscow province officer in the late 1880s; see "Politicheskii obzor Bogorodskogo uezda za 1886," TsGAOR, f. 102, d. 9 (1887). This report is cited extensively in *Rabochee dvizhenie*, vol. 3, pt. 1, 717–35.

82. *Rabochee dvizhenie*, vol. 3, pt. 1, 487–88.

83. "Politicheskii obzor," TsGAOR, f. 102, d. 89, ch. 19 (1888), 9.

they attacked the weaving machinery that threatened their livelihood as hand weavers.[84]

The studies of Western urban disorders offer an interpretation of collective violence that is applicable to the case of Russian worker riots. Eric Hobsbawm's picture of the seventeenth- and eighteenth-century "city mob" in Western Europe bears a close resemblance to the urban and worker disorders in tsarist Russia. He argues that the mob used "direct action—riot or rebellion" to obtain the distribution of food supplies or other necessities in times of shortage. Although "inspired by no specific ideology," the mob expected that its violence would bring results because "the authorities would be sensitive" to the people's grievances and would "make some sort of immediate concession." Hobsbawm referred to such groups as "primitive rebels" because their violent protest was not directed against the existing social and political order.[85]

By employing a form of ritualized violence the Russian workers were in effect adapting the techniques of a less complex age to the social conditions of industrialization and urbanization. The policies of the paternalistic, autocratic state contributed to the expectations of both retribution and redress and the state and its emissaries became thereby both hostile outsiders and agents of reform.

In the last years of the nineteenth century a new pattern began to appear in the workers' protests. The challenge to authority was becoming more openly political. Both the wave of strikes in the 1890s and the new character of worker collective violence, at least in the major urban centers, could be read in this light. The change was visible in the appearance of a new type of worker with a sense of "personal dignity," whom one Petersburg metalworker thought to be the activists responsible for the resistance to "insults to workers by foremen." He asserted that these conflicts were at the heart of "many of the strikes and riots of recent years."[86] One young apprentice from that period later vividly recalled the "type of worker who . . . in every way protested against evil and the existing order of things." He remembered them to be "good workers and people of great willpower" who moved frequently in groups from factory to factory and as a matter of course "sought release in vodka." They resembled the typical migrant laborer in their respect for the person and authority of the tsar but were bitterly hostile to lesser officials: they would beat up a foreman who "tried

84. See Malcolm Thomas, *The Luddites: Machine-Breaking in Regency England* (Newton-Abbot, England, 1970), 75–78.

85. Eric Hobsbawm, *Primitive Rebels* (New York, 1965), 108, 110–11.

86. Timofeev, *Chem zhivet zavodskii rabochii?* 98.

to abuse his power [*pokazat' svoiu vlast'*]."[87] The readiness of such workers to act made them natural leaders of riots, but the anger they felt left no room for the ritual of repentance and redress by the authorities.

Official reports at the end of the century revealed an awareness of the decline of the old ritual of mob action and an increase in social hostility. Writing in the mid 1890s a Moscow factory inspector pointed to the explosive situation created by "the immunity from legal punishment factory authorities enjoy" and by the workers' "silent hatred, which gradually grows and spreads and ultimately erupts in terrible mass disorders that threaten the property and even the lives of the guilty authorities."[88] In 1896 the Moscow police chief issued a warning to district police on the growing number of "disorders" (*volneniia*) in manufacturing and factory enterprises in the city. He blamed "purely local conditions, primarily the discontent of the workers with one or another factory regime" and considered that the consequences of these conditions for public order in the city were ominous.[89] Strikes and riots together posed an unprecedented challenge to Moscow police. I would suggest that the implications for the authorities of the riots were far more serious than earlier riots because they challenged the social order as well as the public order. They introduced into the world of the workers a rebelliousness that undermined the power of the state itself.

The issue of social disorders became an issue of public concern at the end of the century for a different but closely related reason. In the major cities growing fears of crimes against persons and property shifted the locus of violence from city outskirts to the town center. Riots occurred infrequently and largely in outlying neighborhoods where the laboring population was concentrated. Official intervention came relatively quickly and kept the confrontation from moving outside the factory district. These disturbances involved the state and manufacturers on one side and laborers on the other. Only the Jews were seriously at risk and their insecurity was of little moment to most townspeople. Attacks on individuals, however, could not be so readily localized and their randomness threatened all areas of the city. Crime stories were first spread by the popular press in order to attract and to entertain readers. But by the turn of the century, crime assumed more menacing dimensions when reports of street disorders of a random character began to appear. As dramatized in the press, these incidents pitted aggressive "hooligans" against defenseless members of respectable society.

87. K. Mironov, *Iz vospominanii rabochego* (Moscow, 1906), 4–5.
88. Kut'ev, "Dokumental'nye materialy," 118.
89. Ibid., 442.

It is difficult to separate fact from fancy in what quickly became a public cause célèbre. Statistics from various cities on crime rates in the 1890s did not indicate a significant worsening of serious crimes. Occasional reports in newspapers, however, decried indiscriminant attacks of laborers and youth on peaceable citizens. Moscow's tradesmen in the Okhotnyi Riad area, which was located near Moscow University, had long made demonstrating students targets for beatings. But these attacks were explainable in political terms of patriotic (or reactionary) traders versus radical youth. In the 1890s the violence witnessed by Maxim Gorky in the provincial town of Samara had no such easy explanation. In 1894 Gorky used his newspaper column to decry the beating of students in secondary schools by gangs of "toughs" (*gorchichniki*). Their brutality toward the students suggested to Gorky that they hated "everything that in some way or other suggests culture."[90] The violence was no longer an encounter between cohorts of laborers in mass fistfights; rather, it represented a very ominous invasion of the streets by hostile and aggressive gangs that were bent on attacking peaceful townspeople.

At the turn of the century Gorky's "toughs" reemerged in the press of the capitals as "hooligans." They were embellished with more lurid colors and fearsome garb but their activities appeared to express the same anticulturism that Gorky had perceived. The reports from the capitals emphasized that the target for indiscriminate attack were the upper classes (similar to the violence in England, where the press had popularized the term "hooligan" to identify the attackers). In 1903 the violence appeared sufficiently serious to the St. Petersburg police prefect that he issued regulations that banned "the carrying of knives, daggers, and other dangerous weapons" as well as "intentional gatherings of people on the streets of the city."[91] Although the history of Russian "hooliganism" goes far beyond the scope of this study, the emergence of a public debate on this issue is evidence of a moment of transition from the urban conflicts of the late nineteenth century to revolutionary events of the early twentieth century.

The extent to which the hooligan attacks represented a real public danger is debatable. The press and, presumably, its readers took the threat very seriously, as Joan Neuberger makes clear in her study of Russian hooliganism.[92] The explanation for their fears lies in the threat that this

90. M. O. Chechanovskii, ed. *Gor'kii v Samare* (Moscow, 1938), 199–200.
91. "Otchet gradonachal'nika," TsGIA, f. 182, op. 3, d. 545 (1902), 105–6.
92. Joan Neuberger, "Crime and Culture: Hooliganism in St. Petersburg, 1900–1914" (Ph.D. diss., Stanford University, 1985); see also Joan Neuberger, "Stories of the Street:

violence posed to the widespread hopes that had emerged in previous decades for the creation of cities of orderliness and enlightenment. The vision of a civilized city, which educated Russians and officials had espoused, had made an obvious mark on urban life—in the new schooling, the public readings, and the civic improvements that the urban civic elite had promoted. The existence of dangerous places and social violence did not appear to threaten respectable society seriously because these things belonged to a barbaric past and were the product of a backward people. Although we can now see that this attitude was a sorry illusion, the urban elite shared a fundamental conviction that the future belonged to reason and orderliness.

The hooligan disrupted this mode of isolating urban violence. In his public persona he embodied familiar traits that had previously been used to characterize the dissolute and depraved individuals among the laboring population. He was drunken, not sober, preferred the company of prostitutes, and turned his leisure time into exploits of mayhem and violence. One Petersburg paper presented its ongoing accounts of street violence in the capital under the title of "savage customs." The most violent events were labeled "the law of the knife."[93] These customs of "darkest Russia" were no longer restricted to the laboring sections of the city; they now reached into such eminently respectable areas as Nevsky Prospect. Violence among the laboring population was no longer limited to encounters with the police or other fistfighters but now involved peaceful townspeople. One Moscow writer warned that the hooligan acted with "systematic premeditation" in attacking upper-class townspeople.[94] In other words, the hooligan was an updated, modern menace, not an urbanized version of the "dark masses." Thus, he was a perverse link between the migrant city and the images of modernity that had been associated in the previous decades with Russian urbanism. He was inseparable from the city, but his presence subverted the very ideals of orderliness, enlightenment, and civilization, of which the Russian city was to have been the embodiment.

Hooliganism in the St. Petersburg Popular Press, 1900–1905," *Slavic Review* 48 (Summer 1989):177–95.

93. Joan Neuberger, "Crime and Culture," 48–53.

94. A. Pazukhov, "Khuligany," *Moskovskii Listok,* 17 August 1903.

Conclusion

The search for clues to the origins of the revolutionary turmoil of the early twentieth century in Russia has tended to dominate the historiography of the late tsarist period. It has lent an apocalyptic atmosphere even to studies of subjects that are far removed from revolutionary history. The inquiry into the background of the revolution is part of the study of the Russian city. In 1905 urban areas were the arena of strikes and confrontations between workers and tsarist troops. These events confirmed that the decades of tsarist efforts to propagate piety and patriotism and to inculcate orderliness into the urban population had been a failure. It is easy to dismiss the various policies that the tsarist officials introduced as feeble and antiquarian. Although official reports stressed the danger that the migrant city posed to social order and political stability, the state was unable to come to grips with the problem.

Municipal reforms opened an institutional path for the implementation of the urban improvements that civic activists and business interests desired. After 1870, however, the "best people," who were to implement these much needed local reforms, proved to be few in number and deeply divided on the agenda for civic action. Nonetheless, administrative domination ceased to be the rule and municipal responsibilities were no longer an estate obligation or something that a handful of townspeople undertook to achieve personal benefits. In the last decades of the century an active civic leadership took numerous initiatives that were designed to shape and guide the growth of the migrant cities. The social bonds and the ethos that these various municipal practices created were the key ingredients in the emergence of a civil public sphere that had the effect of giving urban affairs an important place in the public life of the country.

Public opposition to the autocracy was a missing motif in municipal debates before 1905. Its sudden emergence that year suggests that it was present earlier but masked by ostensibly benign activities. Volunteer and semiofficial movements, along with municipal activities, had contributed to expanding the urban public sphere. In 1905 its political implications appeared in the public proclamations voted by municipalities in support of the liberal movement and in the incidents that revealed the intimate connection between urban welfare and oppositional politics. One such incident was the meeting in early January 1905 of the Saratov Temperance Guardianship. It was scheduled to hold a literary reading in its cafeteria–reading room but instead hosted a meeting of fifteen hundred people who heard Marxist workers denounce capitalist exploitation and who voted a resolution, passed unanimously, calling for liberty in Russia.[1] For a brief time this organization was part of the revolutionary movement.

In the late decades of the nineteenth century the periodic confrontations between laborers and the tsarist state hinted at the potential for revolutionary upheaval in the cities. The leadership of radical intellectuals and worker militants gave some degree of discipline to popular agitation, but riots and pogroms were also potent forces of popular mobilization in the revolutionary years. The ritualized violence in which the workers appealed to the tsarist officials appears to have vanished. But the practices of communal violence and the images of diabolical forces in urban conflicts added the ugly dimension of ethnic hatred to the solidarity of revolutionary action in 1905. The unity evident among urban populations in the early months of 1905 quickly dissolved in conflict and distrust as municipalities lost their aura of progressive leadership and social conflict undermined political solidarity. With hindsight one finds ample evidence that these tensions had grown and deepened in the previous decades.

To the many Russians attuned to Western precedents the economic expansion of the urban areas seemed to make their cities the center of social and cultural progress. The spread of literacy and learning encouraged them to hope that urban print culture would coalesce around the culturist models of educated Russians. These trends strengthened a tradition, whose origins lay in tsarist city plans, of giving progress an urban face. It took a variety

---

1. Tsentral'nyi gosudarstvennyi arkhiv Okt'iabrskoi revoliutsii (abbreviated TsGAOR), f. Departament politsii, d. 1250 (1905), 3:50–51.

of forms but remained deeply marked by its statist origins. Although Catherine II's hope of turning her capitals and provincial centers into outposts of civilization proved largely illusory, in the next century its heritage shaped official policies and the ideals of educated Russians. Explicit and implicit references to models of the civilized city in municipal reports, the writings of doctors and scientists, and tsarist plans were more than rhetorical tricks and figures of speech. The national expositions of Moscow and Nizhny Novgorod, which were idealized and tangible versions of urban modernity, bore only a very remote resemblance to existing conditions in Russian cities, but in their remoteness they remained faithful to Catherine's precedent. Their shaping of an ideal urban setting around technology and industry reflected a capitalist as well as a statist understanding of urban progress. This understanding was compatible with the hopes of the commercial elite of the country but not with the level or character of most urban economic practices.

One measure of urban crisis in the early twentieth century was the disparity between the vision of what I have termed the "sanitized city" and continued rapid urbanization. The dislocations occasioned by population growth and industrialization differed only in degree from earlier decades; what had changed, however, was the readiness of the urban population to condemn civic leaders for their supposed incompetence and servility. One observer, writing in the early twentieth century, was convinced that "almost all [Russian] cities bear the stamp of neglect, wild growth, and the absence of systematic leadership."[2] His point of view revealed the disillusionment of the reformers, who equated "wildness" with decadence and who believed that leadership was the source of progress. This disillusionment is a prominent theme in the historical literature on the origins of the revolutionary upheaval. It is echoed in Leopold Haimson's theory of the "stability" of the cities, where, as in the past, the privileged estates confronted the hostile laboring population that was moved by the age-old "spirit of *buntarstvo*," that is, rebelliousness. Describing the city as a place of "psychological chasms" that divided "Russia's society of estates," he characterizes urban social relations in a manner more suitable to the mid-nineteenth-century town.[3] At the turn of the twentieth century the cultural and social divisions in the city were profound. Their roots lie, however, not in the stagnation of urban society but in the confrontation

---

2. D. Protopopov, "Sud'ba russkikh gorodov," *Gorodskoe delo* (15 December 1911):1713.
3. Leopold Haimson, "The Problem of Social Stability in Urban Russia, 1905–1914," *Slavic Review* 23 (December 1964):635–36; 24 (March 1965):21.

between the visionaries and the business elite, on the one hand, and the migrant city, on the other.

In another idealized version, the city became a place of culture and learning. The formal and informal campaigns to spread schooling in urban areas reflected both the practical needs of the population and the hopes and expectations of educated Russians. That these campaigns did not achieve their goals is a measure of the obstacles they confronted as well as their own shortcomings. The hopes and disappointments of the Russians who participated in the voluntary associations offered abundant inspiration for literary satire. Chekhov's writings remain a forceful reminder of the great gap that existed between the real and the ideal in the culturist view of society. We may also think of the culturist hopes for enlightenment and technological wonders as a utopian vision of the triumphant city. This perspective reemerged in the imagined cities of Soviet science fiction. The cities were marvels of engineering and social control in these works, but they were nightmarish in Evgeny Zamiatin's novel *We*. His warning that this vision contained destructive intellectual flaws was an implicit criticism of the idealism of previous generations of urban dreamers.

For the agents of planned or visionary urbanism the ideal city looked to the West for its model. In its own way the history of Russian urbanism captures the tensions that Russia's position on the cultural borderland of Europe created. The exaggerated hopes that Russians placed in the civilizing mission of urban centers are best understood if we recall that they believed that the territory beyond the city represented what was variously described as backwardness or barbarism. This manner of constructing a cultural map of the country created invidious comparisons between the capitals and the provinces and the city and the countryside as well as between cultured and uneducated groups. It entailed a broad vision of progress in which the cities had a major role. The Nizhny Novgorod exposition of 1896 and St. Petersburg's Nevsky Prospect, whatever their differences, were bound together by these cultural expectations.

Another form of urbanism was also constructed from popular daily practices in the cities. The accounts of the ways in which the city was incorporated into the lives of the inhabitants, both new arrivals and settled residents, tell a story as significant as those of the proclamations and statutes of officials or the visions of educated Russians. At this level of interpretation the historian confronts two major difficulties. First, our evidence of popular urbanism is largely filtered through the views and assumptions of the officials and intellectuals who compiled written records. Second, much in Russia's urban history is unrecorded because urbanization in the last half of the nineteenth century extended over a vast territory and touched the lives of millions of people. Even the census of 1897 fails the test of comprehensiveness. Still, it offers the only foundation on which to build a general interpretation of Russian urbanization. The model of the migrant city that emerges from a quantitative analysis of the census data reveals that the role of the migrants was crucial in fixing the social profile of the cities.

Two paradigms emerge from the study of nineteenth-century Russian urbanism. One paradigm consists of the idealized visions of tsarist officials and educated Russians; these visions were diverse and even contradictory in substance but all had one thing in common: they were remote from the experience of the population. The other paradigm was apparent wherever economic expansion emerged in urban areas and wherever urban migrants made their presence felt. It focuses on the popular practices, aspirations, fears, and conflicts that were created in the city. It conceives of the city as a place of old customs and new human endeavors where industrialization and temporary migration developed side by side. This amalgam of urban practices is the lived, not the idealized, migrant city. It is an arena of movement and transience and railroad stations and taverns; it is a place where entrepreneurs appeared in the guise of merchants and a city's electric lighting created a "hill of stars" that hid its filth and stench. In this city the townspeople conceived of educational opportunities in a way that suited their expectations of rewards, which were largely determined by the work place and not by elitist culture or tsarist programs of patriotism and piety. Also, the penny press moved into the print culture with messages that appealed to a mass readership and with lurid and colorful accounts of crime and petty affairs.

The domain of the laboring and migrant population bore the cultural and social imprint of their peasant origins. Their relative isolation within the city was a source of their hostility toward the propertied, the cultured, and the powerful. We can partly understand their social animosity as a reaction to the authoritarianism and deep inequalities in wealth and standing that they found in the urban population. But it was also an expression of their own manner of identifying friends and enemies in a world that they defined by their own places—the tavern, factory, and neighborhood—and their own bonds and practices—labor experience, collective fistfights, and the drinking culture. The "fugitive" townspeople of the mid 1800s eventually gave way, at least in part, to an assertive laboring population, some of whom were close to the model proletarian in their social identity and activities but many more of whom were part of the community of migrants, that is, distant from their rural origins but also strangers to respectable urban dwellers. They created their own urban world. In their city the outsiders were those with plans and utopian visions as well as Jews, traders, tsarist officials, and police. The migrant city was a deeply divided place by the end of the nineteenth century: elite fears of popular violence confronted the social antagonism of the laboring population. The gulf separating Moscow's 1882 exposition and the Khitrovka slums remains an abiding symbol of these divisions.

In this history of Russian urbanism tradition and modernity stand as the points of reference by which the Russians gave meaning to the city. The two terms represented temporal markers by which to understand events in a rapidly changing urban world. In the form of custom and myth the past shaped the behavior and attitudes of townspeople, migrants, and laborers. The future, in the shape of dreams and ideals, inspired hopes for learning, visions of technological wonders, and dreams of personal achievement and social justice. The migrant city juxtaposed the old and the new not only in visible, tangible forms but also in the perceptions and expectations of its inhabitants. In this sense the migrant city was a subversive presence. It was not built to any ideal model and it nurtured forces of violence and destruction as well as development and opportunity. In its ambiguities and contradictions the migrant city is a symbol of Russia itself in the late tsarist years.

Appendix

Discriminant Analysis
and Migrant Cities

For the social historian the census of 1897 is an invaluable source with which to explore the characteristics of urban society in late imperial Russia. Although it employs a bureaucratic definition of the term "urban"—essentially the definition used by the Ministry of Internal Affairs—the census provides a detailed picture of the urban population of several hundred towns. The categories of enumeration include a large number of socioeconomic variables, including place of birth (in table A-1 I differentiate between "migrant," "intermediate," and "stagnant" towns on the basis of the proportion of the population that was born outside the city of residence at the time of the census), legal estate, household size, age distribution, literacy, and economic status (that is, self-supporting or dependent).

For the purposes of comparing towns with widely varying populations, these data have to be reduced to percentage values that are calculated on the basis of the appropriate population for a particular city—for example, the total inhabitants—in order to calculate the percent locally born. In the form of percentages the resulting urban profiles are susceptible to statistical analysis to ascertain the characteristics of the typical urban center as well as the characteristics of significant types of urban centers, as grouped by region, size, and—most important for this study—proportion of migrants "born outside their town of residence."

The search for traits that are shared by clusters of towns is particularly important to this study of Russian urban history. In my investigation I make a number of assumptions that affect the manipulation of the data.

The first assumption is that the urban development of Russia is best understood through the pattern—or patterns—of evolution of the cities in general. Moscow and St. Petersburg contained 18 percent of the total urban population of European Russia, but, despite their prominence, they did not by themselves define urbanization in Russia. Although containing no single center rivaling the capitals, the provinces were a vast arena in which the peculiar pattern of Russian urban growth unfolded.

At the other end of the urban spectrum there existed a mass of small towns that, even in the aggregate, represented only a minor presence in the history of the Russian city. The second assumption of this work is that the contribution of these small towns to urban history was so small that for the purposes of statistical analysis they can be excluded from the study. In the initial data collection I only tabulated the urban population for those towns—a total of 144—whose population exceeded fifteen thousand (the procedure previously adopted by Lewis and Leasure in their demographic study of Russia).[1] Even with this restricted group the total population numbered over six million.

Simple descriptive statistical tests (mean, median, range) reveal a wide disparity in social conditions among these urban centers. Although the population of the typical town (median value) was local born by a slight majority, the proportion of local born ranged from 90 percent to 17 percent. As indicated in the text, a Soviet demographic historian has discovered that in fixing the place of birth the census compilers classified an urban area itself as the "local" place only for those cities above twenty thousand population (they included the outlying rural districts in the "local" limits of smaller towns).[2] Although this idiosyncrasy does not distort other variables, it restricts precise study of migrant towns to those centers of over twenty thousand population.

On the borderlands of the empire where non-Russian populations predominated, the social and cultural conditions of the cities were in large part a product of their ethnic composition. They developed in a manner substantially different from the Russian lands.[3] The third assumption of this work, which is important in the statistical analysis as well as in the overall study, is that European Russia represented an area in which urban society

1. Robert Lewis and J. W. Leasure, *Population Changes in Russia and the USSR: A Set of Comparable Territorial Units* (San Diego, 1966).

2. B. V. Tikhonov, *Pereselenie v Rossii vo vtoroi polovine XIX veke po materialam perepisi 1897 g. i pasportnoi statistiki* (Moscow, 1978), 54–55.

3. Studies of several major borderland cities are in *The City in Late Imperial Russia*, ed. Michael Hamm (Bloomington, Ind., 1986).

was shaped by a set of forces that was sufficiently different from the borderlands to merit separate treatment. Administrative divisions determine the boundaries of this territory; the census takers followed these guidelines in their own classification, situating Poland, most of the Baltic lands, Transcaucasia, and Siberia in separate regions. All of these are excluded from my analysis.

This statistical study thus examines a relatively restricted group of towns. Even so, the diversity that existed among these centers extended into many areas of urban life. The population range was enormous, from St. Petersburg's 1.2 million inhabitants to 15,000 in Ranenburg in Tambov province. There was also great economic diversity, from the agricultural community and rail hub of Borisogleb in Kharkov province to the textile center of Ivanovo Voznesensk in Vladimir province. However, a cursory examination of the averages (see table 1) reveals that there were basic similarities underlying this diversity among urban areas. The most notable similarity is that when the proportion of migrants was high, so too were several other social characteristics such as the proportions of self-supporting residents, small households, and hired labor.

This impressionistic observation suggests that as the populations of Russian cities swelled through the influx of migrants, their overall social configuration altered as well. The similarities cannot be explained by a single factor such as migration. Too many forces were at work in the towns to permit such a simple explanation. A more reasonable working hypothesis seems to be that a particular cluster of attributes determined the presence of a distinct type of migrant town.[4] Similarly, the distinctions among the types of towns appears not to be absolute because one might easily shade into another; rather, these types of towns reveal the tendencies for traits that are grouped together in a very approximate manner to appear more or less strongly across a broad social spectrum. The assumption that by the end of the nineteenth century Russian towns had evolved toward identifiable types of population centers, one of which included a large proportion of migrants, led me to undertake a statistical analysis of the census data to uncover the demographic profile of these urban types. The final assumption on which I base my statistical study is that quantitative analysis is a proper tool to uncover "a range of cities formed and functioning under shared

4. In sociological terms the hypothetical groupings do not resemble "monothetic groups," defined such that "the possession of a unique set of attributes is both sufficient and necessary," as much as they resemble "polythetic groups," defined as "a set of attributes such that each entity [in this case, the migrant city] possesses most of the attributes and each attribute is shared by most of the entities." Peter Burke, *Sociology and History* (London, 1980), 36.

circumstances," a grouping that one urban historian has baptized as a "city family."[5]

The initial test of the hypothesis is provided by bivariate correlations that compare the variation in values first for all the cities, then for particular subgroups, across the array of variables compiled from the census. The strength of association, that is, the degree to which two variables are related, is measured by a correlation coefficient whose maximum value is either $+1$ or -1 ($+1$ if the values move in an identical direction across the array of observed units and -1 if they move in opposite directions). The test reveals that a high level of migrants is strongly associated with a number of other traits, especially those mentioned earlier, but also including high literacy rates of the urban estates. The pattern of association is positively correlated among all these variables (the lowest value is .50). In other words, simple bivariate correlation reveals a statistically significant nexus of variables whose strength of association suggests in schematic form a type of urban population—the migrant city—among the 144 towns I studied. The results point to the importance of an urban profile that is closely linked to migration and economic expansion. Statistics confirm what common sense has previously supposed, a reassuring preliminary observation.

The next step in testing the statistical significance of the hypothesis is factor analysis. Having isolated a series of related variables, computer analysis permits the search for a configuration ("factor") to which all these variables are strongly related; computer analysis also makes it possible to determine statistically how well this configuration explains the variance in values of these variables. In factor analysis no one variable is assumed to depend on the others; all are supposed to vary independently from each other. As expected, this test strongly supports the migrant city hypothesis. The variables of age, household size, literacy, migration levels, and percentage of self-supporting population define a factor explaining 70 percent of the variance when all 144 cases (cities) are used.

The final and most meaningful step for historical interpretation is to ascertain whether the individual cities (restricted to those above twenty thousand in population) can themselves be assigned to identifiable urban types that are differentiated by proportion of migrants. Discriminant analysis is a powerful statistical tool to verify similarities among grouped cases as well to classify cases according to the group they most closely resemble.[6]

5. S. G. Checkland, "An Urban History Horoscope," in *The Pursuit of Urban History*, ed. Derek Fraser and Anthony Sutcliffe (London, 1983), 460–61.

6. See William Klecka, *Discriminant Analysis* (Beverly Hills, 1980), 8–11.

Because place of birth appears to be most strongly associated with other variables and identifies relatively distinct groups, I use it as the "discriminant" variable to classify the cases (cities). As I indicated earlier, the cities have values that range from very high to very low proportions of local born (and, conversely, of migrants). No particular value categorically differentiates one group of cities with more or less locally born from another. It seems logical to start from the premise that the common configuration of traits of the "migrant town" grows stronger or weaker as the proportion of local born declines or rises. I therefore separate the cities into three groups that include two "extreme" types, one that is characterized by a high level of local-born inhabitants (above 55 percent) and the other by a low level (below 45 percent). Between these two groups I establish an intermediate group of cities; the level of locally born of the towns in this third group falls in between the values of the other two groups.

Discriminant analysis requires the identification of "discriminating variables" to determine ("predict") how many cases in each assigned group will fit a particular preselected configuration within that group. This procedure permits the precise calculation of the power of the discriminating variables to isolate these unique types. In this case it permits a concrete test of the grouping among certain social characteristics of Russian towns that are selected according to their proportion of migrants.

Discriminant analysis classifies by calculating functions based on the discriminating variables, which in turn provide the values for the calculation of group means. Each case (city) is assigned a value based on its score as measured by the discriminating variables. It is then placed in that group to which its mean value is closest. Correlation coefficients identified the best variables to use. Table A-1 presents the results of this analysis. Discriminant analysis reveals that of the thirty-seven migrant cities, thirty (81 percent) are correctly classified by the discriminating variables and seven are assigned to the intermediate group; of the thirty-eight nonmigrant cities, thirty-one (82 percent) share the unique properties that are isolated by the variables to be classified in this group; only seven are classified among the intermediate group and none with the migrant cities. In the intermediate group twenty-six of the thirty towns are correctly classified, the remaining four falling in the group of migrant cities. Most important to the migrant city model is the fact that no city from either of the two polar groups proves in its overall social configuration to resemble the urban centers in the other group. Overall, 83 percent of the grouped towns fall in the assigned group, a sufficiently high proportion to confirm the presence (in a statistical sense) of two distinct urban types at the polar extremes of a spectrum that is defined by levels of migration.

Table A-1. The Russian Migrant City in 1897

Discriminant Test on Migrant Cities with Population over 20,000 (N = 105)

| | | Predicted Group Membership | | | | | |
| | | 1 | | 2 | | 3 | |
Actual Group	Number of Cases	Num- ber	Percent- age	Num- ber	Percent- age	Num- ber	Percent- age
Migrant city (more than 55% born outside city of residence)	37	30	81	7	19	0	0
Intermediate city (45–55% born outside city of residence)	30	4	13	26	87	0	0
Stagnant city (0–45% born outside city of residence	38	0	0	7	18	31	82

Structure Matrix: Pooled within-groups correlation between canonical discriminant function and discriminating variables

Group	Correlation on first function (98% of variance)
Large households (six members or more)*	−.70
Working age population (ages 20–40)	.47
Distant migrants (outside province) from urban estates	.39
Artel housing*	.32
Local migrants (within province) from urban estates	.28
Salaried workers	.17
Distant peasant migrants*	.16

*Denotes variables with the strongest correlation within the function.

A second advantage to this statistical test is its capacity to assign to specific variables particular values based on their strength of association with the principal discriminant function. The higher the value, the more closely is a variable associated with that function. The most powerful function (indicated by its canonical correlation coefficient—the relatedness between the groups and the function—of .98) includes a cluster of three variables that are related to the demographic profile of the towns: (1) the proportion of large households—smaller in the migrant cities, larger in stagnant towns; (2) the presence of working-age residents (ages twenty to forty) among town residents—higher in migrant towns, lower in nonmigrant towns; and (3) the proportion of residents living in communal (*artel'*) housing—again, higher in migrant cities, lower elsewhere. In addition, other significant variables point to characteristics that I identify with the urban centers that were more or less attractive for outsiders seeking jobs—the proportion of distant and local migrants and the proportion of salaried workers. The statistical findings appear to challenge common sense in one particular respect: the test does not isolate the variable that measures the proportion of peasant migrants that are born in the same province as the city to which they migrate is located in. One might hypothesize that peasant migration into provincial urban centers was a phenomenon so pervasive throughout Russia that in itself it operated regardless of the other factors in urban development.

Two less obvious but significant observations should be pointed out here. First, although the proportion of peasants in these towns is greater than that of any other estate, the migrant city's uniqueness is defined by characteristics that are not specifically associated with peasant demographic traits. Second, in the migrant city model there are no specific indicators of occupations in either manufacturing or trade (these variables are calculated using census employment figures as a proportion of the total self-supporting population). Rather, the significance of economic activity is apparent in the proportion of work-age inhabitants and wage labor in migrant towns. In these quantitative terms late nineteenth-century urbanization was not the result of industrialization.

Regional analysis would present a modified picture. Table 1 indicates the extent to which the cities of the Central Industrial region were distinguished by the importance of manufacturing (which was not limited to factory labor) and by other measures of economic enterprise, particularly the literacy of the urban estates and the proportion of self-supporting residents among the townspeople. Clearly, however, the urban centers of that region did not set the pattern for the rest of the country. Rapid growth marked urban centers in other areas, where opportunities for employment were much less concentrated in manufacturing. The domestic and service jobs available in commerce, manufacturing, and private households, which required no training and employed as many women as men, were particularly prominent in migrant towns. These jobs did not delimit the only important occupational sectors, and their prominence is symptomatic of the diversity of economic activities that distinguished all the migrant cities. In this statistical analysis these cities appear to be primarily centers of an industrious population, the product of decades of urban migration and economic growth.

Selected Bibliography

The array of works, published and unpublished, that is relevant to the study of Russian urbanism in the late tsarist period is vast and tends to vary according to the topic emphasized. My list is intentionally idiosyncratic, indicating the materials that proved either stimulating or useful in my own inquiry.

I. Unpublished Sources

Archival Materials

Tsentral'nyi gosudarstvennyi arkhiv Okt'iabrskoi revoliutsii (TsGAOR) (Central State Archives of the October Revolution)

f. 102 Ministerstvo vnutrennikh del, Departament gosudarstvennoi politsii (Yearly reports from provincial gendarme officers).
f. 109 Tret'e otdelenie (Records of police reform).

Tsentral'nyi gosudarstvennyi istoricheskii arkhiv (TsGIA) (Central State Historical Archives of the USSR)

f. 91 Imperatorskoe vol'noe ekonomicheskoe obshchestvo (Records of the elementary school survey conducted by the Petersburg Literacy Committee in 1894).
f. 207 Glavnoe upravlenie putei soobshchenii (Governmental discussions and plans for the location of railroad lines).
f. 573 Ministerstvo finansov, Departament okladnykh sborov (Records of the 1906 survey of urban real estate).

f. 733 Ministerstvo narodnogo prosveshcheniia (Ministerial reports on the conditions and the development of urban schools).

f. 796 Kantseliariia Sinoda (Yearly reports from the bishoprics of the Orthodox Church).

f. 1149 Gosudarstvennyi sovet, Departament zakonov (Discussions of police reform in the 1870s).

ff. 1263, 1281, 1282, 1284 Ministerstvo vnutrennykh del, Departament obshchikh del (Yearly reports from provincial governors).

ff. 1287, 1290 Ministerstvo vnutrennikh del, Khoziaistvennyi departament (Reports on municipal reforms, elections, and taxes).

f. 1297 Ministerstvo vnutrennikh del, Meditsinskii departament (Reports on sanitary conditions of cities).

ff. 1356, 1391 Gosudarstvennyi senat (Reports of the senatorial investigation of provincial administration of 1880–81).

Dissertations

Bobroff, Anne. "Working Women, Bonding Patterns, and the Politics of Daily Life: Russia at the End of the Old Regime." Ph.D. diss., University of Michigan, 1982.

Bol'shov, V. V. "Kakhanovskaia komissiia (1881–85): K voprosu o vnutrennei politike samoderzhaviia pervoi poloviny 80-kh gg. XIX v." Kandidat dissertation, Moscow University, 1977.

Desjean, Mary Frances. "The Common Experience of the Russian Working Class: The Case of St. Petersburg, 1892–1904." Ph.D. diss., Duke University, 1978.

Esin, B. I. "Russkaia gazeta vtoroi poloviny XIX veka." 2 vols. Doctoral dissertation, Moscow University, 1973.

Hanchett, Walter. "Moscow in the Late Nineteenth Century: A Study in Municipal Self-Government." Ph.D. diss., University of Chicago, 1964.

Hinshaw, Christine. "The Soul of the School: The Professionalization of Urban Schoolteachers in St. Petersburg and Moscow." Ph.D. diss., University of California, Berkeley, 1986.

Kut'ev, V. F. "Dokumental'nye materialy moskovskikh gosudarstvennykh arkhivov po istorii rabochego klassa goroda Moskvy v 90-kh gody XIX veka." Kandidat dissertation, Moscow State University, 1955.

Listengurt, F. M. "Rol' ekonomichesko-geograficheskogo polozheniia v istoricheskom razvitii gorodov Iaroslavlia, Kalinina i Rybinska." Kandidat dissertation, Moscow Pedagogical Institute, 1960.

McGivney, Thomas. "The Lower Classes in the City of Moscow, 1870–1905." Ph.D. diss., New York University, 1978.

McReynolds, Louise. "News and Society: *Russkoe Slovo* and the Development of a Mass-Circulation Press in Late Imperial Russia." Ph.D. diss., University of Chicago, 1984.

Neuberger, Joan. "Crime and Culture: Hooliganism in St. Petersburg, 1900–1914." Ph.D. diss., Stanford University, 1985.

Pavliuchenko, E. A. "Moskovskoe gorodskoe upravlenie v 70–80-kh godakh XIX veka." Kandidat dissertation, Moscow State University, 1956.

Pisar'kova, L. F. "Moskovskoe gorodskoe obshchestvennoe upravlenie s seredina

1880-kh godov do pervoi russkoi revoliutsii." Kandidat dissertation, Moscow University, 1980.

Varaksin, N. B. "Formirovanie belorusskikh gorodov vo vtoroi polovine XIX–nachale XX v." Doctoral dissertation, Minsk Institute of Architecture, 1965.

Vasil'ev, B. N. "Formirovanie fabrichno-zavodskogo proletariata tsentral'nogo pro-myshlennogo raiona Rossii, 1820–1890." 2 vols. Doctoral dissertation, No-vocherkassk Pedagogical Institute, 1972.

Weinberg, Robert. "Worker Organizations and Politics in the Revolution of 1905 in Odessa." Ph.D. diss., University of California, Berkeley, 1985.

Zlatoustavskii, B. V. "Moskovskoe gorodskoe samoupravlenie v period reformy 60-kh godov XIX veka." Kandidat dissertation, Moscow State University, 1953.

II. Published Sources

Primary Sources

Alabin, P., and T. Konovalov. *Sbornik svedenii o nastoiashchem sostoianii gorod-skogo khoziaistva v glavneishikh gorodov Rossii*. Samara, 1889.

Alchevskaia, Kh. D. *Polgoda iz zhizni voskresnoi shkoly*. St. Petersburg, 1895.

Ashukin, N. S., ed. *Ushedshaia Moskva: Vospominaniia sovremennikov o Moskve vtoroi poloviny XIX v*. Moscow, 1964.

Astov, N. I. *Vospominaniia*. Paris, 1940.

Babushkin, I. V. *Vospominaniia*. Leningrad, 1925.

Baikov, A. M. *Obzor deistvii Rostovskogo (na Donu) gorodskogo khoziaistvennogo upravleniia za 1863 g*. Odessa, 1864.

Bakhrushin, S. V., ed. *Moskovskii krai v ego proshlom: Ocherki po sotsial'noi i ekonomicheskoi istorii*. Moscow, 1928.

Belousov, I. A. *Ushedshaia Moskva*. Moscow, 1929.

Buryshkin, P. A. *Moskva kupecheskaia*. New York, 1954.

Chicherin, B. N. *Vospominaniia: Zemstvo i Moskovskaia duma*. Moscow, 1934.

Dolgorukii, V., and V. Anofriev. *Putevoditel' po Moskve i ee okrestnostiam*. Mos-cow, 1872.

Elpat'evskii, S. Ia. *Vospominaniia za piat'desiat let*. Moscow, 1929.

Eremev, I., ed. *Gorod Sanktpeterburg s tochki zreniia meditsinskoi politsii*. St. Petersburg, 1897.

Fal'bork, F. A., and V. I. Charnoluskii, eds. *Nachal'noe narodnoe obrazovanie v Rossii*. 4 vols. St. Petersburg, 1900–1905.

Gerasimov, V. G. *Zhizn' russkogo rabochego: Vospominaniia*. Moscow, 1959.

Giliarovskii, V. A. *Izbrannoe*. 3 vols. Moscow, 1958.

Goroda Rossii v 1904 g. St. Petersburg, 1907.

Gvozdov, S. *Zapiski fabrichnogo inspektora*. Moscow, 1911.

Kanatchikov, S. I. *A Radical Worker in Tsarist Russia: The Autobiography of Semen Ivanovich Kanatchikov*. Translated and edited by Reginald Zelnik. Stan-ford, 1986.

Kiev v 80-kh godakh: Vospominaniia starozhila. Kiev, 1910.

Kokorev, I. T. *Moskva sorokovykh godov: Ocherki i povesti o Moskve XIX v*. Moscow, 1958.

Komissiia dlia issledovaniia zheleznodorozhnykh del. *Trudy.* 4 vols. St. Petersburg, 1880–81.

_____. *Doklad o passazhirskom dvizhenii.* St. Petersburg, 1881.

Krestovnikov, N. *Semeinaia khronika.* 3 vols. Moscow, 1903–4.

Kuchin, Ia. *Putevoditel' po Volge.* Saratov, 1865.

Leikin, N. A. *Apraksintsy: Tseny i ocherki.* St. Petersburg, 1904.

Makashin, S. A. *Rasskazy o starom Saratove.* Saratov, 1937.

Ministerstvo putei soobshcheniia. *Aperçu statistique des chemins de fer et des voies navigables de la Russie.* St. Petersburg, 1900.

Ministerstvo vnutrennikh del. *Ekonomicheskoe sostoianie gorodskikh poselenii evropeiskoi Rossii v 1861–1862 g.* 2 vols. St. Petersburg, 1863.

_____. *Materialy otnosiashcheisia do novogo obshchestvennogo ustroistva v gorodakh imperii.* 6 vols. St. Petersburg, 1877–83.

_____. *Sanitarnoe sostoianie gorodov Rossiiskoi imperii v 1895 g.* St. Petersburg, 1899.

Mironov, K. *Iz vospominanii rabochego.* Moscow, 1906.

Moskovskoe gorodskoe obshchestvennoe upravlenie. *Deiatel'nost' Moskovskogo gorodskogo obshchestvennogo upravleniia po narodnomy obrazovaniiu.* Moscow, 1896.

_____. *Otchet o deiatel'nosti gorodskikh vrachei.* Moscow, 1899.

Naidenov, N. A. *Vospominaniia o vidennom, slyshennom i ispytannom.* 2 vols. Moscow, 1903–5.

Nikiforov, D. I. *Vospominaniia iz vremen imperatora Nikolaia I.* Moscow, 1903.

_____. *Moskva v tsarstvovanii Aleksandra II.* Moscow, 1904.

Nikitin, V. N. *Proidokha: Vospominaniia kuptsa starogo vremeni.* St. Petersburg, 1900.

Novikov, A. *Zapiski gorodskogo golovy.* St. Petersburg, 1905.

Osobaia komissiia dlia sostavleniia proektov mestnogo upravleniia. *Trudy komissii Kakhanova.* 6 vols. St. Petersburg, 1884.

Pushkarev, U. U. *Putevoditel' po Sankt-Peterburge i okrestnostiam.* St. Petersburg, 1848.

Putevoditel' po gorode Kieva. St. Petersburg, 1877.

Putevoditel' po Odesse. Odessa, 1896.

Rabochee dvizhenie v Rossii v XIX veke: Sbornik dokumentov i materialov. 4 vols. Moscow, 1950–63.

Ragozin, E. I. "Puteshestvie po russkim gorodam." *Russkoe obozrenie* 4, no. 7 (July 1891):207–61.

Sanktpeterburgskoe gorodskoe obshchestvennoe upravlenie. *Desiat' let: Doklad.* St. Petersburg, 1883.

Sazonov, G. P. *Rostovshchichestvo-kulachestvo: Nabliudeniia i issledovaniia.* St. Petersburg, 1894.

Semenov, S. T. *Dvatsat' piat' let v derevne.* Petrograd, 1915.

Semenov-Tian-Shanskii, P. P. *Geografichesko-statisticheskii slovar' Rossiiskoi imperii.* 5 vols. St. Petersburg, 1863–85.

Shapalov, A. S. *V bor'be za sotsializm: Vospominaniia starogo Bol'shevika.* Moscow, 1934.

Shcherbatov, A. P. *Otchet Moskovskogo gorodskogo golovy o deiatel'nosti Moskovskoi gorodskoi dumy, 1863–1869.* Moscow, 1869.

Sinitsyn, A. A. "Iz vospominanii starogo vracha." *Russkaia starina* 152 (December 1912):667–73; 154 (June 1913):495–549; 155 (July 1913):140–46.

Slonov, I. A. *Iz zhizni torgovoi Moskvy.* Moscow, 1914.

Smidovich, P. *Rabochie massy v 90-kh godakh.* Moscow, 1930.

Smirnov, I. I. "Brianskie zavody v 80–90-kh godakh." *Letopis' revoliutsii* 4 (1923): 85–94.

Stasiulevich, M. M. *Desiat' let Sanktpeterburgskogo obshchestvennogo upravleniia.* St. Petersburg, 1884.

Timofeev, P. *Chem zhivet zavodskii rabochii?* St. Petersburg, 1906.

Titov, A. A. *Putevoditel' po Iaroslavle.* Moscow, 1883.

Tsentral'nyi statisticheskii komitet. *Pervaia vseobshchaia perepis' naselenii Rossiiskoi imperii, 1897 g.* 89 vols. St. Petersburg, 1899–1905.

Voronov, N. I. *Zapiski o sobytiiakh Vladimirskoi gubernii.* Vladimir, 1907.

Secondary Literature

Abbott, Robert. "Crime, Police, and Society in St. Petersburg, 1866–1878." *Historian* 40 (November 1977):70–84.

Agulhon, Maurice, ed. *Histoire de la France urbaine.* Vol. 4, *La ville à l'âge industriel.* Paris, 1983.

Akademiia nauk SSSR. Institut istorii. *Istoriia Moskvy.* 6 vols. Moscow, 1952–57.

Alexander, John. "Petersburg and Moscow in Early Urban Policy." *Journal of Urban History* 8 (February 1982):145–69.

Anderson, Barbara. *Internal Migration during Modernization in Late Nineteenth-Century Russia.* Princeton, 1980.

Anokhina, L. A., and M. N. Shmeleva. *Byt gorodskogo naseleniia srednei polosy RSFSR v proshlom i nastoiashchem.* Moscow, 1977.

Anuchin, E. *Istoricheskii obzor razvitiia administrativno-politseiskikh uchrezhdenii v Rossii.* St. Petersburg, 1872.

Bagalei, D., and D. Miller. *Istoriia goroda Khar'kova za 250 let ego sushchestvovaniia.* Vol. 2, *XIX i nachalo XX veka.* Kharkov, 1912.

Baidakov, N. N. "Vvedenie Gorodovogo polozheniia 1870 g. v Nizhnem Novgorode i vybory v 1870–90-kh gg." *Uchenye zapiski Gor'kovskogo Gosudarstvennogo Universiteta, seriia gumanitarnykh nauk* 105 (1969):73–78.

Bakrushin, S. V. *Maloletnie nishchie i brodiagi v Moskve: Istoricheskii ocherk.* Moscow, 1913.

Bater, James. *St. Petersburg: Industrialization and Change.* London, 1976.

———. "Transience, Residential Persistence, and Mobility in Moscow and St. Petersburg, 1900–1914." *Slavic Review* 39 (June 1980):239–54.

Berk, Stephen. *Year of Crisis, Year of Hope: Russian Jewry and the Pogroms of 1881–1882.* Westport, Conn., 1985.

Berlin, P. A. *Russkaia burzhuaziia v staroe i novoe vremia.* Moscow, 1922.

Bernstein-Kogan, S. V. *Chislennost', sostav i polozhenie Peterburgskikh rabochikh: Opyt statisticheskogo issledovaniia.* St. Petersburg, 1910.

Bill, Valentine. *The Forgotten Class: The Russian Bourgeoisie from the Earliest Beginnings to 1900.* New York, 1959.

Bliokh, I. S. *Vliianie zheleznykh dorog na ekonomicheskoe sostoianie Rossii.* 4 vols. St. Petersburg, 1878.

Bogdanov, I. M. *Gramotnost' i obrazovanie v dorevoliutsionnoi Rossii i v SSSR.* Moscow, 1964.

Bonnell, Victoria. *Roots of Rebellion: Workers' Politics and Organizations in St. Petersburg and Moscow, 1900–1914.* Berkeley, 1983.

Borisova, E. A. *Russkaia arkhitektura vtoroi poloviny XIX veka.* Moscow, 1979.

Bradley, Joseph. *Muzhik and Muscovite: Urbanization in Late Imperial Russia.* Berkeley, 1985.

Brooks, Jeffrey. *When Russia Learned to Read: Literacy and Popular Literature, 1861–1917.* Princeton, 1985.

Brower, Daniel. "L'urbanisation russe à la fin du XIX siècle." *Annales: Economies, Sociétés, Civilisations* (January-February 1977):70–86.

———. "Urban Russia on the Eve of World War One: A Social Profile." *Journal of Social History* 13 (1980):424–36.

Carstensen, Fred. *American Enterprise in Foreign Markets: Singer and International Harvester in Imperial Russia.* Chapel Hill, N.C., 1984.

Coleman, William. *Death is a Social Disease: Public Health and Political Economy in Early Industrial France.* Madison, 1982.

Corbin, Alain. *The Foul and the Fragrant: Odor and the French Social Imagination.* Cambridge, Mass., 1986.

Crisp, Olga. *Studies in the Russian Economy before 1914.* London, 1976.

de Certeau, Michel. *The Practices of Everyday Life.* Translated by Steven Rendall. Berkeley, 1984.

Didrikhson, A. *Istoricheskii obzor deiatel'nosti Khar'kovskogo obshchestva rasprostraneniia v narode gramotnosti.* Kharkov, 1911.

Dikhtiar, G. A. *Vnutrenniaia torgovlia v dorevoliutsionnoi Rossii.* Moscow, 1960.

Dikson, K. I., and B. E. Ketrits. *Sanktpeterburgskii komitet gramotnosti, 1861–1911: Istoricheskii ocherk i vospominaniia.* St. Petersburg, 1911.

Ditiatin, I. I. *Ustroistvo i upravlenie gorodov Rossii.* 2 vols. St. Petersburg, 1875; Yaroslavl, 1877.

———. *Stat'i po istorii russkogo prava.* St. Petersburg, 1895.

Dyos, H. J. *The Study of Urban History.* London, 1968.

Dyos, H. J., and Michael Wolff, eds. *The Victorian City: Images and Realities.* 2 vols. London, 1973.

Egorov, I. A. *The Architectural Planning of St. Petersburg.* New York, 1969.

Eklof, Ben. *Russian Peasant Schools: Officialdom, Village Culture, and Popular Pedagogy, 1861–1914.* Berkeley, 1986.

Ekzempliarskii, P. M. *Istoriia goroda Ivanova.* Moscow, 1958.

Engelstein, Laura. *Moscow, 1905: Working-Class Organization and Political Conflict.* Stanford, 1982.

Erisman, F. F. *Izbrannye proizvedeniia.* 2 vols. Moscow, 1959.

Esin, B. I. *Russkaia dorevoliutsionnaia gazeta, 1702–1917 gg.: Kratkii ocherk.* Moscow, 1971.

Fedor, Thomas. *Patterns of Urban Growth in the Russian Empire during the Nineteenth Century*. Chicago, 1975.

Fedosiuk, Iu. A. "Moskva sto let nazad." *Voprosy istorii* (February 1968): 209–16.

Fraser, Derek, and Anthony Sutcliffe, eds. *The Pursuit of Urban History*. London, 1983.

Freeze, Gregory. "The *Soslovie* (Estate) Paradigm and Russian Social History." *American Historical Review* 91 (February 1986):11–35.

Frieden, Nancy. *Russian Physicians in an Era of Reform and Revolution, 1856–1905*. Princeton, 1981.

_____. "The Russian Cholera Epidemic, 1892–93, and Medical Professionalization." *Journal of Social History* 10 (June 1977):538–59.

Gan, I. A. *O nastoiashchem byte meshchan Saratovskoi gubernii*. St. Petersburg, 1860.

Gatrell, Peter. *The Tsarist Economy, 1850–1917*. London, 1986.

Gavlin, M. L. "Sotsial'nyi sostav krupnoi moskovskoi burzhuazii vo vtoroi polovine XIX v." *Problemy otechestvennoi istorii* 1 (1973):166–88.

Gindin, I. F. *Russkie kommercheskie banky: Iz istorii finansovogo kapitala v Rossii*. Moscow, 1948.

_____. "The Russian Bourgeoisie in the Period of Capitalism: Their Development and Distinctive Features." *Soviet Studies in History* 6 (Summer 1967):3–50.

Girouard, Mark. *Cities and People: A Social and Architectural History*. New Haven, 1985.

Golovshchikov, K. D. *Gorod Rybinsk: Ego proshedshee i nastoiashchee*. Yaroslavl, 1890.

Grass, V. *Spravochnaia kniga dlia gorodskikh obshchestvennykh upravlenii*. Chernigov, 1900.

Gregory, Paul. "Economic Growth and Structural Changes in Tsarist Russia: A Case of Modern Economic Growth." *Soviet Studies* 23 (1973):418–34.

_____. "Russian Living Standards during Industrialization." *Review of Income and Wealth* 26 (1980):87–103.

Hamm, Michael. "The Modern Russian City: An Historiographical Analysis." *Journal of Urban History* 4 (November 1977):39–76.

_____, ed. *The City in Russian History*. Lexington, Ky., 1976.

_____, ed. *The City in Late Imperial Russia*. Bloomington, Ind., 1986.

Herlihy, Patricia. *Odessa: A History, 1794–1914*. Cambridge, Mass., 1986.

Hittle, J. Michael. *The Service City: State and Townsmen in Russia, 1600–1800*. Cambridge, Mass., 1979.

Hooson, D. J. M. "The Growth of Cities in Pre-Soviet Russia." In *Urbanization and Its Problems*, ed. R. Beckinsab, 254–76. Oxford, 1968.

Ianina, V. L., ed. *Russkii gorod*. Moscow, 1976.

Islavin, M. V. *Obzor trudov vysochaishe utverzdennoi, pod predsedatel'stvom stats-sekretaria Kakhanova, osoboi komissii*. St. Petersburg, 1908.

Ivanov, L. M., ed. *Rossiiskii proletariat: Oblik, bor'ba, gegemoniia*. Moscow, 1970.

_____. "O soslovno-klassovoi strukture gorodov kapitalisticheskoi Rossii." In *Problemy sotsial'no-ekonomicheskoi istorii Rossii*, 312–40. Moscow, 1971.

Ivanov, V. N., ed. *"Obraztsovye" proekty v zhiloi zastroike russkikh gorodov XVIII–XX vv.* Moscow, 1961.

Johnson, Robert. *Peasant and Proletarian: The Working Class of Moscow in the Late Nineteenth Century.* New Brunswick, N.J., 1979.

Jones, Robert. "Urban Planning and the Development of Provincial Towns in Russia, 1762–1796." In *The Eighteenth Century in Russia,* ed. J. G. Garrard, 321–44. Oxford, 1973.

Kabo, E. O. *Ocherki rabochego byta: Opyt monograficheskogo issledovaniia domashnego byta.* Moscow, 1928.

Kabuzan, M. *Izmeneniia v razmeshchenii naseleniia Rossii v XVIII–pervoi polovine XIX vekakh.* Moscow, 1971.

Kazantsev, B. N. *Rabochie Moskvy i Moskovskoi gubernii v seredine XIX veka.* Moscow, 1976.

Kean, Beverly. *All the Empty Palaces: The Merchant Patrons of Modern Art in Prerevolutionary Russia.* New York, 1983.

Khlystov, I. P. *Don v epokhy kapitalizma.* Rostov on Don, 1962.

Kir'ianov, Iu. I. *Zhiznennyi uroven' rabochikh Rossii: Konets XIX–nachalo XX v.* Moscow, 1979.

Kirichenko, E. I. *Russkaia arkhitektura 1830–40-kh godov.* Moscow, 1978.

Kitanina, T. M. *Khlebnaia torgovlia Rossii, 1875–1914 gg.* Leningrad, 1978.

Kleinbort, L. *Istoriia bezrabotnitsy v Rossii, 1857–1919.* Moscow, 1925.

Kotelnikov, A. *Istoriia proizvodstva i razrabotki vseobshchei perepisi naseleniia 1897 g.* St. Petersburg, 1907.

Kovalevsky, Maksim, ed. *La Russie à la fin du 19e siècle.* Paris, 1900.

Kraevskii, A. *Vopros o nishchenstve i ob organizatsii blagotvoritel'nosti v Moskve.* Moscow, 1889.

Krupianskaia, V. Iu., and N. S. Polishchuk. *Kul'tura i byt rabochikh gorne-zavodskogo Urala: Konets XIX–nachalo XX v.* Moscow, 1971.

Langer, Lawrence. "The Historiography of the Preindustrial Russian City." *Journal of Urban History* 5 (February 1979):209–40.

Laverychev, V. Ia. *Krupnaia burzhuaziia v poreformennoi Rossii, 1861–1900.* Moscow, 1974.

Lebedev, V. "K istorii kulachnykh boev na Rusi." *Russkaia starina* 44 (August 1913):323–40.

Lees, Andrew. *Cities Perceived: Urban Society in European and American Thought, 1820–1940.* New York, 1985.

Lewis, Robert, and J. W. Leasure. *Population Changes in Russia and the USSR: A Set of Comparable Territorial Units.* San Diego, 1966.

Lofland, Lyn. *A World of Strangers: Order and Action in Urban Public Space.* New York, 1973.

Lotova, E. I. *Russkaia intelligentsiia i voprosy obshchestvennoi gigieny: Pervoe gigienicheskoe obshchestvo v Rossii.* Moscow, 1962.

McGrew, Roderick. *Russia and the Cholera, 1823–32.* Madison, 1965.

McKay, John. *Tramways and Trollies: The Rise of Urban Mass Transport in Europe.* Princeton, 1976.

Metzer, Jacob. *Some Economic Aspects of Railroad Development in Tsarist Russia.* New York, 1977.

Mikhnevich, V. *Iazvy Peterburga: Opyt istoriko-statisticheskogo issledovaniia nravstvennosti stolichnogo naseleniia.* St. Petersburg, 1886.

Mironov, B. N. "Sotsial'naia mobil'nost' i sotsial'noe rassloenie v russkoi derevne XIX–nachala XX vv." In *Problemy razvitiia feodal'izma i kapitalizma v stranakh Baltiki,* 156–83. Tartu, 1972.

_____. "Sotsial'naia mobil'nost' rossiiskogo kupechestva v XVIII–nachale XIX veka." In *Problemy istoricheskoi demografii SSSR,* 207–17. Tallinn, 1977.

_____. *Vnutrennii rynok Rossii vo vtoroi polovine XVIII–pervoi polovine XIX v.* Leningrad, 1981.

_____. "Gramotnost' v Rossii, 1797–1917 gg." *Istoriia SSSR* (July-August 1983): 137–53.

_____. "Russkii gorod vo vtoroi polovine XVIII–pervoi polovine XIX v.: Tipologicheskii analiz." *Istoriia SSSR* (September-October 1988):150–68.

Mukalov, M. K. *Deti ulitsy.* St. Petersburg, 1906.

Nardova, V. A. "Adres Moskovskoi gorodskoi dumy 1870 g." *Istoricheskie zapiski* 98 (1977):294–312.

_____. *Gorodskoe samoupravlenie v Rossii v 60-kh–nachale 90-kh godov XIX v.* Leningrad, 1984.

Nifontov, A. S. *Moskva vo vtoroi polovine XIX st.* Moscow, 1947.

_____. "Formirovanie klassov burzhuaznogo obshchestva v russkom gorode vtoroi polovine XIX v." *Istoricheskie zapiski* 54 (1955):239–50.

Novosel'skii, S. A. *O razlichiiakh v smertnosti gorodskogo i sel'skogo naseleniia Evropeiskoi Rossii.* St. Petersburg, 1911.

Odesskoe obshchestvennoe upravlenie. *Odessa, 1794–1894.* Odessa, 1895.

Orzhekhovskii, I. V. *Iz istorii vnutrennei politiki samoderzhaviia v 60–70-kh godakh XIX v.* Gorky, 1974.

Ostroumov, S. S. *Prestupnost' i ee prichiny v dorevoliutsionnoi Rossii.* Moscow, 1960.

Owen, Thomas. *Capitalism and Politics in Russia: A Social History of the Moscow Merchants, 1855–1905.* Cambridge, Mass., 1981.

Papkov, A. A. *Tserkovnye bratstva: Kratkii statisticheskii ocherk.* St. Petersburg, 1893.

Pazhitnov, K. A. *Gorodskoe i zemskoe samoupravlenie v Rossii.* St. Petersburg, 1913.

Persits, M. M. *Ateizm russkogo rabochego.* Moscow, 1965.

Pisar'kova, L. F. "Deiatel'nost' Moskovskoi gorodskoi dumy v oblasti meditsiny, narodnogo obrazovaniia i obshchestvennogo prizreniia posle 1892." *Problemy istorri SSSR* 7 (1978):128–43.

_____. *Moskovskoe gorodskoe obshchestvennoe upravlenie: Avtoreferat.* Moscow, 1980.

Plandovskii, V. A. *Narodnaia perepis'.* St. Petersburg, 1898.

Potolov, S. I. *Rabochie Donbasa v XIX veke.* Moscow, 1963.

Pustokhov, P. I. *Perepisi naseleniia.* Moscow, 1936.

Rabinovich, M. G. *Ocherki etnografii russkogo feodal'nogo goroda: Gorozhane, ikh obshchestvennyi i domashnii byt.* Moscow, 1978.

Rashin, A. B. *Naselenie Rossii za 100 let, 1811–1913.* Moscow, 1956.

_____. *Formirovanie rabochego klassa Rossii: Istoriko-ekonomicheskie ocherki.* Moscow, 1958.

Rieber, Alfred. *Merchants and Entrepreneurs in Imperial Russia.* Chapel Hill, N.C., 1982.

Robbins, Richard. *The Tsar's Viceroys: Russian Provincial Governors in the Last Years of the Empire.* Ithaca, N.Y., 1987.

Rodwin, Lloyd, and Robert Hollister, eds. *Cities of the Mind: Images and Themes of the City in the Social Sciences.* New York, 1984.

Rozman, Gilbert. *Urban Networks in Russia, 1750–1800.* Princeton, 1976.

Ryndziunskii, P. G. *Gorodskoe grazhdanstvo v doreformennoi Rossii.* Moscow, 1958.

_____. *Utverzhdenie kapitalizma v Rossii, 1850–1880.* Moscow, 1978.

_____. *Krest'iane i gorod v kapitalisticheskoi Rossii vtoroi poloviny XIX veka.* Moscow, 1983.

Salov, V. V. *Istoricheskii ocherk uchrezhdeniia komissii dlia issledovaniia zheleznodorozhnogo dela v Rossii.* St. Petersburg, 1909.

Semenov, D. D. *Gorodskoe samoupravlenie: Ocherki i opyty.* St. Petersburg, 1910.

Semenov-Tianshanskii, V. P. "Gorod i derevnia v Evropeiskoi Rossii." *Zapiski po otdelu statistiki Imperatorskogo russkogo geograficheskogo obshchestva* 10 (1910).

Sharapov, S. F. "Egor'evskii gorodskoi golova Nikifor Mikhailovich Bardynin, 1872–1901." In *Iz moikh vospominanii,* by S. F. Sharapov, 173–87. Moscow, 1909.

Shishkin, V. F. *Tak skladyvalas' revoliutsionnaia moral'.* Moscow, 1967.

Shkvarikov, V. A. *Ocherk istorii planirovki i zastroiki russkikh gorodov.* Moscow, 1954.

Shreider, G. I. *Nashe gorodskoe obshchestvennoe upravlenie.* St. Petersburg, 1902.

Siegelbaum, Lewis. "The Odessa Grain Trade: A Case Study in Urban Growth and Development in Tsarist Russia." *Journal of European Economic History* 9 (Spring 1980):113–47.

Skorobotov, N. A. *'Peterburgskii listok' za 35 let.* St. Petersburg, 1914.

Smith, Michael. *The City and Social Theory.* New York, 1979.

Solov'eva, A. M. *Zheleznodorozhnyi transport vo vtoroi polovine XIX veka.* Moscow, 1975.

Spasskii, P. Kh. *Istoricheskii ocherk razvitiia putei soobshcheniia v Rossii.* St. Petersburg, 1913.

Subbotin, A. P. *V cherte evreiskoi osedlosti.* 2 vols. St. Petersburg, 1888, 1890.

_____. *Volga i Volgari: Putevye ocherki.* St. Petersburg, 1894.

Thurston, Robert. *Liberal City, Conservative State: Moscow and Russia's Urban Crisis, 1906–1914.* New York, 1987.

Tikhonov, B. V. *Pereselenie v Rossii vo vtoroi polovine XIX veka po materialam perepisi 1897 g. i pasportnoi statistiki.* Moscow, 1978.

Viatkin, M. P., ed. *Ocherki istorii Leningrada.* 3 vols. Moscow, 1955–57.

Vishnevskii, A. G., ed. *Brachnost', rozhdaemost' i smertnost' v Rossii i v SSSR: Sbornik statei.* Moscow, 1977.

Vologodtsev, I. K. *Osobennosti razvitiia gorodov Ukrainy.* Kharkov, 1930.

Von Laue, Theodore. "Russian Labor between Field and Factory, 1892–1903." *California Slavic Studies* 3 (1964):33–62.

Weissman, Neil. "Regular Police in Tsarist Russia, 1900–14." *Russian Review* 44 (January 1985):45–68.

Zaionchkovsky, P. A. *The Russian Autocracy in Crisis, 1878–82*. Translated and edited by Gary Hamburg. Gulf Breeze, Fla., 1979.

Zelnik, Reginald. *Labor and Society in Tsarist Russia: The Factory Workers of St. Petersburg, 1855–1870*. Stanford, 1971.

Zhbankov, D. N. *Bab'ia storona: Statistiko-etnograficheskii ocherk*. Kostroma, 1891.

Zolotov, V. A. *Vneshniaia torgovlia Rossii cherez porty Chernogo i Azovskogo morei v pervoi polovine XIX v.* Rostov on Don, 1962.

_____. *Khlebnyi eksport Rossii cherez Chernogo i Azovskogo morei v 60–90 godakh XIX veka.* Rostov on Don, 1966.

Index

Compositor:	Braun-Brumfield
Text:	Aldus
Display:	Helvetica
Printer:	Braun-Brumfield
Binder:	Braun-Brumfield